Textbooks as Propaganda

Textbooks as Propaganda analyses post–Second World War Polish school textbooks to show that Communist indoctrination started right from the first grade. This indoctrination intensified as students grew older, but its general themes and major ideas were consistent regardless of the age of the readers and the discipline covered.

These textbooks promoted the new, post-war Poland's boundaries, its alliance and friendship with the Soviet Union, and communist ideology and its implementation within the countries of the Soviet bloc. Through a thorough analysis of nearly a thousand archival textbooks, Joanna Wojdon explores the ways in which propaganda was incorporated into each school subject, including mathematics, science, physics, chemistry, biology, geography, history, Polish language instruction, foreign language instruction, art education, music, civic education, defense training, physical education and practical technical training. Wojdon also traces the extent of the propaganda, examining its rise and eventual decrease in textbooks as the totalitarian state began its decline.

Positioning school textbooks and textbook propaganda in the broader context of a changing political system, posing questions about the effectiveness of the regime's educational policies and discussing recent research into political influences on school education, this book will appeal to anyone interested in the history of communist-era propaganda.

Joanna Wojdon is an Associate Professor of History at the University of Wrocław, Poland. Her publications include *White and Red Umbrella: Polish American Congress in the Cold War Era (1944–1988)* (2015); *The World of Reading Primers: The Image of Reality in the Reading Instruction Textbooks of the Soviet Bloc* (in Polish: *Świat elementarzy: Obraz rzeczywistości w podręcznikach do nauki czytania w krajach bloku radzieckiego*) (2015); and *E-teaching History* (2016, ed.). She is the managing editor of the *International Journal of Research on History Didactics, History Education and History Culture: Yearbook of the International Society for History Didactics* (vol. 33–37: 2013–2016).

Textbooks as Propaganda
Poland under Communist Rule, 1944–1989

Joanna Wojdon

NEW YORK AND LONDON

First published 2018
by Routledge
711 Third Avenue, New York, NY 10017

and by Routledge
2 Park Square, Milton Park, Abingdon, Oxon OX14 4RN

Routledge is an imprint of the Taylor & Francis Group, an informa business

© 2018 Joanna Wojdon

The right of Joanna Wojdon to be identified as author of this work
has been asserted by her in accordance with sections 77 and 78 of the
Copyright, Designs and Patents Act 1988.

All rights reserved. No part of this book may be reprinted or reproduced
or utilised in any form or by any electronic, mechanical, or other means,
now known or hereafter invented, including photocopying and recording,
or in any information storage or retrieval system, without permission in
writing from the publishers.

Trademark notice: Product or corporate names may be trademarks or
registered trademarks, and are used only for identification and explanation
without intent to infringe.

First published in Polish in 2000 with the title *Propaganda polityczna
w podręcznikach dla szkół podstawowych Polski Ludowej* by the publisher
Wydawnictwo Adam Marszalek

Library of Congress Cataloging-in-Publication Data
A catalog record for this book has been requested

ISBN: 978-1-4128-6558-6 (hbk)
ISBN: 978-1-315-11427-9 (ebk)

Typeset in Goudy
by Apex CoVantage, LLC

Contents

	List of Figures	vii
	Introduction	1
1	**Primary School Curricula in Poland: 1944–1989**	6
	The Interim Period 6	
	Stalinism 6	
	The 1960s 8	
	The 1970s and 1980s 9	
2	**Primary School Textbook Propaganda: Central Themes**	12
	Periodization 12	
	Geopolitics 13	
	New Way of Dealing with Citizens 17	
	A Socialist Set of Values 26	
3	**Maths and Sciences**	29
	Mathematics 29	
	Science 37	
	Physics 40	
	Chemistry 48	
	Biology 52	
4	**Geography**	63
	Scientific World View 63	
	Economic Issues (Polytechnization) 64	
	The World 69	
5	**Polish Language Instruction**	81
	The Past 83	

vi   *Contents*

The Image of the People's Poland 89
The Image of the Post–World War II World outside Poland 102

6   **History**   108
Periodization and Class Struggle 110
The Revolutionary Movement 113
The Catholic Church 114
Poland between Germany and Russia 116

7   **Foreign Languages and the Arts**   121
Russian Language Instruction 121
French, English and German 125
Art 128
Music 130
Other Subjects 131

8   **Civic and Defense Education**   133
Civic Education 133
Defense Training 136

9   **Conclusion: Primary School Textbooks, Propaganda and the
    Totalitarian State**   140
Deliberate and Systematic Attempt 140
Shaping Perception and Manipulating Cognition 143
Directing Behavior 144
The Propagandist and its Intent 144
Achieving a Response 145

Bibliography of the Textbooks Cited   149
General Bibliography   156
Index   159

Figures

9.1	Total Amount of Propaganda in Primary School Textbooks by Year	141
9.2	Distribution of Propaganda Content Among School Subjects	141
9.3	Distribution of Propaganda Content Among the School Grades	142
9.4	Textbooks with the Largest Percentage of Pages with Propaganda	142
9.5	Total Amount of Propaganda in Primary School Textbooks for Pupils Starting Their Education in Each School Year	143

Introduction

The idea of this book originated from my experience as a pupil of the Soviet primary school. We solved hundreds of mathematical exercises about workers producing "elements" and read countless stories on the Soviet achievements related to all the disciplines of science and all spheres of life. We sang Russian revolutionary songs, and the first poem in English that I learned by heart started with: "There is a well-known portrait upon the classroom wall, we see the face of Lenin so dear and loved by all". A few years later, back in Poland and after the collapse of the communist regime, as a young historian, I decided to check to what extent education in the Soviet-dominated Poland followed the Soviet model.[1]

I chose to analyze school textbooks since they play a crucial role as a dominating teaching tool in Poland. They are widely used both at school and for homework.[2] Many teachers and their students follow them step by step. The term "doing a textbook" was coined to characterize the flow of many lessons. Under communism, some teachers' journals openly discouraged teachers from reducing or enhancing the scope of textbook contents and even from changing the order of topics. A textbook was to serve as a universal guide for both teachers and pupils. Such a position adds to its reliability as a historical source documenting school practices of the time. Unlike oral or written testimonies, diaries or copybooks, textbooks are not limited to the individual experiences of one local school, nor do they depend on memory and its distortions and, unlike school curricula, they not only reflect the model of education desirable by the authorities, but also give an idea about everyday school practices. This model was presented in official documents, but textbooks made it more specific. They transformed the general concepts of the curricula into detailed lesson plans: texts, tasks, exercises. Textbooks, not curricula, were what teachers and pupils actually "did". Of course, there were exceptions: teachers who taught according to their own beliefs and methods and pupils who used their own sources of knowledge. However, I was interested in the rule, not the exceptions. Textbooks, better than other historical sources, provide an insight into the commonly and universally practiced school routines in Poland under communism. They prove without any doubt that the regime wanted school to indoctrinate the young people already from the first grade.

Another feature of the communist system that made my research more meaningful was the uniformity of all spheres of life imposed by the authorities. Since

2 Introduction

the late 1940s there was one dominant political party, one youth organization, one school model, and one officially approved textbook for each subject and grade. Thus, all the pupils in Poland learned from exactly the same teaching materials. The analysis of just one set of textbooks tells us what a whole generation studied during their school years and how their minds were shaped.

I chose primary school textbooks for the sake of reconstructing the universal message of the regime addressed to its youngest citizens. Primary education was compulsory for 7- to 14- and later 15-year-olds. Some researchers prefer to focus on secondary schools because their textbook narratives are more sophisticated. However, I was interested not only in the pattern of indoctrination, but also in its possible influence on society. The audience for primary school textbooks was significantly higher. Moreover, younger readers are much less critical and therefore more susceptible to the propaganda messages.

The uniformity of the textbooks made my research easier. The titles of the approved books appeared yearly (or sometimes twice a year) in the official journal of the Ministry of Education. The journal was, thus, the main source of bibliographical data. I took into consideration all the books accepted for general use at schools, but excluded textbooks for children with disabilities and for national minorities. They are interesting per se, but did not play as crucial a role in the shaping the collective memory, identity and imagination. Some textbooks were in use only for one year, others for more than twenty years. Sustainability and changes could be noticed not only by identifying changing authors, titles and official notes, but also by comparing various editions of a given textbook page by page. Altogether, approximately one thousand non-identical volumes of textbooks were singled out.[3] Out of them approximately sixty, mostly from the late 1940s and early 1950s, turned out to be unavailable in the Polish libraries. Still, 94% formed a sufficient basis from which to draw conclusions.

I did not work on a pre-defined propaganda model to be verified by primary sources. There were no points of reference. It was to a certain extent a pioneering work. There existed some rather descriptive studies on history education in the People's Republic of Poland.[4] John Rodden's *Textbook Reds*,[5] dealing with the political impact on education in the German Democratic Republic, was only being written. As for my methodology, generally speaking, I simply read the books and noted down the instances of what I believed had been inserted for political reasons, that is, points that corresponded either with Marxist doctrine or with the propaganda campaigns of the regime and were useful for its political goals.[6] In some cases, a single occurrence of a certain motive need not have been propaganda, but became one due to its repetitive nature (e.g. a tractor in the fields in the 1950s or transporting goods in railway cars). Some tips on what to pay attention to could be found in school curricula and pedagogical journals as well as in secondary literature dealing with various aspects of education and indoctrination in post-war Poland.

The archival files of the Ministry of Education and of the Censorship Office not only confirmed my intuition of the propagandist character of many inserts and interpretations, but they proved that all the textbook content remained under meticulous multilevel and multilayer influence and control of the regime. Censors demanded certain topics to be omitted (e.g. references to Christianity) and others to be inserted into textbooks, for example, Soviet achievements to illustrate physical, chemical or biological phenomena, or presentation of workers—and especially miners—to exemplify collective efforts of the Poles in support of the post-war changes. Even texts that seem neutral may have had some ideological background; for example, the father of Ala (the main character of the reading primer) in the 1950s could not be an engineer but only a worker. The authorities seemed never to have been satisfied with the quantity and quality of the ideological passages of the textbooks, no matter how saturated the books were.[7]

I have tried to place my impressions in an objective context and calculate the proportion of propaganda content in each book.

To do so, I counted all the pages that included at least one instance of politically loaded text or image. I was aware of the problems such an approach entails, from the subjectivity of the very classification of a word, a sentence or a paragraph as propagandist to taking the whole page as a unit regardless of the length of propaganda-loaded items it contained. However, I believe that longer texts need not mean more influence on pupils. It may be even easier to ignore a whole ideological passage or chapter than to skip a single phrase or sentence of an otherwise neutral text. Spreading propaganda messages all over books instead of concentrating them in separate sections was praised and demanded by policymakers. As for the subjectivity, first, the archival materials proved that I initially underestimated rather than overestimated political influence on textbooks, and things that seemed neutral turned out to be carefully discussed and commented on for political purposes. Second, in returning to the same texts after a considerable amount of time, I came to very similar conclusions about whether they were propaganda or not.

Using percentages, and not just the number of pages, made the books comparable to one another (regardless of their length, format or font) and allowed me to observe changes over time. I took into consideration textbooks for the following disciplines: Polish language (and grammar), Russian language, history, mathematics, science, physics, chemistry, biology, geography, art, music (in 8-year schools) and defense training. Western European languages were excluded from statistics, since they were not compulsory for the greater part of the post-war period, as were civics, physical and technical education books—for their ephemeral character. Songbooks for 7-year school could not be included because many of them are unavailable in libraries, and religious instruction textbooks were excluded even from general analysis. They were approved by the Ministry of Education between 1946 and 1950 but religious instruction was only an optional subject.[8]

In an attempt to operationalize the research topic, I chose to refer to the classic definition of propaganda by Jowett and O'Donnell of "the deliberate and systematic attempt to shape perceptions, manipulate cognitions and direct behavior to

4 Introduction

achieve a response that furthers the desired intent of the propagandist".[9] And although Hannah Arendt claimed that totalitarian movements "do not actually propagate but indoctrinate" for their actions are "inevitably coupled with terror",[10] I am using the terms propaganda and indoctrination interchangeably. Although it seems quite natural that schools intend to shape their pupils according to a desired model, I focused on the manipulations used by the textbook authors, on the strictly political content of the books and on the intent of the propagandist and the propagated system of values that did not necessarily correspond with the intents of other stakeholders in the process of raising younger generations, that is, parents, local communities or the Catholic Church.

The following chapters present qualitative analysis of the propaganda content of school textbooks. Chapter 1 provides a background of the system of education in Poland between 1944–1989 and its political implications. Chapter 2 gives a general overview of the propaganda goals and their implementation in various subject areas. Chapters 3 to 8 are devoted to particular disciplines, grouped into maths and sciences, geography, the Polish language, history, other languages and arts, and civic and defense education. Some quantitative analysis and verification of the findings in reference to the aforementioned definition of propaganda have been put into Chapter 9 that concludes the analysis. The bibliography is divided into textbook and general sections and includes only the works directly cited.

Notes

1 This is a modified English version of a book initially published in Poland: Wojdon, Joanna. 2000. *Propaganda polityczna w podręcznikach dla szkół podstawowych Polski Ludowej* (Political Propaganda in Primary School Textbooks of the People's Poland (1944–1989)). Toruń: Adam Marszałek.

2 It has been recently confirmed in a report: Choińska-Mika, Jolanta, Jakub Lorenc, Krzysztof Mrozowski, Aleksandra Oniszczuk, Jacek Staniszewski and Klaudia Starczynowska. 2014. "Nauczyciele historii". In *Liczą się nauczyciele: Raport o stanie edukacji 2013*, edited by Michał Federowicz, Jolanta Choińska-Mika and Dominika Walczak. Warsaw: IBE, 227.

3 The full bibliography of textbooks can be found in the Polish version of the book (Wojdon, 2000, 292–318) and at www.wojdon.net.

4 An overview of the secondary literature as of 2000 has been provided in its original Polish version. Due to the fact that the literature has been almost entirely published in Poland and in Polish and therefore remains unavailable to most English-language readers, I chose not to provide the details here and to give bibliographical references only to the works directly cited. For further references see Wojdon, 2000 and Wołoszyn, Jacek Witold. 2015. *Szkoła jako instrument politycznej legitymizacji władzy partii komunistycznej w Polsce (1944–1989)*. Lublin: IPN.

5 Rodden, John. 2006. *Textbook Reds: Schoolbooks, Ideology and Eastern German Identity*. University Park: Pennsylvania State University Press.

6 On the textbook analysis methods see Johnsen, Egil. 1993. *Textbooks in the Kaleidoscope: A Critical Survey of Literature and Research on Educational Texts*. Oslo: Scandinavian University Press.

7 The files examined included: Archiwum Akt Nowych. Warsaw. Ministerstwo Oświaty (Ministerstwo Oświaty i Nauki; Ministerstwo Oświaty i Wychowania) and Główny Urząd Kontroli Prasy, Publikacji i Widowisk.

8 In 1961 it was completely banned from schools.
9 Jowett, Gareth and Victoria O'Donnell. 2006. *Propaganda and Persuasion*. Thousand Oaks, CA: Sage, 7.
10 Cited in: Papazian, Elizabeth. 2013. "Literacy or Legibility: The Trace of Subjectivity in Soviet Socialist Realism". In *The Oxford Handbook of Propaganda Studies*, edited by Jonathan Auerbach and Russ Castronovo. Oxford: Oxford University Press, 68–69.

1 Primary School Curricula in Poland
1944–1989

The Interim Period

Education was one of the main points of interest of the communist regime from the very beginning of its rule in Poland. Already the July Manifesto (i.e. the very first document of the communist authorities that were taking power in 1944) guaranteed free schooling to everyone. During the first post-war school year most pre-war regulations remained in force, including school curricula that could be adjusted by local school authorities to the new needs and realities. On a national level, the Ministry of Education demanded in 1944 that schools celebrate the anniversary of the Soviet revolution and present the provisions of the newly introduced agrarian reform to their pupils. These were the first symptoms of the politicization of education.[1]

At the same time, the national authorities worked on a major reform of education. However, the tensions between the Polish Workers Party (i.e. the Communist Party) and the Polish Teachers' Union postponed its total Stalinization. The new provisional curricula introduced in 1945/46 included more anti-German elements than pre-war editions. Friendship and cooperation among all Slavic peoples were promoted, manual labor and technological progress esteemed, working people (i.e. workers, craftsmen and farmers) respected. The Russian language was introduced for the first time as a foreign language to be taught in schools, alongside French, English and German (the latter being rather discouraged). The Russian language curriculum included information about the life of Soviet citizens and the achievements of the USSR. Even more data about the construction of socialism in the Soviet Union and about the Soviet heroes and leaders was to be included in the next school year (1946/47).

Stalinism

The Polish Workers' Party was not satisfied with the changes. As it began to monopolize political, social and cultural life in 1947–1948, the reform project gained momentum. The ministerial instruction of June 10, 1948, introduced a new system of education, with a 7-year primary and 4-year secondary school despite the teachers' postulates of 8-year primary school. The same instruction

Primary School Curricula in Poland 7

contained new curricula. They were based on the principles of a "contemporary, scientific world view", of combining teaching and upbringing, and of the compatibility with the economic and political needs of the People's Poland. The "educational ideals" of the new school contained propaganda slogans of "love of the People's Poland", "love towards all the progressive elements and the traditions of the national culture", "deep respect for work", "attachment to the idea of progress and social justice and resistance against any forms of backwardness and exploitation", and "the feeling of brotherhood towards freedom-loving nations, particularly towards Slavic nations".[2]

As for the contents of the education curriculum, more economic issues were inserted. Cooperatives were to be promoted, especially in the context of selling and buying agricultural products. Fishing, fish processing, poultry farming, chemical industry including metallurgy, and electrification were to be presented.

However, by the end of 1948 the Party leadership criticized both the pace and scope of the newly introduced changes. The Minister of Education noticed the symptoms of "right-wing and nationalist deviation" in the new curricula[3]—thus proving that his critique was part of the broader political and propaganda campaign aimed at eliminating any independence of Polish Communists from the Soviet leadership. The ministry issued directives for new curricula. They included Marxism-Leninism as a philosophical, cognitive, educational and methodological base. The Soviet Union and other countries of the "people's democracy" (i.e. of the Soviet bloc) were to be treated as the "natural allies" of Poland, and Western countries as "natural opponents". The directives encouraged the broader propagation of the achievements of the Soviet science and art, supplementing patriotism with "internationalism" and proposed the inclusion of "the struggle for socialism".[4]

The issue of educational reform was raised during the so-called Congress of the Unity of the Working Class in December 1948 (i.e. on the highest decision-making level). Disdain for capitalism and imperialism was added to the aforementioned list of educational priorities. The speakers announced the struggle for lay education.

The curricular instruction for 1949/50 implemented most of the Party directives.[5] All the school subjects were to promote economic achievements of socialism, especially in Poland and in the Soviet Union. Schools should emphasize the enthusiasm of Poles for the new system and the Polish-Soviet friendship that had started during World War II. The Slavic brotherhood was to be replaced with the community of the socialist-building countries—probably the result of the Stalin-Tito tensions (Yugoslavia was not an ally anymore, though it had a mostly Slavic population) and of the more general ideological turn from a national to class perspective. Teachers were encouraged to familiarize their pupils with state dignitaries, such as president Bierut, Minister of Defense Marshal Rokossovsky and General Świerczewski.

The next year the saturation of curricula with ideological content grew even further. All school subjects were referred to the Six Year Plan, announced in 1950. The curriculum for each subject was published in a separate brochure. The

8 *Primary School Curricula in Poland*

general goals of education were reiterated in introduction. They included the formation of a scientific world view, based on "dialectical and historical materialism" (i.e. Marxism), and of a "socialist morality" with such components as a "true people's patriotism and internationalism", "socialist attitude" towards property, work and "creative scientific thought", and the ability to live in a collective. Graduates were supposed to become active citizens, "vigilant towards the class enemy", proud of the achievements of socialism and of progressive national traditions. They should know and love the "revolutionary and progressive traditions of the working class worldwide", express their solidarity with the socialist camp struggling with "imperialism", love and respect the Soviet Union—"the best friend of the People's Poland, the country of the victorious socialism, the pattern to follow by all the countries and nations", and share the notion of the superiority of the socialist economy over the capitalist one, which was based on "the exploitation and social injustice".[6] Those ideological goals apparently dominated more universal virtues, such as courage, diligence, and conscientiousness that were mentioned at the very end of the list.

The introduction was followed by the detailed contents of lessons, and in the last part of the curricula new chapters were added for "the formation of a materialist world view and ideological education" in a given subject.

The structure of the curricula remained unchanged in 1951/52, but more emphasis was put on including the Six Year Plan in all school subjects. The new curriculum for civic education was introduced, to be replaced just one year later, when the new constitution of the "People's Republic of Poland" was signed into law. As a result, civic education was replaced by "constitutional science", which concentrated on discussing the new law chapter by chapter and stressing its socialist, and thus progressive, character.[7]

The curricular instruction for 1954/55 for the first time did not enhance but limited the content of education. Already in 1952, the first critical opinions about the new curricula and textbooks were voiced. "Trybuna Ludu", the official press organ of the Polish United Workers' Party, published a letter to the editor, allegedly authored by a primary school pupil who complained that he could not grasp most of the texts in his textbooks. The death of Stalin in 1953 did not start de-Stalinization immediately. The official goals of education remained unchanged, as did the ideological remarks, but the teaching material for Polish language instruction, history, mathematics, physics, chemistry, biology, geography and physical education was significantly reduced. In 1955 "constitutional science" was abolished as a separate subject.

The 1960s

The de-Stalinization process brought a new version of school curricula, signed into law in 1959. They were relatively moderate in terms of their ideological content. Schools were supposed to prepare young people for work and life (in that order) and bring them up as "the future hosts and constructors of the socialist fatherland". The values to be promoted included a materialist world view, "socialist consciousness and discipline", tolerance—though the lay content of school subjects was to be preserved, and brotherhood with all those who "wanted peace and the struggle for the social progress in the world".[8]

Thus, the saturation of curricula for 7-year primary schools paralleled the large-scale political changes in Poland. It peaked in the early 1950s and was downsized by the end of the decade, though never reached the level of the 1940s. Key decisions were always made by the Party leadership. Interestingly, they corresponded with the changes introduced in other countries of the Soviet bloc.

The provisions of the new large-scale reform of education, introduced in Poland in 1961, were similar to the solutions adopted in the Soviet Union in 1958, in Bulgaria and the German Democratic Republic (GDR) in 1959 and in Hungary in 1961.[9] They prolonged primary school to eight years and emphasized the role of practical training to prepare young people for productive work. Sciences should provide the pupils with "poly-technical" education and humanities with an ideological base. More attention was to be paid to foreign languages and arts.

The Polish school was to be a lay institution. Religious instruction was completely removed (it returned only after the collapse of the communist regime in 1989). The word "socialism" appeared in the new curriculum more frequently than ever before. There was a socialist school, a socialist morality for graduates, socialist principles for social life, and a socialist work attitude. School was supposed to convince pupils of the social, economic and moral superiority of socialism over capitalism. Internationalism and brotherhood with all those who "wanted peace, the struggle for social progress and the victory of justice", and the scientific world view did not disappear. Geography had more economic and political elements than in 1959. The achievements of the People's Republic of Poland and other countries of the Soviet bloc were to be stressed, while the capitalist world was to be condemned and despised. This can be noticed in the very wording of the document that, in the point devoted to the Soviet Union, read: "Assistance for countries liberated and liberating from colonial oppression" while in reference to the US: "Imperialist policy of the United States—defending the interests of the capitalist countries, keeping poorly developed countries in political and economic dependency. Military bases on all the continents of the world".[10]

Thus, the political and ideological content of the 1961 curriculum did not concentrate so much on topical issues and on the current propaganda campaigns of the authorities. It was full of economic issues; promoted achievements of socialism; expressed trust in the power of science; and promoted its technical usage.

The 1970s and 1980s

The first steps towards the new reform were undertaken in 1968/69. The Party again played a decisive role. Nineteen commissions were nominated "in cooperation with the Section of Science and Education of the Central Committee of the Polish United Workers' Party and with the help of the secretaries of the Party committees at the universities"[11] to work on particular school subjects. But

10 Primary School Curricula in Poland

only minor changes were eventually introduced. New curricula were published in 1970 and 1971, but only for history, Polish language and initial education (grades 1–3). Defense training was introduced as a new, highly politicized, subject. Some smaller corrections introduced by the end of the 1970s eliminated many political and economic elements of science education. Mathematics was almost completely de-politicized and not limited to arithmetic any more.

With the general political changes in Poland associated with the new first secretary of the Communist Party, Edward Gierek, another new educational reform project was launched. This time it was preceded with the report on the state of education in Poland conducted by a team of sociologists, but supervised by the Party's Central Committee. Despite the Party's pressure, the report expressed critical opinions, both in terms of content, staff and the structure of education. It formulated various strategies to overcome these difficulties, but did not give preference to any of them. The decisions were made by the Party leaders again, while other bodies played only limited advisory roles. The key document, titled *For an Active Participation of the Young Generation in the Construction of Socialist Poland—The Tasks of the Party, State and Nation in Raising Youth*, was adopted by the General Assembly of the Party's Central Committee in November, 1972. Its guidelines were developed by the parliament that in October 1973 adopted a bill on the system of national education. Eight years of primary school and four years of secondary education were to be combined into ten years of "uniform high school". As ten years before, similar changes were introduced in other countries of the Soviet bloc.

The process of implementing the new law lasted for years. The first changes pertained to the extracurricular activities of pupils. Beginning in 1973/74, it became compulsory to participate in some "socially useful" activities. School ceremonies were expanded and enjoyed special attention. Schools were encouraged to have their own banners and to open museums (or at least memory rooms), to host scouting groups and student government. New curricula were developed by the mid-1970s. Before being officially introduced, they were tested in selected schools. The first grades of 1978/79 were to become the first grades of the 10-year school.

Two years later, however, the authorities decided not to change the system of education. This was partially due to the expected high costs and economic difficulties Poland experienced at the time, but also as a result of social pressure, including that from the newly formed Teachers' "Solidarity" trade union that had its own vision of Polish education. Keeping the old system of education did not stop the process of introducing new curricula and textbooks which were modified according to the agreements signed between the Teachers' "Solidarity" and the government. The process lasted in primary schools until 1985/86. The curricula contained a large amount of socialist phraseology, often referred to the communist ideology, and emphasized the role of labor and the lay character of education. Ideological goals of education were given priority again. A closer look at particular subjects reveals, however, that the rhetoric of the reforms did not correspond

Primary School Curricula in Poland 11

with the factual content of most disciplines. Most propaganda elements were removed and never returned to Polish schools.

***

The Communist Party strictly controlled the post-war primary school curricula. It had decisive power, while all other institutions could merely approve and implement its guidance. The educational reforms closely corresponded with the general political developments in Poland and with the changes introduced in other countries of the Soviet bloc. In the 1950s school curricula were saturated with communist ideology. Indoctrination never totally disappeared, but, gradually, other factors were also taken into consideration, such as pupils' interests and abilities or the scientific character of particular disciplines.

Notes

1 See Paczkowski, Andrzej. 2003. *The Spring Will Be Ours—Poland and the Poles from Occupation to Freedom*, trans. by Jane Cave. University Park: Pennsylvania State University Press for details on the post–World War II history of Poland.
2 Skrzeszewski, Stanisław. 1948. Zarządzenie Ministra Oświaty z dnia 10 czerwca 1948 r. w sprawie przejściowego program nauczania w szkole średniej na rok szkolny 1948-1949. In: *Dziennik Urzędowy Ministerstwa Oświaty [Journal of the Ministry of Education*, hereinafter referred to as *Dziennik*], no. 7, item 127, 271–272.
3 Skrzeszewski, Stanisław. 1948. *Podstawowe zadania oświatowe*. Warsaw: PZWS. Accusations of the "right-wing and nationalist deviation" were used at that time in the internal Communist Party struggles aiming at eliminating the activists who claimed that Poland did not have to follow the Soviet patterns in all aspects of life.
4 Archiwum Akt Nowych, Warsaw. Files of Departament Reformy Szkolnictwa Ministerstwa Oświaty, no. 108/4, cited in Mauersberg, Stanisław. 1974. *Reforma szkolnictwa w Polsce w latach 1944–1948*. Wrocław: Ossolineum, 239.
5 Jabłoński, Henryk. 1949. Zarządzenie Ministra Oświaty z 2 sierpnia 1949 r. w sprawie przejściowego programu nauczania w 11-letniej szkole ogólnokształcącej na rok szkolny 1949/50. *Dziennik*, no. 12, item 209.
6 Jabłoński, Henryk. 1950. Zarządzenie Ministra Oświaty z 28 lipca 1950 r. w sprawie programu nauczania w 11-letniej szkole ogólnokształcącej na rok szkolny 1950/51. *Dziennik*, no. 13, item 173.
7 Jarosiński, Witold. 1951. Zarządzenie Ministra Oświaty z 16 czerwca 1951 r. w sprawie instrukcji programowej i podręcznikowej dla 11-letnich szkół ogólnokształcących na rok szkolny 1951/52. *Dziennik*, no. 11, item 135.
8 Ministerstwo Oświaty. 1959. *Program nauczania w szkole podstawowej*. Warsaw: PZWS.
9 Pęcherski, Mieczysław and Antoni Tatoń. 1963. *Więź szkoły z życiem w krajach socjalistycznych*. Warszawa: PZWS, 5–35.
10 Ministerstwo Oświaty. 1964. *Program ośmioklasowej szkoły podstawowej (tymczasowy)*. Warsaw: PZWS, 2nd ed.
11 Maciaszek, Maksymilian. 1980. *Treść kształcenia i wychowania w reformach szkolnych PRL*. Warsaw: Książka i Wiedza, 79.

2 Primary School Textbook Propaganda

Central Themes

Periodization

The main goal of the political propaganda in the primary school textbooks of the People's Poland was to present the new post–World War II Polish realities in the most positive way. Pupils were expected to get acquainted with and to accept those realities and to actively engage in the ongoing changes. This main goal did not change throughout the whole period of 1944–1989, although the detailed content and means of propaganda were modified. One can distinguish five main periods, with the years 1949, 1957, 1965 and 1980 as symbolic turning points, though it took a couple of years until the desired changes were introduced in all textbooks.

In the first five years (1944–1948), the propaganda content was relatively moderate, and concentrated on the Polish language instruction books only. It included joy at the end of the World War II, the new borders of Poland, and the first reforms introduced by the communist authorities: the agrarian reform, the nationalization of industry and the enhancement of social care. Enthusiasm for post-war reconstruction was also emphasized.

In 1947, the first steps were made to include more political content in the textbooks for all subjects. This trend continued in 1948. In 1949, the propaganda role of many textbooks started to dominate their other functions. In many instances, both the style and content of the texts resembled propaganda brochures of the time. The textbooks dealt with a wide scope of issues not related to disciplines of knowledge, but only to current propaganda campaigns. The saturation of textbooks with propaganda increased every year until 1952, remained at its peak until 1955, and then gradually diminished. The mere erasing of passages dealing with Stalin and Bierut, with the details of the Six Year Plan and shortening references to Soviet examples, gave textbooks a totally different character.

Detailed descriptions of technological processes, enthusiastic remarks on the technological and civilizational progress, and other issues related to the developing economy of Poland under the communist regime remained in post-Stalinist textbooks. Some of them were even expanded in the 1960s when the notion of making education more practical gained popularity. Practice meant production, not just everyday life.

Primary School Textbook Propaganda 13

The last turning point is the least apparent. Already in the mid-1970s mathematics textbooks contained almost no propaganda, while the humanities had never achieved that level of freedom. However, the discussion initiated by the Solidarity trade union in 1981 and the demands presented by the Teachers' Solidarity group resulted in significant changes in history, geography and Polish language instruction books that were introduced in the 1980s, despite the fact that Solidarity itself had been delegalized upon the introduction of martial law in December 1981. In general, the textbooks published in the last years of the People's Republic of Poland dealt predominantly with the issues of their respective disciplines, and not with the political campaigns of the regime. They started to discuss scientific, moral and existential questions, and "everyday life" referred to the pupils' experiences at home or at school, and not at factories, construction sites or collective farms. The achievements of the People's Republic of Poland were still promoted, but some shortcomings and weaknesses were also mentioned (and often excused).

All textbooks (and propaganda in the People's Republic of Poland in general) presented July 22, 1944, as a turning point in the history of Poland, the beginning of the new era. The July Manifesto, officially proclaimed on that day, and the other regulations of the new communist authorities that followed, were claimed to be the fulfilment of the eternal dreams of the Polish people, and especially of the Polish working class. The revolutionary changes that were said to have been introduced in the post-war period could be attributed to three areas: Poland's new geopolitical situation, the new way of dealing with citizens and their problems, and a new system of values. All these spheres were affirmed in school textbooks.

Geopolitics

The new geopolitical situation in Poland was determined by its new borders and new alliances. Immediately after World War II these were the issues of the utmost interest and concern to the whole Polish society, but the textbooks promoted only one attitude: unconditional acceptance of the post-war changes.

New Borders

New borders were presented in the geography textbooks—quite naturally—but also in history, Polish language, mathematics and biology, even though they do not necessarily belong at the core of those disciplines. In Gdańsk, Szczecin, Opole and Wrocław monuments were described testifying to the Polish, or at least Slavic heritage of those cities, which had belonged to Germany for more than six hundred years, and "returned" to Poland only after the war. The toponyms were also said to confirm the Polish past of the so-called Recovered Territories (this term was used in the official propaganda outside school as well). The economic benefits of their inclusion in Poland were stressed, especially broad access to the sea and the incorporation of the whole of Silesia (not only part of it, as in the pre-war years) into the Polish economic system. The Soviet Union,

14 *Primary School Textbook Propaganda*

the Red Army and the "people's" Polish Army were presented as the guardians of border integrity.

The textbooks dealt with the resources that Poland gained in the "Recovered Territories", both natural, such as coal, ores and forests, and man-made, from agricultural infrastructure and the railway system to the regulated Odra River and numerous spas. Coal mines and metallurgical plants of Upper Silesia and the ports of the Baltic coast enjoyed the particular attention of textbook authors, as did PaFaWag, a railway car factory located in Wrocław. The images of coal on its way to Polish cities and abroad accompanied those of transports of ore to the Silesian steelworks. The miners and metallurgists enjoyed their holidays in the Polish mountains and at the seaside. The "Recovered Territories", according to the textbooks, gave a solid base for the economic development of the country and for the well-being of its citizens.

In the early post-war years, textbooks described the details of the Polish settlement and reconstruction of the area. Gradually, they mentioned more and more newly created post–World War II facilities, such as the cement factory in Opole, the steelworks in Stołczyn near Szczecin, the fertilizer-producing plant in Police, factories of the Masuria lakes region, shipyards, harbors and later the copper basin of Legnica and Głogów. Thus, the People's Republic of Poland was said to be multiplying the potential it had gained.

New Alliances

The new international situation of Poland, and especially its relations with neighboring countries, were presented in the most positive way. Never had Poland been so safe, according to the school textbooks.

Czechoslovakia was not problematic for textbook authors. At first, it was appreciated as a fraternal Slavic country. Traditional cooperation between the Poles and Czechs dated back to the legendary times of Lech, Czech and Rus—the brothers who were said to be founders of the three countries: Poland, Czechoslovakia and Russia. From the end of the 1940s their common political system seemed to be more important than common history. Czechoslovakia became one of the socialist friends of Poland. Lech, Czech and Rus remained in Polish language textbooks, but political cooperation and especially economic exchange were what mattered most.

Relations with **Germany** were much more complicated. Initially, Germany was portrayed as an eternal and lethal enemy of Poland—which should come as no surprise after the events of World War II. Nazis (or rather Hitlerites) were presented as the direct successors of the Teutonic Knights and Prussians who had wanted to destroy Poland from the very outset of mutual relations. Germans were said to have always attacked, while the Poles had only defended themselves. The Germans were accused of destroying Poland, both militarily and economically (e.g. pre-war German factory- and mine-owners exploited Polish workers, miners and farmers). When the GDR was founded in 1949 and recognized the western border of Poland on the Odra and **Nysa** Rivers, anti-German rhetoric began to disappear from textbooks, except in those for history and geography. The border between Poland and the GDR was always called "the border of peace" (no other border bore this name). In the 1950s textbooks, portraying the conflict between social classes was given general priority over conflicting nations, so the German businessmen became a part of the international bourgeoisie which slowed down the development of Poland, while the common German people were seen to have sympathized with Poles in the past. The Federal Republic of Germany (FRG) was, as a rule, simply omitted in textbooks with the exception of history and geography. The anti-German tone of the latter changed only in the 1970s, probably due to the treaty of December 1970 between the FRG and Poland and the work of the bilateral textbook commission. Cooperation between Poland and the GDR was stressed already in the 1950s and exemplified with the correspondence and meetings between the Polish scouts and East German pioneers.

The **Soviet Union** enjoyed the most attention of all foreign countries. Not only was it the largest neighboring country (and the largest country in the world), which safeguarded Polish borders, but first and foremost it was the leader of the socialist camp and served as a model to be followed by Poland. Everything in the USSR was the largest and best in the world. The USSR appeared in textbooks for all school subjects.

Polish and Russian language, history and geography textbooks dealt with the history of Russia. Episodes were selected to present the country in the most positive light. Other issues were either totally omitted or excused, usually based on the Russian raison d'état. The October Revolution was presented in the most detailed way. It was said to have started a new era, not only in the history of Russia, but also that of the whole world. Whatever happened after the revolution was depicted in the best possible light (only a few history books mentioned Stalin's abuses). In the 1950s Lenin and Stalin were presented as the leaders of the entire progressive world. Later only Lenin remained in subjects other than history.

All textbooks mentioned Soviet economic achievements. They admired the exploration and transformation of the natural environment in the USSR that made Russia an exporter of many natural resources which had been imported in the tsarist times. The Soviets were constantly praised for reaching territories in the far North and East, building new cities and expanding the railroad system. They constructed dams, canals and power plants to better use their rivers. They could grow cotton and cereals on the steppes thanks to the watering system and foresting that prevented the damage caused by eastern winds. In the 1950s those issues were presented in geography, biology, mathematics, and Polish and Russian language textbooks. The electrification of the Soviet Union, decreed initially by Lenin, was supposed to serve as a pattern to follow in Poland. Soviet investments were enumerated by name. Lots of statistical data was cited to prove the power of the Soviet economy. No negative elements, such as the exploitation of forced labor in the Soviet economy or the lack of everyday products, were ever mentioned.

Textbooks presented Soviet and Russian achievements in various scientific disciplines. Thus, Ivan Michurin was regarded as the greatest biologist ever, and

16 *Primary School Textbook Propaganda*

Trofim Lysenko was presented as his successor. Texts about Lysenko disappeared in books published after 1960, while passages regarding Michurin, albeit shortened and moderated, survived until the collapse of the communist regime. Both were praised for transforming plants so that they could better serve human needs, particularly in the severe climate conditions of the Soviet Union. Unlike the tsarist regime, the Soviet authorities recognized the significance of Michurin's research. His achievements were subsequently implemented in kolkhozes and sovkhozes.

Chemistry textbooks praised Mikhail Lomonosov, who was credited with formulating the principle of mass conservation (it was admitted that Lavoisier came to similar conclusions in France), and Dmitri Mendeleev for his periodic table of elements. In physics, the Russians were regarded as the inventors of the electric bulb (Lodygin), radio (Popov) and television (Zvorykin). In geography, the Russian explorers Papanin and Cheluskin were presented. The Soviet polar exhibitions and meteorological observations served as examples of "planned science" and contrasted with the "unplanned" Western research. The Soviet achievements in the exploration of space appeared for obvious reasons from the 1960s, but they occupied many textbooks, starting with physics, geography (as proof of the Earth's shape) and including Polish and Russian language (short stories about Gagarin's emotions) and mathematics.

The Soviet Union was supposed to be not only admired, but also followed. The Soviet political system was said to have introduced ideal equality of all citizens, abolished all forms of exploitation and created broad opportunities for social and cultural advancement, especially for the primitive tribes of Siberia and the far North. Soviet authorities were also praised for securing good living conditions for all their citizens. They provided healthcare, vacation opportunities and supplied food and other goods for the working class. They offered learning and professional training opportunities to young people. In return, Soviet citizens were ready to make every sacrifice for their country. During the war they had fought on the front and worked devotedly on the home front. In peace time the working foremen of the Stakhanov movement served as role models for Poles.

The Soviet economic system was also presented as a model to copy in Poland. The previously mentioned Soviet achievements were possible thanks to central planning and state and cooperative property in both industry and agriculture.

The USSR was said to offer its satellite states (or rather brotherly countries) help and advice in implementing Soviet models. Soviet support for Poland enjoyed particular interest and dated back to the time of the war. The Soviet Army was said to have liberated Poland. The Soviets helped reconstruct the war-devastated country and fulfill the Six Year Plan (in particular, to build the metallurgical plant in Nowa Huta near Cracow and the Palace of Culture and Science in Warsaw). In the 1970s Soviet oil was transported through the "Friendship" pipeline that was constructed by the Comecon countries.

The People's Republic of Poland could, therefore, feel safe in the socialist camp where all her neighbors belonged. Even the distant countries of the Soviet bloc enjoyed more attention from textbook authors than, for example, Western

Europe, with whom Poland had traditionally kept cultural, political and economic ties. France and England were mentioned as war allies, but only in the 1940s. By the end of the decade the textbooks divided the world into two opposing camps: "good" socialist and "bad" capitalist (often called imperialist), which were compared and contrasted in the 1950s. The United States was accused of devastating the natural environment (the Americans were felling forests while the Soviets planted them), of using nuclear energy for military goals (while the Soviets had nuclear reactors only for energy production and moving mountains), and of discriminating against its black population at home and in the former European colonies abroad. Solidarity with the exploited black population, especially children, was expressed in the Polish textbooks until the collapse of the regime.

Generally, starting from the 1960s, textbooks simply tended to ignore the Western world. The problems of the Far East (China, Korea, Vietnam) seemed to be closer to pupils' interests than those of Western Europe. If Western countries had to be mentioned (e.g. in geography), they were presented in a very reserved and factual manner which contrasted with the enthusiasm of the paragraphs devoted to the socialist states.

New Way of Dealing with Citizens

The political system of the People's Republic of Poland—called a "people's democracy" (*demokracja ludowa*)[1] was, according to the textbooks, the best and the most just in Polish history. It fulfilled the dreams of the once-oppressed classes. The portrayals of socialism and capitalism began in reading primers and were developed as children grew older. Each school subject played its part in this process, at least until the 1970s when mathematics and sciences gradually began to concentrate on purely scientific issues. The excellence of this "people's democracy" expressed itself in the harmonious cooperation between the people (usually called citizens) and the authorities. Each side fulfilled its obligations ideally and complemented the achievements of the other, thanks to which the country flourished.

The Authorities

One aspect of the image of the authorities presented in the textbooks was true: their totalitarian character. The authorities influenced all spheres of life, both public and private. This influence was regarded as a positive symptom of their care for the country and its citizens. The authorities were always right. Textbooks concentrated on their declarations (promising a great deal) rather than on the implementation of the resolutions, not to mention the far-reaching results of their actions.

The very words and legal acts had power. The Six Year Plan illustrates this phenomenon. The expected results of the plan were presented as if they had actually been achieved, and after the six years passed, the plan was hardly ever mentioned

18 *Primary School Textbook Propaganda*

again. This can be partially attributed to the changing character of the textbooks (which did not deal so much with the current political issues any more), but probably also to the tendency to avoid uncomfortable topics. The issue of fulfilment of the plan was doubtlessly one such topic. Its best results were in heavy industry, while light industry, coal mining, food production and agriculture lagged behind the schedule. Work efficiency was also low—despite all the efforts made to encourage labor competition—because of poor stimuli to increase it (i.e. the policy of full employment and relatively equal wages disregarding personal engagement and achievements). Textbooks presented only the positive sides of the plan.

The way in which the textbooks dealt with environmental protection serves as another example of how overrated the official regulations were. Environmental issues were totally ignored when the textbooks presented industrial investments. Smoking chimneys symbolized economic development, not air pollution. For many years, the very existence of legal regulations and organizations promoting environmental protection sufficed to prove that the authorities took proper care of the natural environment. Citizens obviously obeyed the rules and the environment was safe. The planned economy was said to prevent any ecological problems that the capitalist world experienced—yet more proof of the superiority of one system over the other. Only in the 1980s did the environmental problems of Poland, not only of Western countries, start to be noticed. Still, the textbook narratives were rather calm and measured, while independent observers were raising the alarm about water and air pollution. The quality of most Polish rivers fell below any standards, and acid rain destroyed hectares of forests in the mountains along the Polish-Czechoslovakian border.

Economic issues occupied a great deal of space in the textbooks. The main characteristics of the socialist economy included state or social (these two categories were often used interchangeably) ownership of means of production, priority for heavy industry, central planning and central management.

The superiority of collective ownership over private ownership was stressed particularly in the 1940s and 1950s. Later, private companies simply disappeared from textbooks (except private farms, as discussed later).

Large-scale industry was given priority over small private firms. In the 1940s children in textbooks visited craftsmen and factory workers to learn that factory production was more effective and of better quality than the work of individual small-scale enterprises. Gradually, craftsmen's workshops disappeared from the books entirely. Only factories remained, sometimes described in great detail. The industrialization of Poland under communism was openly praised. Pupils were told that heavy industry formed the basis for the further development of the whole economy and that volumes of coal, steel and energy production indicated the level of economic development of a given country. These indicators could make Poles proud: they were much higher than before the war, constantly growing, and favored Poland as compared to other countries. Statistical data was amply provided, but always selected to serve propaganda purposes.

The very amount of space that textbooks allocated to heavy industry showed its importance. Physics, chemistry and, to a certain extent, science and biology described the technological processes related to the disciplines they covered. Geography mentioned the location of particular industrial installations or whole branches of industry in Poland. Industry was present in mathematical tasks, and in readings and grammar exercises for Polish and foreign languages.

Metallurgy and coal mining were particularly popular, followed by the chemical industry and shipyards, which Poland had never had before. The automotive industry and fishing were also developing. Textbooks presented particular factories and construction sites that were changing over time. In the 1950s the most popular were the Nowa Huta steelworks near Cracow and the railway car factory (PaFaWag) in Wrocław, while in the 1970s the oil refinery in Płock enjoyed the attention of both the press and textbooks.

Tracing the changes of economic topics over time, one can notice that in the 1940s, post-war reconstruction dominated the textbook narratives, alongside the first reforms introduced by the communists in Poland: agrarian reform and the nationalization of industry, and the "battle for trade" that had just started.

The speed and scope of post-war reconstruction must have impressed readers. The aptness of the authorities' decisions was stressed, especially regarding Warsaw, where the government resided from the moment of the liberation of the city despite the ruins and the other effects of the German occupation. The authorities immediately decided to reconstruct bridges and precious monuments; construct new wide transport routes; build beautiful residential districts for workers to replace old, unpleasant working class houses; and to bring other fresh ideas in urban development to life. The reconstruction of Warsaw was linked to almost every school subject. In physics it illustrated phenomena otherwise related to construction work and water supply; in chemistry, the use of various substances such as metals in construction works; in mathematics, calculating construction parameters and the efficiency of the workers. Geography books provided general descriptions of the city. Music textbooks published songs about Warsaw, Polish language textbooks discussed the aspects of construction and use of rebuilt objects, while foreign language texts usually stressed the immensity of the war devastation and expressed pride at the speed and scope of the reconstruction. In the following decades, admiration for Warsaw and its reconstruction was limited to geography, science and languages. The administrative functions of the city as the Party and government headquarters were always mentioned. The Palace of Culture and Science (the tallest building in Warsaw, built in the 1950s as a gift of the Soviet nation to the Polish people), for many years was the place where such natural phenomena as atmospheric pressure, the horizon or elevator speed could be observed and many calculations performed—apparently better than anywhere else, according to the textbooks.

The nationalization of industry was regarded as an important factor that accelerated the reconstruction of industry and its further development after the war damage. These reforms were praised beginning in books for the 1st grade. Both arguments of social justice and economic efficiency were used. Factories and mines did not bring profits solely to their private owners anymore. The owners used to be foreigners who had exploited Polish workers—claimed the textbooks

20 *Primary School Textbook Propaganda*

for sciences when dealing with the issues of mining and metallurgy. Polish language readers were presented with vivid images of exploitation. Once the factories became state-owned, they were called "our" or "common". The profits went to the state treasury: in other words, all citizens benefited. The state looked after the development of each and every factory, entire industries, the economy of Poland and the well-being of the workers. Nationalization was said to have facilitated management. Textbooks claimed that the socialist economy made it possible to easily predict the performance of individual companies, to enforce certain decisions and to invest in long-term or costly endeavors that private proprietors could not afford. As a result, the authorities ensured the harmonious economic development of the country.

Agrarian reform was presented as the very first reform of the "people's" government, introduced immediately after the "liberation" of the first Polish territories following the war. It was said to fulfill the eternal dreams of Polish farmers that had been largely ignored by the nobility and state authorities. Thus, the new government cared for its citizens more than any previous one. This enthusiasm was expressed in Polish language, history, geography and mathematics textbooks.

The so-called socialization (*uspołecznienie*) of trade and services started in the 1940s. So did the general and textbook propaganda that supported the process. Trade was presented in the most detailed way. Apparently, the textbook narratives corresponded with the propaganda and political campaign called "the battle for trade" emerging in the late 1940s and early 1950s. The word "cooperative" replaced "shop" in Polish textbooks well into the 1980s. In the 1940s, when privately owned shops were quite common, textbooks persuaded pupils to shop at cooperative and state-owned establishments. First of all, profits did not go to private owners, but benefited every member of the cooperative or society as a whole. They were usually invested in order to further develop the business. Second, textbooks praised the quality of service and prices at collectively owned firms. Private shops were characterized as dirty, untidy, poorly supplied and expensive. Cooperative shops, on the other hand, always provided a fresh assortment of high quality goods at moderate prices and obeyed all the rules of hygiene. Shop assistants were polite, neat and honest, unlike their counterparts in private businesses. High profits were not the primary goal of those shops. Serving customers' needs was their priority. As a result, people in the countryside did not have to travel to town to do their everyday shopping anymore. But if by any chance they went to the city, they could enjoy newly opened "Public Department Stores". In the 1940s and 1950s they were promoted particularly in textbooks for the youngest readers, beginning in reading primers. Pupils were to be impressed by their size, decoration, choice of goods, affordable prices, long opening hours and nice, professional service. Mothers and children were proud that the "people's authorities" cared about the time and money of ordinary people.

The beginning of the 1950s was the period of the "construction of socialism" in Poland. The primary goal was to fulfill the Six Year Plan. Its main provisions included even faster industrialization, the collectivization of agriculture, the reconstruction of the country and the "battle for trade". The plan was presented in textbooks for all school subjects. It testified to the ambition, courage and wisdom of the government which had elaborated its details. Textbooks stressed how hard large-scale planning was and what wonderful benefits the plan would bring.

The Six Year Plan was preceded by the Three Year Plan of post-war reconstruction scheduled for 1947–1949. In 1947 textbooks were relatively free of propaganda and not involved in contemporary political campaigns. More and more data was introduced toward the completion of the plan. They proved that the results exceeded expectations, which testified to the value of planning, to the wisdom of the planners, the potential of the country and the progress achieved in a relatively short period as compared not only to post-war damage, but also to pre-war times. The year 1938 served as a point of reference for many indicators.

Five year plans that were introduced after 1956, in the Soviet manner, usually were not discussed in textbooks—probably in part because the books stopped changing every year and were not as engaged in current political issues as under Stalinism. However, they still presented a great deal of statistics to show the progress of the People's Republic of Poland in various fields.

Collective farms were actually never introduced in Poland on a large scale, but were constantly promoted in school textbooks. The campaign peaked in the early 1950s, but was continued until the 1980s. Whole separate chapters of books presented the advantages of collective farming. It was connected with all the school subjects. State-owned and cooperative farms were said to implement "scientific" methods of agriculture, such as the selection of seeds and the care of plants (biology) with chemical fertilizers (chemistry). Mechanization was praised in physics textbooks, while the benefits of joining the collective farms (higher crops and farmers' income) were calculated in mathematics. Readings described how the everyday life of farmers changed in the collective farms. They enjoyed access to culture, and had modern houses equipped with electricity, radio and various amenities that individual farmers usually could not afford. Some modern technologies—such as tractors—could not be implemented in small private farms.

The tractor enjoyed particular attention, and even reverence, in the eyes of textbook authors. It exemplified work, power and energy in physics; fuel production and use in chemistry; while in mathematics pupils were asked to calculate how many people and horses a tractor could replace. The subject appeared also in science and biology textbooks. Songs and poems about tractor drivers were to be learned by heart in music and Polish language lessons. Being a tractor driver was the dream profession of textbook children.

The collectivization campaign was discontinued after 1956, at least on the political level, but individual farmers did not return to school textbooks. Generally, agriculture enjoyed less attention—which could be due to the fact that the country had industrialized and farming was not as important as in the 1940s, but most likely also due the lack of achievements of collective farming. In reality it turned out that privately owned farms were more effective, but the textbooks still claimed that state-owned farms used the best, scientifically proven contemporary technologies, and offered help to individual farmers.

22 Primary School Textbook Propaganda

Industry was still present in textbooks after 1956. Mining, metallurgy and machine production were discussed and the chemical, shipbuilding and automobile industries were presented as developing and modern. New places were mentioned, such as the copper mining basin near Legnica and Polkowice, the "Friendship" pipeline, oil refineries in Płock and Gdańsk, and the Gdańsk Northern Harbor. Texts concentrated on the technological processes in those areas rather than on praising communist authorities for developing industry, but the pupils were still shown the image of a flourishing country enjoying continual economic growth.

Social care was another important sphere of activity for communist authorities. Not only did they care about macro-economic progress, but also about the well-being of all citizens. The People's Republic of Poland was often compared to pre-war times, and always performed better.

In the 1940s and 1950s the newly introduced welfare system was presented. At that time it was an important argument in support of the communist regime. Textbooks for various subjects portrayed workers at construction sites and families moving to new apartments. The apartments were equipped with electricity, gas, running water and central heating. The details of the construction process were described in Polish language readings that also emphasized the happiness of the new residents. Biology used the example of the newly constructed apartments when healthcare was discussed. Physics described how their water supply worked. Geography characterized the industrial cities. Mathematics calculated the parameters of the new houses.

Similarly, the development of healthcare and of the education system were discussed. The authorities were said to care deeply about working conditions, wanting to build more and more schools to make it possible for thousands of people to obtain education for free (though in reality, Poland still lagged behind Western European countries in the percentage of people completing higher education), to secure summer holiday facilities for miners and shipyard workers (though other people had problems finding a place to stay during holiday due to an insufficient number of good-quality hotels). Textbooks praised cultural and service facilities in the countryside and in the newly constructed residential districts in the cities, but in many cases this was wishful thinking rather than a reflection of reality.

Electrification was rightly regarded as a condition for progress in the countryside. In the 1940s and 1950s science, geography, physics, mathematics and Polish language textbooks presented its implementation in detail. The number of villages and households with electricity grew much faster than in the pre-war years. It was regarded as proof of the superiority of the planned socialist economy over the capitalist economy, and of the care that the new authorities took of farmers. Once a village was electrified, its residents could benefit from radio, libraries, and daycare, as well as new household appliances, such as washing machines, refrigerators, irons and vacuum cleaners, and from agricultural machines. Since the machines made work easier and faster, people could enjoy more free time and could more easily participate in social and political activities.

Textbooks constantly stressed the role of the "people's" authorities in civilizational changes. The government was said to have initiated and coordinated all those endeavors and to take care of its citizens. Until the last years of the People's Republic of Poland, textbooks published statistics that showed the development of education and healthcare and of the availability of electrical appliances and cars, and compared them to pre-war levels.

State policy towards women and children was also dealt with until the collapse of the regime. The model of the "working woman" was promoted. Female engineers, teachers and sometimes other professionals were presented. Working forewomen were the mothers of textbook children. The socialist state offered them free childcare: nurseries and kindergartens (sometimes located in or near factory buildings), schools and daycare, summer camps and healthcare.

Thus, the socialist state took care of various groups of citizens which had been previously discriminated against, but each group was treated separately. There were benefits for workers, women and children, but not for families. The model of summer holiday is symptomatic in this regard: each parent and every sibling spent holiday separately, in a different time and place. The state did not help parents bring up their children; it sought to replace parents. As it took care of its citizens, the state wished to prevent them from initiating any activities on their own. The authorities were said to know better how to organize people's lives and direct them, and were proud of the results.

Representatives of the State

The state or state authorities, sometimes the government, appeared in textbooks as a collective body, not as individuals. At the beginning of the 1950s some leaders were portrayed, especially Bolesław Bierut. His cult did not reach the level of the leaders of other countries of the Soviet bloc, such as Stalin in the Soviet Union, Tito in Yugoslavia or Hoxha in Albania. One can hardly find any mention of post-1956 Party leaders. Collectively ministries, "national councils" (local governments), district committees, police, army or anonymous mayors personified state authority.

The army appeared from time to time in textbooks for various subjects, but one could not speak of military propaganda in those books, with the exception of military training and some Polish language textbooks. They presented the origins of the People's Army, its military path and its role in the post-war years, creating the myth of an army that served ordinary people and helped them in need (e.g. during harvest or in case of floods). Soldiers always received a warm welcome from textbook children and adults.

The People (or Citizens)

The authorities were in charge of the People's Republic of Poland, but the people were also an indispensable part of it. Textbooks wrote either about the citizens or about the Polish nation, and emphasized its unity and cohesion. Very seldom,

24 *Primary School Textbook Propaganda*

only in the upper grades and only in Stalinist times, were class enemies mentioned as those who tried to oppose the ongoing reforms (e.g. calling the builders of Nowa Huta names or sabotaging collective farms). In general, however, following the principle of presenting expectations as reality, all textbook characters actively supported the new system and the new authorities. The idealization of society, ignoring any problems, protests or doubts was another instrument of political propaganda in the textbooks.

What is striking is that the textbook society consisted only of workers and farmers. Workers especially were omnipresent. When someone was picking up a stone in an example in a physics textbook, it was not just a man, but a worker picking up a stone. Workers, not just people, saved money in mathematics, were sick and recovered in biology, or worked with lime in chemistry. They appeared in numerous poems, stories and songs. Farmers were popular in the first post-war years, but later appeared only occasionally. Professionals were represented by engineers, and sometimes also by teachers and doctors.

Positive attitudes towards socialist Poland could be expressed by ordinary people in the form of interest, acceptance or engagement.

Both adults and children in textbook readings **were interested** in the Polish economy and politics. The authorities must have expected a similar interest among pupils, hence the saturation of books for all the subjects and grades with those issues. Textbooks were extremely serious and did not even try to hide the intentions of policymakers. One could wonder, however, if the tone and content of the texts evoked pupils' interest or rather wearied them.

The attitude of **acceptance** was promoted in similar ways. Lots of textbook narratives expressed enthusiasm for post-war Poland. The same was expected from readers. Textbooks left no doubt about how to judge reality. They did not refrain from clear, one-sided opinions and commentaries, and did not just present facts.

Textbooks gave numerous examples of citizens **engaged** in the country's life. They also asked questions and gave direct recommendations to readers, urging them to get involved in various events, activities, organizations, cooperatives and so forth. What is noticeable is that the activities of the textbook characters were seldom spontaneous. They were usually initiated and directed by the authorities and supported the system.

Most examples of engagement came from organizations and institutions. Youth organizations were particularly promoted. Their members attended meetings and school events, helped the old and the weak or farmers on collective farms, and participated in excursions, camps and bonfires. All these activities were presented in a positive light, with the apparent goal to encourage pupils to follow and join the organizations. Textbook adults were mostly just individuals, sometimes members of trade unions, but only sporadically of the Communist Party. Surprisingly, the Party generally did not appear in the books. The government took credit for all the positive changes in Poland, though in fact decision-making processes took place within Party structures.

Forms of citizens' engagement changed with time. In the 1940s they participated in the post-war reconstruction, especially of Warsaw, of factories and schools. Many texts presented settlers coming to the "Recovered Territories" in the West and North. They emphasized the benefits of resettlement. Any difficulties were mentioned only in the past tense. The characters of the 1940s textbooks fulfilled their civic duties (such as taxes or payments in kind) and volunteered to spend time and money on extra activities. In those times there was still room for some grassroot projects initiated by local communities, such as construction or renovation of a road or a bridge, planting trees, draining meadows, and so forth.

In the 1950s fulfilment of the Six Year Plan became the top priority of good citizens. Textbooks were full of working foremen, mentioned by name (miners Pstrowski and Markiewka were the most popular, followed by bricklayers Krajewski and Poręcki) or by profession (miners, metallurgists, female weavers). Other people just did their jobs, but always keeping in mind their duties and the plan. Labor competition, "rationalization" (i.e. inventing new, more effective methods of work) and thriftiness became the main virtues of the time. They were promoted by many disciplines, usually in relation to the economic issues discussed. In the decades to follow, textbooks promoted similar values, but not so intensively.

In the countryside of the 1950s good citizens were expected to join the so-called production cooperatives (i.e. the collective farms), or even better to establish one and encourage others to join. They enthusiastically welcomed electrification and mechanization of their farms and households, and sent their children to school and vocational training.

Even children participated in the Six Year Plan. Any activity could be regarded as participation in this project, such as going to school and getting good grades, not to mention such extra activities as planting trees during the forest festival, collecting waste paper or rugs, or taking potato beetles from the fields. Children organized their own cooperatives at schools, which sold stationery and food and had the same characteristics as the "adult" cooperative shops: good management, honest and nice shop assistants, high-quality goods, and convenience for pupils who could buy what they needed without leaving the school premises. Profits from the cooperative supplied the school with funds.

Both children and adults participated in various mass events where they could publicly express their support for the government, for its leaders and for the People's Republic of Poland. Important holidays (such as May 1st, International Workers' Day; July 22nd, the anniversary of the communist takeover; and November 7th, the anniversary of the October Revolution in Russia) were usually preceded by so-called campaigns (*czyny*) when workers did something special (e.g. completed the plan ahead of schedule or took on some extra duties). Special events, such as Party Congresses or Stalin's birthday, were celebrated in a similar way. Libraries, schools and farms benefited from the "campaigns".

Even after the Six Year Plan had been completed, a professional career remained the main occupation of textbook adults. They spent their spare time on some so-called socially useful works—as volunteers in some community projects. Children followed their example.

In the 1960s and 1970s there were even more celebrations than before. The main holidays did not change, and included May 1st, May 9th (V-Day celebrated

26 Primary School Textbook Propaganda

according to Soviet regulations), and July 22nd (the anniversary of the July Manifesto of the Polish Committee of National Liberation that gave power to the Communist Party in Poland after World War II). Miners' Day, Women's Day and Children's Day were also mentioned on a regular basis. It seems that in the case of celebrations, the main goal of putting them into school curricula was not to generate support for the government, but to form a new lay calendar of holidays and patterns of celebrations in order to replace Christian traditions.

Starting in the 1960s, good citizens (and good pupils) were interested in and supportive of space flights, especially Soviet ones. They were also fond of new technologies and their implementation in Poland.

In the 1980s only some community projects remained, such as caring for one's school and neighborhood, or collecting waste paper. Celebrations were described only in Polish language readings, and were limited to the ones that took place at schools. Students' self-government was a new phenomenon in textbooks.

A Socialist Set of Values

Textbooks tried to replace traditional Catholic values with new socialist ones. Even if some of the new virtues were not explicitly mentioned, their main elements were apparent.

A "scientific world view" was openly promoted, with its two main aspects of atheism and human omnipotence. Textbooks for all school subjects, and especially for the sciences, tried to persuade readers that the world was entirely material and wholly cognizable. However, many natural phenomena were too difficult to explain at the primary school level, and pupils had to trust the authors that scientific explanations existed and were better than other (e.g. religious) ones.

The examples of human power were probably more convincing. Numerous images of man transforming the world were presented, such as "taming" nuclear energy in physics, designing new organic compounds with desired characteristics in chemistry, growing new kinds of plants and animals in biology and large-scale projects for transforming the natural environment in geography (e.g. foresting the steppes or reversing the flow of Siberian rivers). Information about these kinds of projects was usually accompanied with enthusiastic statements of human potential.

Textbooks repeated over and over again that the exploration, use and transformation of the environment helped overcome prejudices that had grown for ages. The Catholic Church was presented as a bastion of these prejudices. In the 1950s and 1980s the word Church was spelled with a small "c". When irrational superstitious explanations of natural phenomena were mentioned, it was usually emphasized that they had been recognized by the Church for many, many years. Textbooks discussed how the Church had persecuted such illustrious scholars as Giordano Bruno, Galileo or the first aviators.

Two factors are worth noticing with regard to the way that scientific evidence and the Catholic Church were presented. First, scientific research and theories were usually labeled as either progressive or backward, just as many other aspects of life. Whatever was approved by contemporary science was regarded as progressive. All theories that were eventually rejected were ridiculed or labeled as backward from the very beginning. The main "progressive" theories included Darwinism in biology, the atomic theory in physics and chemistry, and the Copernican model of the universe in geography. Not only did the textbooks disapprove of any alternative scientific theories or views, but they denied any academic recognition or even respect for their authors and supporters (both past and present). Researchers could not make mistakes. Whoever accepted false theories was regarded as a fool.

Second, the Church appeared in the textbooks as an extremely one-sided, political institution. Its religious role was simply omitted. Policymakers avoided any philosophical debates that could raise doubts or encourage independent reflection. Therefore, the very existence of God or other religious issues was not mentioned at all. As a political or scientific institution, the Church must have seemed outdated, silly and unnecessary. This was enough to question the authority it enjoyed among the Polish people—if the Church was wrong in the case of science and politics, why should it be right about other issues?—and it seemed to satisfy the propaganda needs of the regime.

Another method of propaganda implemented in regard to the Church was ignoring some (troublesome) aspects of reality. Thus, any references in literature or art to Christianity, or to God and faith, were totally ignored. Greek and Roman myths were cited in the Polish language textbooks, but the Bible was not. Writers and poets seemed to deal only with social or political issues, sometimes also with the beauty of nature, but never with philosophical or religious issues. They never raised any doubts or reflected on the meaning of life. Contemporary characters in textbooks had no reflections or religious activities either. Christian culture disappeared from textbooks in the late 1940s.

The scientific world view meant eliminating all non-material phenomena. All elements of fantasy were subsequently removed from textbooks, starting with fairy tales and magical characters from the school readers. The world of textbooks was frightfully realistic.

Individuals in the textbooks were dominated by the state and society. Books made it clear that the common good was much more important than personal interests. Textbook characters always played some social role. They were workers, members of various organizations, representatives of the authorities. Their family roles appeared only in the background, if at all. Each individual, not only prominent politicians or researchers, should sacrifice his or her private life for a professional career.

In order to serve society, individuals should be active. Therefore, the textbooks promoted activism. Their characters never philosophized. They had no time for existential doubts. In the black-and-white world of textbooks the right decisions were obvious. People did not debate or reflect. Everybody had a task to fulfill and worked hard to accomplish it. Job completion brought true satisfaction. Fulfilling the plan or serving others were shown as the life goals of most textbook characters.

28 *Primary School Textbook Propaganda*

Last but not least, textbooks promoted the so-called people's patriotism and internationalism. Readers were to identify with Poland under communist rule and with the Soviet bloc. Friendship with other nations was also mentioned, but often in the context of the "struggle for peace". Friends and allies in the struggle were quite limited in scope and included the Soviet bloc, the working class, and oppressed and exploited peoples of the world.

Let us put aside our general discussion on the nature of textbook propaganda and of the educational goals of the communist regime, and commence a detailed analysis of each of the school subjects in question.

Note

1 According to a popular joke, the difference between democracy and people's democracy resembled the difference between a chair and an electric chair.

3 Maths and Sciences

Mathematics

Most post–World War II textbooks for arithmetic in primary schools were authored by Antoni Maria Rusiecki and Wacław Schayer. Rusiecki died in 1956 and Schayer in 1959, but the last edition of their book for the 1st grade appeared as late as 1975. Rusiecki was a pre-war textbook author who worked in the PZWS publishing house. Schayer worked in the Ministry of Education and reached the rank of vice minister. Textbooks for higher grades were usually authored by academics, though Bolesław Iwaszkiewicz, an algebra textbooks author, was also politically active. He was a member of parliament, an alderman in the city of Wrocław and co-organizer of the Mathematical Olympiad in Poland. Only the mid-1970s brought deeper changes in the concept of teaching mathematics at primary school, and in the team of textbook authors. The textbooks were no longer just sets of tasks, but devoted much more space to presenting theory and thus limited the amount of propaganda content. In the 1980s experimental textbooks were introduced and two sets of books (not just one) developed for the early stages of education.

One could think that mathematics as a "pure science" would be free from propaganda. History shows us, however, that this is not necessarily the case. Lisa Pine discussed, for example, the impact of the Nazi regime on German textbooks for this subject and cited examples of military planes and bombs to count and of disseminating Nazi ideology.[1] John Rodden presented excerpts from GDR textbooks dealing with production issues and the activities of pioneers, but also with some military-related examples.[2] Textbooks from the People's Republic of Poland were not militaristic, but they did refer to propaganda issues from the school curricula and Party guidance. The authors were praised by ministerial officials and by the censorship office for including political elements in their works. According to the curriculum from the 1950s,

> practice material should be based on statistical data pertaining to the economic reconstruction and achievements of industrialization, mechanization and electrification of rural areas, increasing work efficiency, production volumes, the development of culture etc. Continual mention of topics related to

30   Maths and Sciences

production cooperatives in agriculture, department stores, cooperatives and other forms of economy of the socialist country will acquaint young people with current issues in the country and will help prepare them for participation in social and political life. Exercises discussing planning deserve special attention.[3]

In the 1960s and 1970s the explanation was shorter, but still "An appropriate understanding and mastering of the teaching material by pupils requires [. . .] particular examples taken from practical life, from technology and the economic achievements of the People's Poland and of natural phenomena that pupils are familiar with".[4] Eventually, in the 1980s "by including problems related to social and economic life in the exercises, [the teaching of mathematics] should contribute to the learning and understanding of the issues involved in the country's development".[5]

Exercises were sometimes grouped according to the political, not mathematical, issues they dealt with. Titles were added to these groups such as "In the workers' day room", "In the factory city", "In the cooperative shop", "In the coalmine", "July 22nd—a Holiday of Independence and Rebirth", and so forth. The language of the exercises included vocabulary and phrases used in communist newspapers. Some other words were eliminated and replaced with "politically correct" ones (e.g. shops were called cooperatives, and the word "profit" was replaced by "surplus").[6] Some exercises contained long introductions or comments completely unrelated to mathematics, such as: "On the fields of a state-owned farm, a combine-harvester is working. It cuts the grain and simultaneously threshes it. The threshed grain is collected by cars".[7] There was no mathematical content in these two sentences at all. A similarly lengthy technological description referred to a "huge port crane". Sometimes the questions asked in the exercises had no connection to mathematics whatsoever. For example, in one exercise about Szczecin, a 1965 textbook asked "Why do you think the port in Szczecin is developing so fast?"[8] After comparing pre- and post–World War II production volumes of potatoes and sugar beetroots in Poland, a student was asked: "What caused the increase of this production? Try to find out what our industry does with the beetroots and potatoes that are not allocated for consumption".[9] Another exercise started with "Czechoslovakia, Poland and Sweden produce 93 tons of aluminum" and ended with "Do you know where our aluminum smelter is located?"[10]

Arithmetic was more likely to include propaganda content than geometry, but in the 1950s and 1960s even geometry took examples from the "real life" of propaganda. So, for instance, the surface area of Constitution Square in Warsaw was to be calculated, and the length and width of the State Planning Commission building or of the Party Headquarters were to be read from the plans presented in the textbooks. Younger children compared the heights of the chimneys in the "famous coal mine Zabrze-East" and of the houses along the newly constructed East-West Route in Warsaw.

Illustrations in mathematics textbooks were sometimes also propagandist either in content or in aesthetics, resembling socialist realism-style posters. Some

Maths and Sciences   31

of them did not help in understanding mathematical issues, but presented socialist themes such as farming, road construction, roofers or welders at work.

Sometimes a particular exercise was not necessarily propagandist, but the accumulation of similar exercises turned them into propaganda. At the end of the 1940s we may observe how, without changing the numbers, the content of the books changed so that they became more related to politics and the economy. Therefore, instead of the dwarves who lived in a cave (sixty dwarves left the cave while four remained inside), there were cars leaving a garage after being washed (thirty had already left while four remained to be washed). The pots that a potter was selling were transformed into pots on display in a department store.[11]

Three main propaganda issues can be identified in the content of mathematics textbooks: the economic progress of the People's Poland, the progress of civilization and propaganda regarding the engagement of the citizens of the People's Republic of Poland in the country's life.

Economic Progress of the People's Poland

Economic issues were the most thoroughly explored. Poland was presented as a country with a vibrant economy. Exercises presented state farms, state machinery centers, production cooperatives (collective farms) and other kinds of cooperatives: dairy, egg, food, school or clothing cooperatives. Shops were presented not as just shops but either as "cooperatives", or as "Public Department Stores" (*powszechne domy towarowe*) or as shops of the Ministry of Retail. There were also fish distribution centers, cowsheds, hatcheries, various types of factories (producing textiles, clothes, cars, trains, shoes, bags, balls, furniture, porcelain, soap, vinegar, ice, meat products, canned food, sugar), bakeries, mills, brickyards, power plants, coal mines, steelworks, glassworks, ports, factory canteens, storages, wholesale markets and libraries. Some places were mentioned by name, such as Nowa Huta near Cracow, the Automobile Factory in Warsaw (FSO), Petrochemia (oil refinery) in Płock and the coal mine Zabrze-East. In the exercises they produced various goods from the raw materials they received. The goods were then transported to storage and wholesale stores and either appeared in the shops or were used as material in the production of other goods. Transporting things from one place to another was one of the most popular themes of the exercises. The transported goods included such items as milk, eggs, flour, sugar, wheat, cheese, herring, horses, geese in coops, salt, candies, tomato pulp, tea, apples, oil, lard, alcohol, cement, roof tiles, lime, wood, coal, hay, straws, fertilizers, scrap, screws, iron beams, electric poles, paper, newspapers, glasses, soap and so forth. Workers, soldiers and children were also transported from one place to another.

The textbooks stressed that the goods were produced by state- or cooperative-owned companies. They were later placed in state- or cooperative-owned storage or shops, often just called cooperatives. In some textbooks the word "shop" did not appear at all, and was totally replaced by "cooperative".

Workers, farmers and soldiers appeared most often in the exercises. Soldiers almost never fought, but generally took part in parades, rode trains, or were drilled

32 Maths and Sciences

to form various shapes. Children often pretended to be soldiers and marched or were drilled. Craftsmen were replaced with various kinds of cooperatives.

The exercises promoted new collective forms of economy and of work. An exercise about roofers who laid 41.85 m^2 of roof per day followed one about a state-owned construction company that had a team of roofers who, according to the norm, was able to lay 88.5 m^2 of roof, but when they joined a labor competition they covered 112 3/4 m^2 of roof during the first day and 127.8 m^2 during the second day.[12] The superiority of collective versus individual work was stressed. In some exercises, pupils were openly asked to compare the effectiveness of an individual worker with that of a team: "One worker produces 7 concrete plates in a quarter of an hour, while a team of three workers in the same time produces 30 plates. How many more plates does a worker in a team produce than if he worked individually?"[13]

In the countryside, state-owned farms and cooperatives were compared with private farms. In Stalinist times, the conclusions were sometimes explicitly written in the exercises themselves:

> Thanks to more sophisticated cultivation methods a production cooperative collected 160 bushels of wheat from 1 hectare, while individual farms collected only 12 bushels from 1 hectare. The cooperative earned 105 zlotys for a bushel of its wheat, while individual farms 100 zlotys for one bushel. Calculate how much more money from 1 hectare the wheat brought in the cooperative than in the individual farms.[14]

Usually, however, individual farms were simply neglected and agricultural issues were identified either with state-owned or collective farms. Pupils calculated field surface and livestock, estimated mechanization or planned investments. In the villages of the state-owned farms, new houses and new roads were constructed, new schools opened and electrification was in progress. Machines did a lot of work in the fields.

In Stalinist times, when the collectivization of agriculture was most intensively promoted, some exercises illustrated the benefits it brought to a family who joined the cooperative:

> A farmer joined a new type of production cooperative. There were 4 people working in his family. Their daily wages brought 14,800 zlotys, while the daily wages of their pair of horses and a plough brought 2400 zlotys. 1600 zlotys came from the land contribution. The annual income of the family turned out to be higher by 1/3 than that of an individual farm. Calculate how much more money the family earned after joining the cooperative than it would have with an individual farm.[15]

When presenting the economic development of the whole country, textbooks used real statistical data, especially about the production of various industries; these included mining, metallurgy, automobile and sugar factories; about the

Maths and Sciences 33

transportation of goods; a 1980 textbook even discussed birth rates (in that decade Poland experienced its second post-war baby boom). In the 1950s some outstanding workers were mentioned by name. For instance, 7th graders did the following exercise:

> In response to the famous appeal of Wiktor Markiewka, a miner who, in January 1950, invited Polish workers to take part in a long-term work competition, drivers from Warsaw made a long-term commitment. A female driver, Maria Kolska, committed herself to drive 72,000 kilometers in her Renault car without an overhaul, which is 1/6 more than the norm for this car.[16]

The data referred not only to achievements, but often also to economic plans, especially the Three and Six Year Plans. Pupils were supposed to calculate the expected results of the plan, for example in the productivity of farm land after mechanization and with better supplies.

Sometimes anonymous factories which had increased their productivity thanks to "rationalization" of production were presented.

> In a railway workshop a brigade spent 4.5 hours examining one locomotive. After the implementation of a rationalizing idea by one of the workers, that time was shortened by 1/6. How many more locomotives were examined by that brigade during 45 hours of work?[17]

The main goal of some exercises seemed to be to impress pupils with the output of the Polish economy and with the numbers that the planners were dealing with, as in the following examples: "A workers' brigade made a commitment to put 27,500 rivets in a bridge in a 4-day time span",[18] or "In a state-owned farm 21,600 eggs were placed in hatching machines" out of which 19,872 chickens were hatched.[19] Still other examples: "An automatic nail-machine makes 6 nails per second",[20] or

> During a production meeting a coal mine crew made a commitment to achieve productivity of 1482 kilograms of coal per worker per day. Calculate how many 15-ton railway cars of coal this mine will produce during 30 days if it has a crew of 2250 people.[21]

The textbooks also presented technological processes and technical parameters of various branches of industry. For example, they told how much sugar could be obtained from sugar beetroots, flour and bran from grain, heat or electricity from coal, and starch from potatoes. Pupils learned how heavy a liter of spirit or a piece of sheet metal was. They familiarized themselves with the loading capacities of various types of railway cars or ships; the size of various types of bricks or pavement plates; the distance between telephone or electricity poles or between train track underlays; the numbers of rivets, pads and underlays used in the tracks; and the proportions of ingredients of petroleum, cement and various

34   Maths and Sciences

types of chemical fertilizers. The parameters of Polish cars, such as the Syrena, Fiat 126p or Star-20 (a truck), as well as tractors (Ursus, Zetor, Staliniec) were also presented.

Soviet spaceflights were portrayed as achievements of the socialist economy. Yuri Gagarin, Valentina Tereshkova and Herman Titov were mentioned by name. Apparently, mathematical issues were not the most important in the exercise about Sputnik:

> The second artificial satellite to orbit the Earth weighed 508 kg, while the first one was 425 kg lighter. How much did it weigh? The first satellite was launched from the territory of the Soviet Union on October 4, 1957, while the second one on November 3, 1957. Who was the first cosmonaut? When did his flight take place?[22]

Progress of Civilization in the People's Republic of Poland

The progress of civilization in the People's Republic of Poland consisted of several factors. One of them was improved living conditions: more apartments were built, and they were of a higher standard. Numerous exercises asked pupils to calculate the number of windows in the new houses, the number of new apartments, their surface areas, the amount of materials used or the time spent on the construction of new houses. These exercises were often accompanied by pictures.

The progress of education was also acclaimed. The number of new schools available to everybody grew. Tables presenting the number of pupils in various types of schools in pre-war and post-war times served as an illustration of this phenomenon. One non-mathematical task was given as "Think about why so many young people can be educated today".[23] Libraries of various kinds (local, school, factory) were presented. New libraries were organized and their collections grew. "There were 746 books in a local village library. The workers from a nearby factory donated 178 books. The funds from an education week fundraising made it possible to buy some number of books".[24] Day rooms and houses of culture for the workers were operating.

The development of healthcare in the People's Republic of Poland was praised. Statistics presenting the number of people per doctor or the production of pharmaceuticals before and after the war were used.

The state used various ways to show its concern for workers. They were offered managerial positions.

> During the three years from 1947 to 1949 in the coal mines of the People's Poland, 837 miners were promoted to managerial positions as directors and deputy directors, and to positions in mid- and high-level technical supervision. Out of this number, 817 miners were promoted in 1949.[25]

Workers were offered loans or installment plans, if needed, and vacation in the summer. The Employee Vacation Fund (*Fundusz Wczasów Pracowniczych*), founded in 1949 by a special bill of parliament and managed by the trade unions, was promoted. The Fund monopolized the holiday infrastructure in Poland. Workers had to have special referrals from their companies to be able to take advantage of the FWP's offer. Textbooks did not mention any of these obstacles, but simply presented the offer of the Fund and the growing number of employees who used it. According to one of the textbooks, in 1949 it encompassed 504,000 workers, forty-two times more than in 1945.[26] It is remarkable that the textbooks always presented the individual holiday of a worker or of a pupil, but never of a family.

The progress of civilization in the countryside included electrification and activation of radio and telephone services. Many exercises presented the mechanization of agriculture, the melioration of land or the use of chemical fertilizers. Their positive influence on crops was shown, but also on the quality and speed of farmers' work. The harvest before and after melioration was to be compared, the consumption of grain in manual sowing and by a mechanical seeder, the speed of plowing using horses and tractors. Pupils were told how many horses, men or older machines could be replaced by new equipment: for example, in the process of tillage, a tractor did the work of twenty horses, while "a big Soviet tractor" did the work of thirty.[27]

Engagement of the Citizens

Many exercises tried to shape the moral character of the citizens of the People's Republic of Poland. They promoted their engagement in the country's life.

Patterns to follow were set out. Workers who took part in labor competitions and exceeded plans, people undertaking community work, such as road construction or forestation, or being engaged in the cultural development of their neighborhood, served as good examples. The founders and members of agricultural cooperatives were also praised.

School cooperatives, where pupils could buy mostly stationery and sometimes also other products, were promoted. The exercises illustrated the growing membership of such cooperatives, presented the work of their treasurers and cashiers, asked pupils to calculate their daily balance sheets and other financial documents, and discussed sales and product acquisition. Exercises about food cooperatives (i.e. food shops) raised similar issues.

The volunteer work of pupils at school was also presented, such as tending the school garden, planting trees, cleaning the area around the school, organizing events—especially May 1st and Children's Day—and competitions in collecting waste paper. Schoolchildren were members of the scouting organization: "What does it mean that 100% of sixth-graders are scouts?" one of the exercises asked.[28] The activities of the scouts were also calculated: their meetings, summer camps, excursions. During Stalinist times, "Service for Poland" (*Służba Polsce*), a communist paramilitary youth organization, was also presented in the most positive light.

Saving money in general and particularly in the "School Savings Fund" (*Szkolna Kasa Oszczędności*) was promoted. Thrift was a virtue in mathematics

36 *Maths and Sciences*

textbooks, with respect to both schoolchildren and adults. "Poland has about 24 million inhabitants. Calculate how many zlotys everyone would save annually if they all saved 1 *grosz* [cent] daily".[29] Textbook children and adults saved money to buy something, or just to compete in saving.

The model of the worker's spending was presented in some exercises. He paid his rent, bought food and sometimes clothes, spent some money on his "cultural needs", and always saved something. A pupil could see that workers' wages in the People's Republic of Poland exceeded their basic needs, which was, however, a mere piece of propaganda. Marek Hłasko, in his novel about the 1950s, wrote that his earnings as a driver hardly allowed him to survive. He could not even buy a suit, not to mention an apartment.[30]

Dates

Propaganda in school mathematics was also related to Roman numerals, which, in the Polish language, replace the names of months in dates. The dates of holidays were used to practice this notation, especially July 22nd (the anniversary of the establishment of communist rule in Poland, officially presented as the Holiday of Independence and Liberation, Holiday of Independence and Rebirth and later the Holiday of the Rebirth of Poland), as well as May 1st. Other holidays thus used included V-Day, celebrated in Poland as in the Soviet Union on May 9th, and November 7th—the anniversary of the October Revolution in Russia. They appeared in exercises and were printed either in bold or in red font, or displayed on pictures (e.g. of pages from a calendar), with some explanation of the character of a holiday. In the first post-war years religious holidays were also mentioned, but they were then either replaced with other holidays (e.g. New Year replaced Christmas, or it was simply omitted).

Pupils were supposed to recognize the holidays in the calendar or to calculate the day of the week, or were assigned other chronological tasks. They also calculated the deadlines of the production plans, the dates of future anniversaries (e.g. of the founding of the People's Poland or the establishment of the Polish United Workers' Party). Holiday celebrations were also mentioned, such as military parades on July 22nd, lectures and labor competitions, for example: "In a workers' housing estate 20 houses are being built. For the 1st of May celebrations seven of them were completed; for the 22nd of July, six more. How many houses remain to be completed?"[31] or "Three scouting teams promised to make 6 flying models of gliders before May 1st, and made 9 models more".[32]

For many years the following exercise was used: "Marysia is as old as the New Poland, since she was born in Chełm on July 22, 1944. How old is she now?"[33] In 1968 it was changed to "Ewa's uncle is as old as the New Poland". Interestingly, Chełm was one of the two cities where the July Manifesto of the communist regime was displayed in the first days of communist rule, while it obviously had no relation to the age of either Poland or Marysia. Nevertheless, it was mentioned.

***

In mathematics textbooks of the People's Poland one can observe how pre-war content was gradually abandoned in the 1940s. Exercises corresponding with young pupils' knowledge, abilities and interests were replaced with production-related tasks that dominated the Stalinist period. At the end of the 1950s some themes were eliminated (such as the Six Year Plan). However, until the 1970s textbooks were dominated by economy-related content. In the 1980s the total number of exercises decreased, including propaganda-related ones. As a result, the youngest pupils in the People's Republic of Poland had less contact with propaganda in mathematics.

Science

Science was taught as a school subject in various grades, depending on the time period. Until 1963, in the 3rd grade it served as an introduction to physics, chemistry, biology and geography, all of which were taught as separate subjects to older pupils (from 4th, 5th, 6th or 7th grade, depending on the subject). Between 1963 and 1980 science was continued also in the 4th and 5th grades and only in the 6th grade separated into physics, chemistry and biology (while geography was taught separately already in the fourth grade). Starting from 1978, science accompanied the "three r's" from the first until the third year of school, geography and biology started in the fourth grade, physics in the sixth and chemistry in the seventh.

In all grades and periods of time, one of the educational goals of the school subject "science" was to develop students' pride in the post–World War II achievements of Poland. The government, or more generally "the authorities" of the People's Poland were given credit for them. It was said that they cared for the harmonious development of the country, both its industry and its agriculture. Emphasis was also placed on workers' input: in the 1950s, textbooks addressed to students as early as the 3rd grade wrote about the participation of workers in the management of large enterprises, as well as how those workers expanded their competencies (owing to in-service training provided by the government and trade unions), labor competition and efficiency drives.

Coal-mining, metallurgy and residential construction were the most extensively portrayed branches of industry. The role played by coal and steel for the rest of industry was stressed. Children read that "Just as a man needs air and water to live, industry needs iron and steel".[34] Textbooks presented the interior and exterior of mines and steelworks alongside discussions of the work done by miners and metallurgists and how production levels in both branches were increasing. They described how building materials were produced and houses were built, and enumerated the building-related professions: engineers, bricklayers, carpenters, glaziers and others. All of them were said to enjoy the care of the state.

Science textbooks also dealt with various means of transport: car, train, airplane and water. In the 1980s, the automobile industry was noticed. Polish car makes were mentioned, and the Warsaw automobile plant (FSO) served as an example of a factory.[35]

38   Maths and Sciences

As for agriculture, the government's engagement included contracting deliveries of certain products (particularly pigs and flax).

Textbooks drew students' attention to changes in their neighborhoods. One of the popular techniques was to compare old, sometimes very old, tools and household appliances to new ones. Mechanization of both agriculture and industry was presented in detail. Industrial machines were shown in order to convince young pupils that factories were more efficient than craftsmen's workshops. The work of the individual craftsman was characterized as mundane, old-fashioned, unprofitable and lagging behind the growing needs of contemporary society. Factory workers enjoyed better working conditions, worked faster and more efficiently since each of them performed only one task while working together. The example of spinners versus textile factories was used.

> The work [of a female-spinner] is very slow and arduous. The spinner spins all evening but hardly makes any thread. The spinning department of a factory is so different! Hundreds of spindles rotate at a time at a speed beyond the reach of manual labor. [. . .] You must understand by now that work in a factory has to be far more efficient than in a village spinning workshop, and that one factory worker makes more thread to weave than hundreds of spinners could make on spinning-wheels at home".[36]

The textbooks tried to persuade students that the countryside was another place where efficient work was only possible in state-owned and collective farms, engaged in collective, mechanized production managed by educated specialists.

> Today, at state-owned farms the soil is processed by tractors. The tractor turns its wheels, the ploughs turn the soil, and the work proceeds rapidly. Agricultural cooperatives also have tractors. One tractor works in the fields of the cooperative members. The machinery centers house various tools. They are available to farmers from the nearby villages.[37]

The collectivization of agriculture was promoted in science textbooks mainly in the 1950s, just as in other school subjects. Later on, state-owned and collective farms were treated as the vanguard of progress in agriculture that slowly reached private, individual farms as well.

The "Farmers' Self-Reliance Union" (*Związek Samopomocy Chłopskiej*) was said to be the forerunner of progress, providing farmers with professional consultants, access to carefully selected seeds and purebred livestock, as well as to infrastructure, such as hatcheries, dairies and agricultural machines. As an illustration of the progress that had been made, old dirty wooden cottages were juxtaposed with clean, new brick houses on the pages of the textbooks. The same method was applied when placing old dark hovels alongside bright new spacious chicken farms, cowsheds and pigsties.

The cooperative shops operated by the Farmers' Self-Reliance Union were always clean, neat and well-stocked with products, in contrast to street vendors and privately owned shops, which were portrayed as dirty and empty, concentrated

Maths and Sciences 39

on bringing profit to the owners rather than on meeting customers' needs. As one of the textbooks advertised in 1951, "Every farmer should belong to the cooperative. Nobody will cheat him there, neither in buying nor selling, and the profit of the cooperative becomes the property of all members".[38] In the cities, the science textbooks promoted state-owned department stores in a similar manner.

The textbooks encouraged readers to establish cooperative libraries in the villages, where everybody would donate books that their fellow countryside inhabitants could later read. Other activities promoted in this manner included an annual rat extermination week in the 1940s, saving food and growing pigs, fighting the potato beetle, collecting scrap metal and growing corn; the most popular of them was the so-called Forest Festival, an annual tree-planting campaign.[39] The role of forests for nature and for the economy was stressed, as well as the devastation they had experienced during World War II and in pre-war Poland as a result of the "unplanned economy". The ecologically friendly plans of the communist authorities were highlighted.

As time passed, ecology occupied increasingly greater space in textbooks. However, the narratives concentrated solely on the legal regulations introduced by the regime. New parks and gardens were mentioned. Schoolchildren were encouraged to join the League for the Protection of Nature, and to get involved in the League's activities, which mostly consisted of following regulations and propagating the idea of protecting the natural environment.

Among the multitude of achievements of People's Poland, various accomplishments were promoted such as the breeding of new varieties of poultry and cattle, development of the automotive industry and railways, the country's leadership (second in the world after the USSR) in potato production, healthcare and improving living conditions of the population, and progress in electrification of the countryside.

Another area of interest for textbooks was the development of fruit orchards in Poland. Progress was noted, but also regarded as insufficient. The Soviet Union was set as an example to follow, and Ivan Michurin in particular was praised. The way he was presented in 3rd grade textbooks at the end of the 1950s illustrates the continual expansion of propaganda content in school textbooks of that period. In 1949, his achievements were mentioned in just two short sentences: "Frost-resistant fruit trees that do not freeze even during very cold winters were grown by the Soviet researcher I. Michurin. He engineered them to make their fruit beautiful, juicy and large".[40] In 1951, the paragraph was extended:

> You have probably heard about the famous Soviet researcher and gardener Michurin, who grew frost-resistant pears and many other valuable fruit trees and shrubs. He wanted every child in his country to have apples, even in the regions with long frosty winters. Thanks to his work, trees producing tasty apples and pears can grow and bear fruit in cold northern regions.[41]

In 1952, almost an entire page was devoted to the topic, with a large portrait of Michurin placed on the opposite page.

> There is one country where those obstacles have been overcome. In this country, there lived a man who found a way to have tasty fruit ripen everywhere.

40   *Maths and Sciences*

This country is the Soviet Union, and the man was the researcher and gardener Ivan Michurin. The Soviet Union is a huge country. [. . .] Ivan Michurin decided to grow fruit trees and bushes that would not freeze, even during the coldest frosts. He wanted every child to eat tasty fruit all year round. He devoted his whole life to this work, and achieved his goal. He succeeded in growing frost-resistant trees. Nowadays, in all the regions of the Soviet Union there are orchards where apple, pear and cherry trees grow and bear tasty, beautiful fruit. The children of the Soviet Union love the researcher-gardener and try to follow his example. In this way, they learn about how plants live and how to take care of and improve fruit trees. There also should be plenty of fruit in our country. We have to make sure that all children, in the cities and in the countryside, have enough fruit to eat. We are setting up large orchards in state-owned farms and production cooperatives. Year after year we have more and more fruit trees.[42]

In the 1980s, schoolchildren in the first three grades were acquainted not only with their neighborhood and the country, but also with the international position of Poland. A chapter titled "Cooperation with Other Countries" in the 3rd grade science textbook dealt with the lively relations between Poland and other socialist countries.[43] The benefits mentioned included the "Friendship" pipeline bringing petroleum from the Soviet city of Kuybyshev—a guarantee of defense and friendship. On the other hand, Polish sugar plants in Cuba were mentioned, alongside refineries and cement plants in Libya and roads in Iraq.

The core message of the "science" textbook was the superiority of communism over capitalism, of post–World War II Poland following the Soviet example over pre-war Poland, and of the collective versus individual work, whether in industry or agriculture. The accents and examples evolved over time, and included major themes of communist propaganda emphasized during particular periods: the "battle for trade" and collectivization of agriculture of the early 1950s gave way to the new automobile industry and Polish expansion into developing nations in the 1970s.

Physics

Over forty different primary school textbooks for physics were published in Poland between 1946 and 1989. Between 1946 and 1955, this subject was taught in grades 5–7 (in the 5th grade together with chemistry), from 1956 to 1965 in grades 6–7 and later in grades 6–8. Before 1950 there were two alternative textbooks for grades 5 and 6. Later there was a monopoly of one textbook for each grade, and all the editions until the 1970s were written by the same authors: Czesław Fotyma and Czesław Ścisłowski, who were joined at the end of the 1960s by Stefan Bąkowski.

Fotyma was an editor of the teachers' journals *Fizyka w Szkole* (*Physics at School*) and *Fizyka i Chemia* (*Physics and Chemistry*). His own articles dealt with physics teaching methodology, stressing the "polytechnisation" of education (i.e. closely connecting education with production technologies) and the ideological aspects of education. Ścisłowski started his career as a teacher in a Warsaw secondary school. Later he taught methodology of teaching physics at Warsaw University. He also chaired the Polish Physics Olympiad.

The new authors of the 1970s came from the Institute of School Curricula of the Ministry of Education and Marie Curie University of Lublin. In the late 1980s they were joined by Jerzy Ginter from Warsaw University. One of the authors, Witold Dróżdż, chaired the primary school subcommittee of the curriculum committee in the Ministry of Education. The committee was established in 1969 with the task of developing new school curricula and textbooks.

Almost all the physics textbooks included some propaganda content. Only the very last ones, from the late 1980s, concentrated on physics in everyday life rather than on production and the economy. They are a bit more difficult, but at the same more interesting than the earlier ones.

Students could find three aspects of propaganda in their physics textbooks. First, according to the principle of "polytechnization", the authors were obliged to illustrate physical phenomena with examples taken from industry and the economy, and to show the correlation between science and industry. Second, physics was supposed to be instrumental in building children's "scientific world view". Third, there were political incursions into textbook narratives that had little or no relation to physics.

Political Incursions

Let us start with the political content. Particularly in the 1940s and 1950s, textbooks started with lengthy introductory chapters that tried to convince readers how important and useful it was to learn physics. They concentrated, however, not on physics but on political issues, on production plans and on the achievements of the socialist economy. The notions of plan fulfillment, work competition, work foremen and rationalizers of a scientific world view appeared already in those introductory chapters and were later expanded.

The introduction for the 6th grade textbook in 1950 can serve as an illustration:

> Our country was severely destroyed during the last war. From the very moment of regaining independence, which we owe to the heroism of Polish and Soviet soldiers, a lot has been done to rebuild the country [. . .] All this was done by Polish workers. For Poland is being rebuilt by herself, with significant help from the Soviet Union. Polish workers understand what an important task they have to fulfil and thus spare no effort to reconstruct Poland. They take part in these noble labor competition and deeply desire that factories produce more and better goods than before, that more buildings, bridges, railways and roads are constructed, that more coal is mined than before. In this noble labor competition for the reconstruction of Poland, Polish workers, technicians, engineers and teachers achieve splendid results and this is why the people honor and respect them. This toil of the Polish worker helps keep peace on earth. For in Western Europe and in the United

42   Maths and Sciences

States there are active war instigators who would like to unleash the ravages of war in order to make huge profits from the misery and death of millions of people. The working masses all over the world oppose these instigators. Under the leadership of the Soviet Union, the peace camp, whose power is growing by the day, has been organized. This camp protects the interests of the working class against the attempts of imperialists and capitalists to initiate the new war. The ranks of workers, technicians, engineers, teachers, doctors and other employees must constantly grow. Our nation is depending on you, young friends. It is counting on the fact that after proper training you will join the ranks of those who work for the development of a socialist Poland. You will work not for the foreign and indigenous capitalists who get rich on the work of others, but for yourselves, for your own country, for your own well-being. The more knowledge you acquire at school, the more valued your work will be. Do keep in mind that with your work, you are building a Poland of social justice, where one man cannot exploit another. A Poland of social justice is a socialist Poland.[44]

Some exercises in the 1950s also concentrated on political issues and were only loosely related to physics. Surface areas to calculate were the areas of fields in a production cooperative or of a lot for a school to be built by local authorities. The Palace of Culture and Science in Warsaw had elevators with specific speeds to calculate, a problem of transporting water to upper floors to be solved, and Torricelli's experiment with pressure changing with altitude to observe. Uniform motion was to be observed on the escalator in the Central Department Store in Warsaw or at the East-West Route, both constructed after World War II.

Physical phenomena were often only a pretext for a broad presentation of political issues. For example, every time electricity was dealt with in textbooks, the issue of the electrification of Poland was raised. The role of electrification in the general economic development of Poland and in the construction of socialism was emphasized. Even Lenin's words were cited that communism is Soviet power plus the electrification of the whole country. The electrification of the Soviet Union was to be continued by Stalin—on his initiative new power plants were built (some of them were called by name). Poland was supposed to follow this model. The textbooks assured pupils that the people's government took this problem very seriously and had established special departments to deal with it.

It was stressed that electrification occupied one of the top positions in the economic plans of the People's Poland. In the early 1950s a whole lengthy paragraph dealt solely with a political explanation of electrification, having nothing to do with physics.

The government of the People's Poland has made the total electrification of the country one of its priorities. Poland is building a socialist system. In this system there is no room for illiterate people; on the contrary, books and newspapers must reach every household. A factory worker, a farmer and a white-collar worker must all have clean and well-lit apartments where they can rest after work in comfort. Factories, agricultural production cooperatives that are emerging in larger and larger numbers in Poland, must be electrified. It is thus understandable that in the Six Year Plan, whose implementation is connected with building the foundation of socialism in Poland, the issue of electrification has been particularly taken into account.[45]

The textbooks focused especially on the electrification of rural areas. At first, its rapid progress was stressed. Books mentioned that it occupied an important position in both the Three and Six Year Plans, that in the 1960s it was going to be completed, but even in the 1980s there were questions on the current situation of electrification. Apparently, the issue remained unresolved.

Statistics on electrification were compared with pre–World War II data. It looked quite natural in the 1940s or 1950s when the speed of electrification was presented: 450 newly electrified villages in the two inter war decades were juxtaposed to the 460 wired up in 1946 alone.[46] However, the pride expressed in 1981 that the production of electricity far exceeded levels in 1939[47] seems to be somewhat unjustified.

Pre-war Poland was criticized for other reasons as well. A textbook from the 1950s mentioned that it was ruled by foreign capitalists, who did not care about the working and living conditions of workers. In the People's Republic of Poland, on the other hand, workers worked for everybody and the people's government guaranteed their safety at work through special regulations. It also ensured pleasant free time thanks to light, spacious apartments equipped with water supplies and central heating. Pre-war authorities were accused of neglecting the development of the Polish fleet, and of overlooking necessary investments in the automobile and aviation industries that flourished under socialism. Volumes of coal mining and steel production, and even the numbers of new drillings in search of natural resources were compared, always to the advantage of the post-war years.

The era of the People's Republic of Poland in physics textbooks was a time of hard work, but also of the constant and rapid economic development of the country. Only the positive aspects of life were noticed, in accordance with the recommendations of the Ministry of Education and of the censorship office, which did not permit even the slightest suggestion of hardship or difficulties. Immediately after the war, the huge destruction wrought on the country was mentioned, for which the Germans were blamed. Such remarks were always followed by information that reconstruction was in progress thanks to the efforts of Polish workers and the planned policies of the people's government.

The Three and Six Year Plans were mentioned, with the former usually discussed *post factum*: it had been completed and even exceeded. The culmination of the Three Year Plan was the Congress of the Unity of the Working Class in 1948. Textbooks mentioned that the shipyard workers accelerated their work on two colliers (coal and ore carriers): *Jedność Robotnicza* (Workers' Unity) and *Sołdek*, to commemorate the congress. The term collier was explained on this occasion, and the "work foreman" Stanisław Sołdek was introduced.

The Six Year Plan was presented in more detail. Not only were its achievements described, but also its goals, in part likely due to the fact that some of them

44   Maths and Sciences

had never been accomplished. Ways to fulfill the plan were proposed: people should save resources, introduce new "rational" methods of work, and compete with others. Examples were taken from the branches of industry that could be related to physics. "Rational" methods were, for example, taken from construction sites where collective efforts based on Soviet patterns made it possible to build houses in just a few days. Technological improvements were presented and workers-inventors praised, such as one who improved a filter used in the process of oxygen condensation, which in turn increased daily production levels by five bottles of oxygen. "It saves half a million zlotys yearly", read one textbook.[48] Sawdust briquettes made use of huge amounts of sawdust which would otherwise be wasted.

One miner, Markiewka, was celebrated as a forerunner who promised to mine 1620 instead of 540 tons of coal during three months in 1950 and called on others to join him in competition.[49] Bricklayers tried to fulfill plans for two and a half years in just twelve months.

Polytechnization

Industry and Construction Sites

Coal mines, shipyards, construction sites and power plants appeared most frequently in the physics textbooks. Some were mentioned in the abstract, while other examples used specific names and locations. Privileges for their workers (e.g. priority in obtaining apartments or places in summer resorts) were presented as an example of the government's care. Nobody asked why such special privileges were needed, or why workers could not get those benefits on a regular basis.

Statistical data about coal mining was accompanied by detailed descriptions of drilling methods in the mines, of mineshaft construction and excavating technologies. Pupils learned where coal deposits in Poland were located (though some data was censored by the censorship office), what happened to the coal once it was mined, where Polish coal was exported to and what Poland could buy for it.

The Archimedes Principle was illustrated with shipyards and stories of Polish access to the sea that had been restored to Poland thanks to the Soviet Army and the Polish People's Army—as if such stories had anything to do with physics. The tonnage of the Polish fleet and commercial ships donated by the Soviet Union were also mentioned on this occasion. Textbooks stressed that Poland had to develop both a navy and a merchant fleet.

Construction sites were used to illustrate all kinds of simple machines and measurements. Lifts were used together with other various physical instruments. Construction workers (not just people) carried various tools, bricks or rubble (not just things) using force, energy and power to be calculated. In the first post-war years the texts mentioned reconstruction; in Stalinist times they concentrated on collective methods of work and work competition, while beginning in the 1960s they simply presented construction sites.

The refrigeration industry was also mentioned for many years, though a bit more briefly than mining or construction sites. It served the needs of Polish

Maths and Sciences 45

agriculture by enabling it to export food. The huge freezers of Gdańsk, Gdynia and Szczecin were described.

Transportation and automobile industry descriptions were initially focused on the Soviet Union, which had donated some trucks for the reconstruction of Poland. Soviet workers were said to be able to buy cheap, high-quality cars, such as the Moskvich and Pobyeda. Later, Polish automobile factories in Warsaw and Lublin were also mentioned. The role of the automobile and aviation industries in the case of war was stressed. As for Polish aviation, schoolchildren were assured of its total safety and regular flights thanks to "perfect pilots and well-maintained machines".[50]

Agriculture

Not only industry was presented in the physics textbook, but also agriculture; particularly so in the context of its mechanization, which could be related to the implementation of achievements of physics. The advantages of mechanization were enumerated and increasing tractor production volumes were meant to make pupils proud. Illustrations also presented other machines, such as five-furrow plows, a "sowing unit (set of machines)" or a "potato harvest unit".[51]

In the early 1950s, similarly to other school subjects, physics promoted production cooperatives (collective farms) as the vanguard of technological progress. They had all kinds of machines and instruments, radios included. At the end of the 1950–1951 edition of the textbook for 6th grade pupils a special chapter was added about the superiority of collective farms over individual farms, the increasing number of the cooperatives based on the Soviet kolkhozes and their bright perspectives.[52] It had no relation to physics at all, and rather served only to encourage farmers to join the cooperatives.

Only after 1956 did textbooks remark that machines were used also by individual farmers, but by that time they generally paid less attention to agriculture than before.

The Soviet Union and Other Countries

The presentation of the Soviet Union was of an undoubtedly propagandistic nature. Soviet help during the war was mentioned, with the role of the Red Army stressed in particular. The USSR provided Poland with cars, ships and models of production and electrification to follow. The achievements of the planned Soviet economy were presented. Particular construction projects, such as Dneprostroy (a power plant on the Dnepr River) and other power plants, as well as the White Sea–Baltic (Belomor) Canal and the Volga-Don Canal were mentioned by name.

Russian inventors replaced other nationalities. Before 1949 textbooks expressed no doubt that the electric light bulb was invented by Thomas Edison. In 1950, he was replaced by a Russian researcher named Alexandr Lodygin. Edison was mentioned as someone who improved on his invention. The textbook used for the 8th grade from 1966–1971 said on page 5 that Lodygin's bulb could not be used in practice and was further developed by Edison, yet on page 112 it

46   Maths and Sciences

mentioned that Edison and Lodygin worked independently. This last statement was repeated until the 1980s, in history textbooks as well.

Other Russian inventors mentioned in physics textbooks included Richmann (his German origins were mentioned), who worked on the lightning rod at the same time as Benjamin Franklin; Alexandr Popov, who built the first radio, later elaborated on by G. Marconi; I. Polzunov preceded James Watt in his work on the steam machine; Petrov and Yablochkov implemented the electric arc. The work of Vladimir Kosma Zvorykin was presented as crucial in the development of the television. His Russian name suggested his nationality, but it was never mentioned that Zvorykin had emigrated from Russia after the revolution of 1917 and lived in the United States until his death in 1982.

Other inventors were appreciated in the textbooks for their lower-class background. Michael Faraday was presented as the son of a smith who earned his living as a bookbinder; Georg Ohm as the son of a locksmith; Robert L. Stephenson was self-educated; Isaac Newton was born into a peasant family.

Soviet superiority was also presented in aeronautics. American achievements were also mentioned, but Soviet ones evoked much more emotion. When it came to nuclear energy, however, it turned out that only the Soviets used it in a proper, peaceful way: in the world's first nuclear power plant, operating since 1954, and in the icebreaker "Lenin". The Americans and the entire "imperialist camp" were fond only of its military applications, "to subdue nations who want to live on their own". In the 1950s a very emotional passage was included:

> The imperialists strive for natural resources and energy to be kept by a very few nations, because it would let them subdue other nations. There is a struggle between these two camps. It is sure, however, that the Camp of Peace, Democracy and Justice will win in this struggle. Poland is proud to be a member of this camp. She wants peace and free development. She wants to establish the conditions which will make it possible to work peacefully on the reconstruction and development of the country.[53]

In the years that followed, textbooks continued to concentrate on nuclear energy, while still arguing that the Soviet Union guaranteed its better and more peaceful implementation (as if the Soviets did not have nuclear weapons, and the Americans did not develop power plants).

The USSR and United States were juxtaposed in other areas as well. Physics textbooks followed other disciplines in presenting the Soviets' plans for foresting vast parts of the land—in contrast to the United States, where the forests were thoughtlessly exploited to fulfill the demands of an unrestrained economy.

In 1950–1951 the United States and Great Britain were criticized for failing to adopt the metric system, which was introduced by the French Revolution and therefore progressive; those two countries were said not to "follow the course of progress",[54] complicating the everyday lives of their citizens. On the contrary, the Soviet Union had abandoned its own system of measures long ago, as had Poland.

Maths and Sciences 47

Capitalism and socialism were juxtaposed in more general ways as well. Capitalism was said to serve the needs of proprietors—landlords and factory-owners—and to exploit workers, who were taken care of under socialism. This description was placed in a chapter devoted to machines. In capitalism, machines eliminated workers from factories, disregarding their needs. In socialism and in the countries building socialism "every citizen has the right to work and cannot be deprived of a job, and all technical improvements improve people's working conditions".[55]

Machines

Machines were treated with the utmost reverence in textbooks, especially in the 1950s. They were said to be especially important in industrializing the country. Modern man was to know and understand machines. Mechanization was praised for accelerating the fulfillment of economic plans. Machines were treated like living organisms that should be taken care of: cleaned, repaired, oiled when necessary. Otherwise they could break down and remain idle for long periods of time. As a result, the production of vital industrial or agricultural goods, and sometimes even of food, would be stopped. Plans would fail. Workers, such as car, train and tractor drivers and miners who competed to see who could take better care of their machines, were presented.

In the 1960s the amount of political commentary decreased, but "polytechnization" (i.e. relating physics to industry and production) survived, and the "scientific world view" was promoted even more rigorously than before. For example, a long passage from a 1971 textbook presented the possible uses of hammers and drills,[56] while forces seemed to be observed only in industrial or agricultural production.

Scientific" World View

The power of science was stressed. The tragedy of the Titanic "is unthinkable today since modern technology makes it possible to detect icebergs from long distances",[57] as one textbook assured. Science, according to the books, could explore everything and tried to make use of these explorations. Lightning and rainbows did not need supernatural explanations, the textbooks claimed, though both phenomena were said to be too complicated for pupils to understand (who simply had to believe their textbooks). Eclipses were also presented as predictable by science, while the nearest one was expected "around the year 2100".[58]

The modern scientific world view was contrasted with the dark past, in which Egyptians were kept in ignorance by the priests who wanted to secure power for themselves, where "witches" were burnt on the stake for their knowledge (one of the textbooks suggested that the knowledge of an average 6th grader would be enough to see him burnt alive in the Middle Ages[59]), Copernican theory was condemned by the Church and the pioneers of aviation accused of contacts with evil. But science and progress will always win out over prejudice", according to one of the textbooks.[60] Atomic theory was presented as "progressive". Its evolution was

48　*Maths and Sciences*

described, beginning with Democritus, while its supporters were praised and its critics ridiculed.

***

For the better part of the history of the People's Republic of Poland, physics at school was closely related to production and only very loosely to everyday life or to pure science. This did not change until the 1980s.

Chemistry

The first chemistry textbook in the People's Poland was not published until 1949. Prior to that, pre-war books for lower secondary schools were used. Chemistry textbooks were among the most enduring. A textbook composed by Halina Grodecka and Barbara Winnicka had twenty editions between 1965 and 1984, with changes introduced only once, in 1976. Another, by Jan Matysik and Andrzej Rogowski, was initially designed for the 7th grade, but then was used in the 8th grade between 1959 and 1975. The new 8th grade textbook did not change for ten years (1975–1984), and two of its authors also wrote the 7th grade book used between 1985 and 1989.

Władysław Lewicki, who wrote during the Stalinist period and whose book was edited almost every year, was a pre-war textbook author and teacher. After World War II he continued his career as a teacher, but was also a school headmaster, a school inspector at the Ministry of Education, and later a professor of chemistry education methodology at the Warsaw School of Pedagogy and Warsaw University. He was also a member of the editorial board of teachers' journals for chemistry teachers. Andrzej Rogowski was a secondary school teacher and a professor of chemistry education methodology, at the Marie Curie-Skłodowska University in Lublin. He was a member of the editorial board of the teachers' journal *Chemia w szkole* (*Chemistry at School*). Jan Matysik was his university colleague. Halina Grodecka worked as a secondary school teacher in Sosnowiec in Upper Silesia.

Chemistry was taught for only one or two years at primary school: in the Stalinist times (1950–1955) in the 5th grade combined with physics and in the 7th grade as a separate subject; between 1956 and 1965 only in the 7th (last) grade while in the 8-year school (in 1944–1949 and 1966–1989) in the 7th and 8th grades. Acquiring knowledge of this extensive discipline in such a short time posed a challenge not only to students, but also to their teachers and textbook authors. The criteria for selection of teaching material included political goals of education, such as forming a "scientific", materialist world view, and the "politechnization" of education.

Scientific World View

The basis of this scientific world view was, in the case of chemistry, atomic theory. The textbooks presented its history beginning from ancient times, remarked that its supporters suffered persecution at the hands of the Catholic Church in the

Middle Ages, and announced its triumph in the modern world. The supporters of atomic theory were regarded as heroes, while those who denied it were portrayed as dilettantes. The textbooks claimed that the scientifically proven uniform nature of the Earth and the entire universe, which consists of the same atoms, was evidence of the material (not supernatural) character of the world and laid the foundations of the scientific world view. As John Rodden stated about the teaching of physics in the GDR, "when they [the schoolchildren] studied the atom, they learned about materialism and atheism".[61]

Achievements in research on atoms and molecules, such as determining their size, weight and specific features, testified to the power of the human mind owing to its ability to describe phenomena that could not be directly observed. This also proved the value of science and its potential in studying "the mysteries of nature". Other manifestations of the power of chemistry and chemists were plastics—with predefined parameters "created" by humans—and the use of nuclear energy.

Polytechnization

One of the most important practical issues where the achievements of chemistry could be implemented was rustproofing. Textbooks persuaded readers how important it was: almost a quarter of the yearly iron production in Poland was destroyed by rust. Rustproofing was presented as if it was a military endeavor: "science becomes a weapon in the struggle against the devastating power of oxidation"; "people are increasingly successful in the struggle against oxidation and losses are getting smaller".[62]

In the introductory chapters, other examples of the practical use of chemistry were enumerated: in the army, in medicine, in food production and in various branches of industry. The industrial implementation of the achievements of chemistry was regarded as proof of their significance. This is why textbooks concentrated on the chemical industry and its technological processes.

Until the 1980s, when introducing particular chemical elements, textbooks explained where they could be found in Poland, how they were obtained and used commercially; meanwhile, their chemical characteristics were only briefly mentioned. Illustrations presented numerous factories both from the inside and outside. To cite John Rodden again: "chemistry [. . .] became not just a science but a history and sociology of DDR [and in case of Poland, of the People's Republic of Poland] industries related to chemistry".[63]

Iron was presented in great detail, starting with the kinds of iron ore and the way they are mined. Then steelworks were described: how furnaces were constructed and how they operated, how steel was tempered and rolled and how the final products were made. Particular steelworks were mentioned. Nowa Huta near Cracow, a flagship plant of the Six Year Plan, appeared most often, especially in Stalinist times. Its gigantic size was mentioned, Soviet assistance in its construction was stressed, and its production plans were presented. The Bierut steelworks in Częstochowa and the Soviet plant of Magnitogorsk also appeared in

50 *Maths and Sciences*

the Stalinist textbooks. In the 1960s, the construction of the Warsaw steelworks was shown.

The technologies of **zinc** and **lead** production were also discussed, as was copper refining. The composition of various alloys was presented together with their implementation. Interestingly, aluminum was said to be used in aviation. The total volume of production of Polish iron, zinc, lead and copper smelters was cited.

Carbon was to be found almost exclusively in the form of coal. The pupils were to know its origin, where it could be found, mining technologies and its economic significance. They were also expected to appreciate the toil of miners, who were taken care of by the government. Chemical processing of coal in gasworks and coking plants was described. The dry distillation of wood was also mentioned and plants in Gryfin and Hajnówka were presented.

Immediately after the war, **sulfur** was presented predominantly as a raw material for the production of matches. The match industry was said to be of strategic importance for Poland. Thanks to the state monopoly, the profits from selling matches served the whole society and not only a small group of mostly foreign capitalists, as before World War II. In the 1960s new sulfur mines near Tarnobrzeg, a city in southeast Poland, were mentioned.

For many years, the dominant context regarding the presentation of sulfur in chemistry textbooks was the production of sulfuric acid as an indication of the development of the chemical industry in the country. Textbooks described the industrial processes involved in making sulfuric acid and various industrial implementations of the chemicals. The factory in Wizów in Lower Silesia, constructed after the war, enjoyed the interest of textbook authors.

Nitrogen and phosphoric acids were presented in a similar, albeit usually briefer, manner. **Azote and phosphorus**, alongside various salts, were discussed as raw materials for chemical fertilizers. Polish mines and plants using these substances were enumerated in the textbooks. Their production volumes were compared to pre-war levels.

The subject of fertilizers gave authors an opportunity to deal with agriculture. The textbooks said that chemical fertilizers were best used in large state-owned or cooperative farms. These farms were also better electrified and mechanized. They used the "scientific methods" of soil examination and "planned sowing". Only one textbook, from 1955, mentioned that individual farmers also used chemical fertilizers and machines.[64]

Petroleum processing was another industrial theme mentioned in chemistry textbooks. Polish petroleum resources in the Carpathian region were mentioned (one of the first in the world to be extracted). In the 1960s the majority of attention was focused on Soviet petroleum transported from Siberia to Poland, and further on to Germany, via the "Friendship" pipeline which was brought online in 1964. It was then refined in the petrochemical plant in Płock. The Polish automobile industry was also associated with petroleum in the school textbooks.

Another chemical element discussed in chemistry textbooks was **calcium**, which was presented as a component of limestone rocks, a source of building

Maths and Sciences 51

materials. The process of burning limestone and extracting lime was described. Bricks, cement, concrete and reinforced concrete were presented alongside their production processes and plants where they were made. Achievements in housing by the People's Republic of Poland were discussed on this occasion, too. The topic of housing was also portrayed in relation to metals: "Iron is used more and more in the construction of factories and houses. The entire framework of the Palace of Culture and Science in Warsaw is made of iron beams".[65] The Polish glass industry was also sometimes linked to calcium.

Oxygen and hydrogen were also presented in relation to their production and use, such as in welding and in the oxygen masks used during rescue missions in coal mines.

In the 8-year primary school system, **organic chemistry** was taught in the 8th grade. The paper industry was mentioned along with the technology of cellulose and paper production. The necessity of saving paper and collecting wastepaper was stressed, especially since the demand for cellulose exceeded the production capacities of Polish industry. New plants were constructed and old ones modernized. According to textbooks, the situation should have rapidly improved: a 1966 textbook expected paper production to increase fourfold.[66] We know, however, that paper shortages were a permanent problem of the socialist economy in Poland, and decisions on paper allotment were made by the censorship office; they served as a means of exerting political pressure on the publishers.

Plastics were another example of the achievements of organic chemistry. This technology was presented only very briefly, but production plants were enumerated in detail. Household chemicals and margarine were only briefly mentioned.

Statistics

Discussions of the chemical industry were not only focused on technologies, but also the production volumes of particular plants and appreciation of its workers, as illustrated in this 1949 book: "Thanks to the generous work of our miner and founder, and despite the many deficits in materials and manpower, we managed to produce about 900,000 tons of pig iron and 1,500,000 tons of steel already in 1946".[67] Even more was expected in 1950. The Six Year Plan was to produce 600,000 tons of chemical fertilizers, including 200 tons of nitrogen fertilizers. In 1955, Poland was expected to have 60,000 tractors with the capacity to plow 40% of its farm land. Other elements of the Six Year Plan mentioned in chemistry textbooks included 100 million tons of coal mined, 16,000 tons of potassium fertilizers from Poland's own potassium resources, and 35 "modern mechanized ore mines" that would bring 3 million tons of ore, comprising 30% of the country's iron production.[68]

The sevenfold increase of sulfuric acid production in Poland was also presented, beginning in 1937, with volumes cited for 1947, 1949, 1955 and 1960, ending with the plans for 1965. Similar trends were to be observed in steel production in 1938–1965. Textbooks explained that more steel was needed due to the growing scope of construction work. Other "big numbers" included the production

52 Maths and Sciences

of concrete, which exceeded 4,000,000 million tons annually in the 1960s, the production of cured vegetable oil (150,000 tons), half a million tons of paper, 30 million tons of window glass, 250,000 tons of glass containers (bottles and jars), 20,000 tons of household glass, 12 tons of porcelain, 15 tons of technical porcelain, 5000 tons of table faience, 5000 tons of technical faience, over 2,500 million bricks, 15 million hollow cement blocks, 80 million roof tiles and 150 million drains. This data, and numbers such as "340,000 chests with 5000 match boxes each" or 100 million meters of natural textile fabrics, were meant to impress young learners.[69]

***

The selection of branches of industry and the way they were presented in chemistry textbooks closely corresponded with general political trends. In the 1940s, damage from the war was presented in the greatest detail, especially in coal mining and metallurgy. Improving working conditions as compared to pre-war years were also stressed. The Three Year Plan was laid out.

In the early 1950s the Six Year Plan dominated all textbook narratives with its statistics, labor competitions, increasing production norms, and with the Soviet Union serving as a model and offering assistance. "Socialist" science was juxtaposed with "imperialist" science in both chemistry and in physics. Marxist ideologists were cited, such as Friedrich Engels on atomic theory, or Minister of Economy Hilary Minc on the role of the dry distillation of coal.[70]

The 1955 edition of Lewicki's textbook was twenty pages thinner than the 1954 version, but nothing had changed in terms of chemistry. The removed material related solely to propaganda and politics.

In the following years the authors concentrated on industrial technologies and presented how they implemented achievements in chemistry. The goal of chemistry education was to prepare pupils to work in the chemical industry and to make them proud of the achievements of the People's Republic of Poland in this area.

In the mid-1970s, textbooks started noting environmental pollution caused by the chemical industry, but at the same time mentioned the possibilities that chemistry offered for protection of environment.

Only at the end of the 1980s did chemistry textbooks concentrate on chemistry in the everyday life of pupils and families rather than on workers in the chemical industry. The kitchen replaced the factory as a place where chemical reactions could be observed.

Biology

Biology was taught at Polish schools starting from the 4th grade in 1949–1955 and 1981–1989, from the 5th grade in 1956–1962 and from the 6th grade in 1944–1948 and 1963–1980. Unlike in case of physics and chemistry, biology textbooks and textbook authors changed quite often and stabilized only when the 8-year primary school was introduced in the early 1960s. Initially, many

Maths and Sciences   53

pre-war authors continued their work, but either on their own or with the help of new editors adjusted their books to the political demands of the time. January Kołodziejczyk, a recognized botanist, died in 1949 but new editions of his textbook appeared until 1961. They were "elaborated by Janina Lubecka" and hardly resembled the original work. Henryk Raabe was a professor of biology and rector of the Marie Curie-Skłodowska University of Lublin, but at the same a political activist of the regime. He was a socialist already before World War II, and then, in 1944 actively supported the communist government, became its ambassador to Moscow and a member of the parliament. Raabe died in 1951, but the last revised edition of his book appeared in 1955. Stanisław Feliksiak was a director of the Polish Zoological Museum. He co-authored zoology textbooks from the first post-war years. His longest-lasting co-author was Włodzimierz Michajłow, a parasitologist from Lublin and a ministerial official who edited the official journal of the Ministry of Education and supervised higher education, holding the rank of vice minister. He was actively involved in promoting Lysenkoism in Poland. Their books were regarded as too difficult for schoolchildren and not always following the school curriculum, but politically acceptable and engaged in promoting socialism.

Jan Żabiński (1897–1974), who authored both pre- and post-Stalinist textbooks on the human body, had the most interesting biography of all the authors of biology textbooks. He was a founder and long-time director of the Warsaw Zoo. In this capacity during World War II he rescued Jews from the Warsaw ghetto, hiding them in the buildings of the zoological garden.[71] In 1965 he and his wife Antonina were recognized as "Righteous Among the Nations" by Yad Vashem Institute in Jerusalem. He also organized clandestine education during World War II and took part in the Warsaw Uprising in charge of a Home Army platoon. He was wounded and taken as a prisoner of war. After returning to Poland in 1945 he resumed his job as zoo director and achieved widespread popularity for his radio programs about animals. However, as a person engaged in the Home Army and thus loyal to the Polish government in exile, he could not keep his position as director of the zoo under Stalinism, and had to resign in 1951. Only after 1956 was he allowed to co-author school textbooks with Janina Wernerowa, a biology teacher who collaborated with Żabiński also in his radio programs.

The set of textbooks developed for the 8-year school lasted for almost twenty years. Its authors came from institutions of higher education and ministerial departments. Tadeusz Gorczyński (5th grade) was a professor of the Higher School of Agriculture (*Szkoła Wyższa Gospodarstwa Wiejskiego*), a member of numerous botanic scientific societies, an editor of scientific journals, a pre-war secondary school teacher and teacher of courses for adults, co-author of post-war academic textbooks, and a member of ministerial commissions on school curricula and textbooks. Aniela Podgórska (6th grade) was a secondary school teacher, professor at a teacher's college and the head of the Department of Teaching Aids at the Ministry of Education. The authors of books for the last two grades, Zofia Wójcik and Wanda Stęślicka-Mydlarska, were academics.

The textbooks of the 1980s were collective works by teachers and academics.

54   Maths and Sciences

Biology textbooks generally dealt with science, not with politics. Some of them, especially in the Stalinist period, presented in prefaces the role of plants and animals in industry (mostly as raw materials) as an encouragement to learn biology. They also stated that knowledge of the rules of nature helps improve the quality and quantity of agricultural products. However, unlike physics or chemistry, biology textbooks paid little attention to technological processes and economic issues were usually discussed in separate chapters.

On the other hand, political propaganda in biology textbooks was not limited to some extra passages dealing with political issues, separate from the core narrative. Quite the contrary, the very science itself was dominated by politics; one example is the acceptance of unproven Soviet theories developed by Ivan Michurin and Trofim Lysenko, loosely based on Darwinism.

Scientific World View (Soviet Darwinism)

Darwinism was, according to the textbooks, a cornerstone of the scientific world view, together with the atomic theory so thoroughly discussed in physics and chemistry. It offered the only acceptable "scientific" explanation of the origins of contemporary living organisms, including human beings.

The evolution of humans enjoyed particular attention. The similarities between man and ape were always stressed, both in texts and with the help of sketches, photographs and diagrams. In accordance with Marxist doctrine, the role of labor in the progress from apes to humankind was explained. "Labor made man" read the title of one subchapter.[72] The first tools were, according to Marxism, the turning point in the evolution from an animal herd to a human society.

The evolution of other species was mentioned rather generally, with more attention paid only to the origins of livestock animals. Pictures presented the ancestors of today's horse or cattle. The remarks for teachers in the 1951 curriculum asked them to stress the similarities between the species and to skip over the differences which pupils would notice anyway.[73]

The so-called creative Darwinism developed by Soviet biologists assumed human intervention in the process of evolution in order to accelerate it and steer it to the benefit of mankind. "Creative Darwinism" served as proof of the power of the human race and a symbol of man's control over nature. The names of Ivan Michurin and Trofim Lysenko were associated with creative Darwinism in the 1950s.[74]

Michurin was regarded a precursor of this trend. His name was mentioned in school textbooks long after the theory of creative Darwinism was abandoned. It appeared whenever fruit trees and orchards were presented, but in the most detail during Stalinist times. His work on one kind of apple tree was presented year by year, with special emphasis placed on his motivation: to provide as many people as possible with fresh fruit. His biography proved that only the Soviet government made it possible for Michurin to concentrate on large-scale research. His career was compared with that of the American researcher Burbank, who received no governmental support; his works fell into oblivion and his orchard was auctioned after his death. The capitalists did not recognize Burbank's achievements, while later Soviet researchers continued the work begun by Michurin. Moreover, all the Soviet findings were regarded as extensions of Michurin's theory.

Trofim Lysenko was proclaimed Michurin's successor. He promoted "vernalization", that is, converting winter wheat into spring wheat, which would bring as much crop as the winter one but prevent freezing of the seeds if planted in spring. He was also said to develop a special method of growing potatoes (though textbooks did not provide any details except the information that it was effective) and *koksagyz* (a rubber plant). Other Soviet researchers were said to follow Michurin and Lysenko and "produce" new varieties of rice, cotton, pigs (grown by Ivanov), hens (leghorns), sheep (Caucasian merino) and cows (from the Karavayevo *kolkhoz*) that were resistant to severe climates but at the same time produced high-quality meat, wool or milk.

What the textbooks did not mention was that neither Lysenko nor his followers could scientifically prove their hypotheses, that Lysenko rejected both Mendel's genetics and the existence of DNA, and thanks to Stalin's confidence that he enjoyed, other scientists who did not share his views were not allowed to pursue their research. Promoting Lysenkoism was a political decision, but was not grounded in scientific research. It started in Poland in 1949 when all textbooks— from primary school to the university level—had to be changed, and ended in the late 1950s when Lysenko's name simply disappeared, with no discussion of his previous influence on Soviet and Polish science. Of the Russian researchers, only Michurin and Ivan Pavlov and his experiments on animal behavior remained in Polish textbooks.

Another biology-related political topic was the potato beetle. It came to particular prominence at the turn of the 1950s, when the theory was developed that it had been dropped by American aircraft on East Germany and then transmitted to Poland. The regions of Poland "attacked" in 1946/47 were enumerated, and measures undertaken by the government described with the conclusion that despite all the efforts made to counter it, the problem still persisted; fields had to be observed, and in case the beetle was spotted the authorities should be informed. Schoolchildren were asked to take active part in these endeavors. Statistical data was used to impress readers. According to one of the textbooks, 7,965,000 hectares of land was inspected multiple times, which took 13,772,000 working days. One hundred seventeen tons of chemicals were used.[75] Textbooks also informed about legal regulations concerning the potato beetle and administrative structures dealing with plant protection; even as late as 1982 they gave information about the existence of special "anti-beetle troops" at schools and other institutions, well-trained and ready to be used in action.[76]

Achievements of the Socialist System

Polish and Soviet achievements in the areas that could be related to biology teaching was another aspect of propaganda in school textbooks.

The Soviet Union was presented as a leader whose models should be followed in Poland. Kolkhozes and sovkhozes were presented as vanguards of agriculture

56 Maths and Sciences

where cooperation between farmers and researchers was possible. Textbooks explained that such cooperation was possible only in a socialist economy where the individual profit of a farmer was less important than food production for the benefit of all citizens. They assured that socialism would bring "wellbeing and a happy life" to the Polish people,[77] so they should follow Soviet solutions in areas like "seeding stations" that offered the best seeds, "scientific" methods of livestock selection, and gigantic chicken farms with huge incubators of fifty thousand eggs.[78]

The achievements of Soviet sportsmen were also considered part of biology. They were possible thanks to the popularity of sports among schoolchildren, young workers and farmers who were offered professional assistance.

Sometimes the passages devoted to the Soviet Union look as if they were added without consideration of the main text. For example, statistical data on the number of chickens in Poland in 1949 was followed with two sentences: "In 1949–1951 chicken production developed in the collective and state-owned farms of the Soviet Union. 1800 new hatching stations were founded there".[79]

Polish Agriculture

Polish achievements in botany were related to orchards and fruit production. According to textbooks, in pre-war Poland the situation was difficult, production insufficient, and trees often suffered during frosty winters. The "planned development" of the Polish orchards helped overcome those difficulties. The Institute of Skierniewice was mentioned which worked on new varieties of apples; the various kinds of fruit trees in Poland were also detailed, while children were encouraged to plant fruit trees at schools and to take part in foresting the country.

Agriculture and crops, especially cereals, potatoes and sugar beetroots enjoyed considerable attention. Textbooks promoted chemical fertilizers and claimed that they were used predominantly in state-owned and collective farms. Unlike the individual farmers, they implemented the most recent achievements of science, used machines and chemical fertilizers under the supervision of specialists, and developed infrastructure such as libraries, schools, kindergartens, shops and culture institutions. It was not mentioned, however, that individual farmers did not resist those solutions, but simply were denied access to them.

Biology textbooks promoted collectivization of agriculture longer than most other books. Already in 1955 they remarked that Polish agriculture did not generate sufficient crops "despite the efforts and special care of the Party and Government",[80] but in 1961 still claimed that "Socialization [i.e. implementing socialist methods] in agriculture increases the wellbeing of the country".[81] Even in 1976 the "chicken breeding teams" organized by female farmers were said to achieve better results than individual farms thanks to modern equipment and breeding methods.[82]

Zoology textbooks mentioned Polish cattle and chicken breeds, superior to the mixed-breed animals. A textbook from the early 1960s explained that new and better breeds were developed thanks to the work of scientists, all of which helped build socialism in Poland.[83]

Statistical data was, as in other subjects, particularly rich in regard to the Six Year Plan. Growth prognoses were presented: the horse population was to grow by 18% in 1955 compared to 1949, cattle by 49%, pigs by 72% and sheep by 134%. Cows were supposed to produce 27% more milk, and the average weight of cattle was to increase by at least 4% "thanks to the collective effort of farmers and scientists". Numbers of eggs and chicken (purebred and mixed-breed) exceeded one million.[84] In the decades that followed, statistics usually referred to the number of poultry (with ducks, hens and geese sometimes given separately), as well as the amount of meat, milk or eggs produced. They were usually presented in tables.

Even school textbooks were forced to admit that in order to produce enough pork the government had to rely on individual farmers. The so-called H-action (*akcja H*) was to encourage them to breed more pigs in order to produce more meat. The government's role was to buy the meat and to ensure its high quality. Pupils were warned against buying meat from unsecure sources where it was not properly inspected (buying meat from unauthorized farmers was a quite common practice considering the permanent shortages of meat in official shops).

Other Branches of the Polish Economy

Fishing was another area of the economy related to biology. In the first postwar years textbooks concentrated on presenting the necessity of and preparations for creating the Polish fishing fleet with appropriate specialists and equipment. The government assisted fishermen's cooperatives. As time passed, plans were replaced with achievements. The volumes of various fish catches and tonnage of the fleet were presented. Pupils were to recognize various types of fishing ships. Fish canning and processing was also discussed.

Other biology-related branches of the economy included the food industry: fruit and vegetable processing, oil and sugar factories, but also distilleries and pharmaceutical manufacturing. Lumber mills and coal mines were associated with trees.

Environmental Protection

In the 1970s the issue of environmental protection appeared in both botany and zoology textbooks. However, just as in textbooks for other subjects, the authors concentrated on the legal solutions adopted by the People's Republic of Poland, which were said to be among the most progressive in the world. All citizens had to do was simply to follow those regulations, such as those concerning the protection of air and water.

The protection of forests enjoyed special attention. Their exploitation in the unplanned economy of pre-war Poland and wartime losses were described and contrasted with the planned solutions adopted in the People's Republic of Poland. Only the minimum amount of wood absolutely necessary for the Polish

58 Maths and Sciences

economy was cut, according to the textbooks. However, a 1976 textbook mentioned that in order to satisfy economic needs, eighty-year-old pine trees could be cut, not only hundred-year-old trees as under previous regulations.[85] Foresting was frequently promoted and schoolchildren were encouraged to participate in "Forest Festivals".

In 1975, for the first time a passage on air and water pollution caused by factories and the fines they had to pay was placed in a textbook.[86] It must have been overlooked in the approval process, since it disappeared in the next edition of the book, published in 1976.

Healthcare

In reference to human biology, the achievements of the People's Republic of Poland in healthcare were mentioned. The textbooks assured that the government paid extensive attention to workers' health. New, light, clean houses, equipped with indoor plumbing, bathrooms and laundries were mentioned along with the network of healthcare centers and summer holiday facilities for workers and pupils; these facilities provided them with opportunities to enjoy their rest in good conditions and in the most beautiful places. The demand for an annual holiday in a resort was said to be made already before the war, but in the capitalist system it went unmet.

Legal regulations protecting workers' health were mentioned, such as the eight-hour working day or special privileges for women and youngsters at work.

Regulations on maternity and child care in the People's Republic of Poland were presented. The available forms of healthcare were enumerated, maternal leave, nurseries and pre-school facilities praised, and in the 1950s the so-called Jordan gardens—playgrounds with instructors supervising children—were discussed. Compulsory school education provided by the government was also regarded as an achievement of the People's Republic of Poland.

At the same time, the textbooks mentioned that after finishing school it was a duty of young adults to repay the money that the government had invested in them. They should work and undertake other activities, and participate in the economic and cultural development of the country.

The People's Republic of Poland was said to have implemented strong policies on the prevention and treatment of diseases. Tuberculosis enjoyed special attention in textbooks. The progress of the living conditions of the working class in Poland was presented compared to pre-war times, and was viewed as the main factor in eliminating tuberculosis. Large, well-lit apartments, information, prevention, healthcare and holiday resorts were all said to help in the fight with this disease. Medical issues, such as vaccines and antibiotics, were totally ignored. Antibiotics were mentioned only in chapters devoted to bacteria, and even as late as in the 1970s were presented as "recently developed".

Trachoma, malaria and venereal diseases were also mentioned. Curing them was presented as a citizen's duty. Generally, disease was not a private issue, but a social problem. Only healthy people were fully productive. Illness could have a

Maths and Sciences 59

negative impact on the production results of an entire team, and curing diseases generated costs for all of society. A good citizen should start his therapy as early as possible.

He should also pay attention to proper nutrition and save food. In the 1950s saving food was interpreted as consuming the minimal amount of calories and other nutrients as proven necessary by scientists. More proteins, fats or carbohydrates would not benefit the body, and "in a situation of limited food resources such wastefulness is socially harmful, since valuable nourishment is wasted while other people are starving, that is, they receive portions below norms".[87]

Presentation of the role of the socialist state in the hygiene of its citizens was also observed in East German textbooks by John Rodden.[88]

Combating the problem of alcohol abuse was also presented as a citizen's duty. The social rather than personal effects of drunkenness were presented:

> Alcohol use diminishes one's ability to work and the efficiency of work performed. As a result of injuries and diseases caused by drunkenness many workers prematurely go on disability pension. In this way the large number of alcoholics leads to the general impoverishment of society.[89]

Textbooks stressed the role of the entire society in preventing alcoholism. The failure of Prohibition in the United States was mentioned. The misguided priorities of the pre-war state monopoly on alcohol aimed at bringing maximum revenue to the budget. Socialist Poland was to control alcohol production and gradually limit its consumption. However, statistical data was not presented in this case, and the pre-war situation was not discussed. Surprisingly, the 1950s textbooks gave Soviet solutions as a model to follow (although alcoholism in the Soviet Union was a large and unsolved problem). Poland under communism was notorious for its extremely high and constantly growing consumption of alcohol and the role of textbooks was minimal if not non-existent in preventing this situation.[90]

***

Generally, biology textbooks had to deal with areas where the People's Republic of Poland and the Soviet Union lacked particular achievements. Food shortages, poor healthcare, insufficient housing stock (the expected waiting time for a new apartment in some larger cities in the 1980s exceeded forty years) were visible even to schoolchildren. Praising achievements in those areas could easily undermine the authority of textbooks. It made the task of the authors of biology textbooks more complicated than in other disciplines.

Notes

1 Pine, Lisa. 2010. *Education in Nazi Germany*. Oxford, New York: Berg, 51–52.
2 Rodden, John. 2006. *Textbook Reds: Schoolbooks, Ideology and Eastern German Identity*. University Park: Pennsylvania State University Press, 181–187.

60   Maths and Sciences

3 Ministerstwo Oświaty. 1949. *Program nauki w 11-letniej szkole ogólnokształcącej. Projekt. Matematyka.* Warsaw: PZWS, 41.

4 Ministerstwo Oświaty. 1964. *Program nauczania ośmioklasowej szkoły podstawowej (tymczasowy).* Warsaw: PZWS, 409.

5 Frycie, Stanisław (ed.). 1985. *Programy szkoły podstawowej. Zbiór dokumentów.* Warsaw: WSiP, 122.

6 Głowiński, Michał. 1990. *Nowomowa po polsku.* Warsaw: OPEN discussed the practices of censorship in the People's Republic of Poland, which forbade the use of certain words with the intention of removing the existence of the phenomena they were related to from the collective consciousness and memory of society—for example, the word "censorship" could only be used regarding the pre-socialist past of the countries of the Soviet bloc and the Western world as if it did not exist under communism; the same was the case of "strike", which was referred to as a "work stoppage", while price increases in Poland were called "price regulations".

7 Rusiecki, Antoni M. and Wacław Schayer. 1965. *Arytmetyka III.* Warsaw: PZWS, 168.

8 Ibid., 70.

9 Rusiecki, Antoni M. and Wacław Schayer. 1968. *Arytmetyka z geometrią. IV.* Warsaw: PZWS, 96–97.

10 Białas, Aleksander. 1967. *Matematyka. 8.* Warsaw: PZWS. 23.

11 Rusiecki, Antoni M., Adam Zarzecki, Zygmunt Chwiałkowski and Wacław Schayer. 1948 and 1949. *Arytmetyka II.* Warsaw: PZWS, 10, 17, 21.

12 Abramowicz, Tomasz and Mieczysław Okołowicz. 1967. *Matematyka. Dla klasy V.* Warsaw: PZWS, 141–142.

13 Rusiecki, Antoni M. and Wacław Schayer. 1965. *Arytmetyka. III.* Warsaw: PZWS, 45.

14 Rusiecki, Antoni M., Adam Zarzecki, Zygmunt Chwiałkowski and Wacław Schayer. 1951. *Arytmetyka. VI.* Warsaw: PZWS, 90.

15 Ibid.

16 Iwaszkiewicz, Bolesław. 1950. *Algebra. Klasa VII.* Warsaw: PZWS, 110.

17 Abramowicz, Tomasz and Mieczysław Okołowicz. 1967. *Matematyka. Dla klasy V.* Warsaw: PZWS, 179.

18 Rusiecki, Antoni M., Adam Zarzecki, Zygmunt Chwiałkowski and Wacław Schayer. 1951. *Arytmetyka z geometrią. IV.* 1951. Warsaw: PZWS, 79.

19 Ibid., 120.

20 Rusiecki, Antoni M. and Wacław Schayer. 1965. *Arytmetyka. III.* Warsaw: PZWS, 195.

21 Abramowicz, Tomasz and Mieczysław Okołowicz. 1959. *Arytmetyka z geometrią. Dla klasy V.* Warsaw: PZWS, 44.

22 Rusiecki, Antoni M. and Wacław Schayer. 1968. *Arytmetyka z geometrią. IV.* Warsaw: PZWS, 90.

23 Ibid., 97.

24 Rusiecki, Antoni M. and Wacław Schayer. 1965. *Arytmetyka. III.* Warsaw: PZWS, 172.

25 Iwaszkiewicz, Bolesław. 1953. *Algebra. Klasa VII.* Warsaw: PZWS, 131.

26 Rusiecki, Antoni M., Adam Zarzecki, Zygmunt Chwiałkowski and Wacław Schayer. 1953. *Arytmetyka z geometrią. V.* Warsaw: PZWS, 46.

27 Rusiecki, Antoni M., Adam Zarzecki, Zygmunt Chwiałkowski and Wacław Schayer. 1951. *Arytmetyka. II.* Warsaw: PZWS, 53, 125.

28 Białas, Aleksander and Stanisław Straszewicz. 1972. *Matematyka. Kl. 6.* Warsaw: PZWS, 86.

29 Abramowicz, Tomasz and Mieczysław Okołowicz. 1948. *Arytmetyka z geometrią. Podręcznik dla klasy IV szkoły podstawowej.* Warsaw: PZWS, 133.

30 Hłasko, Marek. 1966. *Piękni dwudziestoletni.* Paris: Instytut Literacki.

31 Rusiecki, Antoni M., Adam Zarzecki, Zygmunt Chwiałkowski and Wacław Schayer. 1953. *Arytmetyka I.* Warsaw: PZWS, 93.

32 Rusiecki, Antoni M., Adam Zarzecki, Zygmunt Chwiałkowski and Wacław Schayer. 1951. *Arytmetyka II.* Warsaw: PZWS, 67.

Maths and Sciences 61

33 Rusiecki, Antoni M. and Wacław Schayer. 1964–1976 (all editions). *Arytmetyka z geometrią. IV.* Warsaw: PZWS, 176.

34 Ziemecki, Stanisław. 1956. *Nauka o przyrodzie. Dla klasy IV.* Warsaw: PZWS, 118.

35 Krośkiewicz, Wiesława and Elwira Szylarska. 1980. *Poznaję swój kraj. Środowisko społeczno-przyrodnicze. Kl. 3.* Warsaw: WSiP, 31.

36 Zalewska, Zofia and GustawWuttke. 1951. *Poznaj swój kraj. Podręcznik przyrody i geografii dla klasy III szkoły podstawowej.* Warsaw: PZWS, 63–66.

37 Rościszewska-Gąsiorowska, Zofia. 1949. *Poznajemy rośliny i zwierzęta. Podręcznik dla klasy III. Książka ucznia.* Warsaw: PZWS, 113.

38 Zalewska, Zofia and GustawWuttke. 1951. *Poznaj swój kraj. Podręcznik przyrody i geografii dla klasy III szkoły podstawowej.* Warsaw: PZWS, 116.

39 Apparently, the idea of the holiday was neither Polish nor communist. Elena Tabacchi at ISCHE in 2010 presented a paper on the Italian tradition of an annual foresting campaign.

40 Rościszewska-Gąsiorowska, Zofia. 1949. *Poznajemy rośliny i zwierzęta. Podręcznik dla klasy III. Książka ucznia.* Warsaw: PZWS, 22.

41 Wernerowa, Jadwiga. 1951. *Biologia. Dla klasy III.* Warsaw: PZWS, 20–21.

42 Gąsiorowska, Zofia and Jadwiga Wernerowa. 1952. *Biologia. Dla klasy III.* Warsaw: PZWS, 38–39.

43 Krośkiewicz, Wiesława and Elwira Szylarska. 1980. *Poznaję swój kraj. Środowisko społeczno-przyrodnicze. Kl. 3.* Warsaw: WSiP, 78.

44 Fotyma, Czesław and Czesław Ścisłowski. 1950. *Fizyka. Dla klasy VI szkoły ogólnokształcącej.* Warsaw: PZWS, 4–5.

45 Fotyma, Czesław and Czesław Ścisłowski. 1951. *Fizyka. Dla klasy VII.* Warsaw: PZWS, 176.

46 Bąkowski, Stefan. 1949. *Fizyka i chemia. Wiadomości wstępne. Podręcznik dla V klasy stopnia podstawowego szkoły jednolitej.* Warsaw: PZWS, 166.

47 Mazur, Bolesław and Marian Wessely. 1981. *Fizyka. Dla klasy VIII.* Warsaw: WSiP, 159.

48 Fotyma, Czesław and Czesław Ścisłowski. 1952. *Fizyka. Dla klasy VI szkoły ogólnokształcącej.* Warsaw: PZWS, 120.

49 Fotyma, Czesław and Czesław Ścisłowski. 1950. *Fizyka. Dla klasy VI szkoły ogólnokształcącej.* Warsaw: PZWS, 126.

50 Fotyma, Czesław and Czesław Ścisłowski. 1948. *Fizyka. Podręcznik dla VII klasy szkoły podstawowej.* Warsaw: PZWS, 69–70.

51 Bąkowski, Stefan, Czesław Fotyma and Czesław Ścisłowski. 1961. *Fizyka. Dla klasy VI.* Warsaw: PZWS, 211–216.

52 Fotyma, Czesław and Czesław Ścisłowski. 1950. *Fizyka. Dla klasy VI szkoły ogólnokształcącej.* Warsaw: PZWS, 225–226.

53 Fotyma, Czesław and Czesław Ścisłowski. 1951. *Fizyka. Dla klasy VII.* Warsaw: PZWS, 183.

54 Fotyma, Czesław and Czesław Ścisłowski. 1950. *Fizyka. Dla klasy VI szkoły ogólnokształcącej.* Warsaw: PZWS, 8.

55 Ibid., 211.

56 Fotyma, Czesław and Czesław Ścisłowski. 1971. *Fizyka. Dla klasy VI.* Warsaw: PZWS.

57 Fotyma, Czesław and Czesław Ścisłowski. 1950. *Fizyka. Dla klasy VI szkoły ogólnokształcącej.* Warsaw: PZWS, 183.

58 Bąkowski, Stefan, Czesław Fotyma and Czesław Ścisłowski. 1957. *Fizyka dla klasy VII.* Warsaw: PZWS, 34.

59 Bąkowski, Stefan. 1949. *Fizyka i chemia. Wiadomości wstępne. Podręcznik dla V klasy stopnia podstawowego szkoły jednolitej.* Warsaw: PZWS, 225.

60 Fotyma, Czesław and Czesław Ścisłowski. 1952. *Fizyka. Dla klasy VI szkoły ogólnokształcącej.* Warsaw: PZWS, 72.

61 Rodden, John. 2006. *Textbook Reds: Schoolbooks, Ideology and Eastern German Identity.* University Park: Pennsylvania State University Press, 155.

62 Matysik, Jan. 1951. *Chemia. Dla klasy VII szkoły ogólnokształcącej.* Warsaw: PZWS, 21; Bogucki, Anatoliusz. 1959. *Chemia. Podręcznik dla uczniów klasy VII szkoły ogólnokształcącej.* Warsaw: PZWS, 33.

62   *Maths and Sciences*

63 Rodden, 2006, 155.
64 Lewicki, Władysław. 1955. *Chemia. Dla klasy VII*. Warsaw: PZWS, 69.
65 Bogucki, Anatoliusz. 1959. *Chemia. Podręcznik dla uczniów klasy VII szkoły ogólnokształcącej*. Warsaw: PZWS, 5.
66 Matysik, Jan and Anatoliusz Rogowski. 1966. *Chemia. Dla klasy VIII*. Warsaw: PZWS, 64–69.
67 Lewicki, Władysław. 1949. *Chemia. Dla klasy VII szkoły jednolitej stopnia podstawowego*. Warsaw: PZWS, 60–61.
68 Lewicki, Władysław. 1950. *Chemia. Dla klasy VII szkoły ogólnokształcącej*. Warsaw: PZWS, 110; Lewicki, Władysław. 1953. *Chemia. Dla klasy VII*. Warsaw: PZWS, 85, 80, 99.
69 The data come from the textbooks by Jan Matysik and Anatoliusz Rogowski.
70 Lewicki, Władysław. 1950. *Chemia. Dla klasy VII szkoły ogólnokształcącej*. Warsaw: PZWS, 102–103, 124.
71 These activities have been presented in Diane Ackerman. 2007. *The Zookeeper's Wife*. New York: W.W. Norton. A movie based on the story was released in 2017.
72 Raabe, Henryk. 1950. *Biologia. Kl. VII. Nauka o człowieku*. Warsaw: PZWS.
73 Ministerstwo Oświaty. 1951. *Program nauki w 11-letniej szkole ogólnokształcącej. Biologia. Projekt*. Warsaw: PZWS, 67.
74 See also DeJong-Lambert, William. 2009. "The New Biology in Poland after the Second World War: Polish Lysenkoism". *Paedagogica Historica* 45, no. 3: 403–420.
75 Feliksiak, Stanisław and Włodzimierz Michajłow. 1952. *Zoologia dla kl. VI*. Warsaw: PZWS, 80.
76 Wójcik, Zofia. 1982. *Zoologia dla klasy VII*. Warsaw: WSiP.
77 Kołodziejczyk, January. 1950. *Botanika. Dla klasy V*. Warsaw: PZWS, 82.
78 Feliksiak, Stanisław and Włodzimierz Michajłow. 1950. *Zoologia dla kl. VI*. Warsaw: PZWS, 312.
79 Feliksiak, Stanisław and Włodzimierz Michajłow. 1955. *Zoologia dla kl. VI*. Warsaw: PZWS, 155.
80 Kołodziejczyk, January. 1955. *Botanika. Dla klasy V*. Warsaw: PZWS, 128.
81 Kołodziejczyk, January. 1961. *Botanika. Dla klasy V*. Warsaw: PZWS, 128–129.
82 Wójcik, Zofia. 1976. *Zoologia dla klasy VII*. Warsaw: WSiP, 169.
83 Feliksiak, Stanisław and Włodzimierz Michajłow. 1963. *Zoologia. Dla klasy VI*. Warsaw: PZWS, 210.
84 Feliksiak, Stanisław and Włodzimierz Michajłow. 1952. *Zoologia dla kl. VI*. Warsaw: PZWS, 279.
85 Podgórska, Aniela, Tadeusz Gorczyński and Halina Pomirska. 1976. *Botanika. Dla klasy VI*. Warsaw: WSiP, 61.
86 Podgórska, Aniela, Tadeusz Gorczyński and Halina Pomirska. 1975. *Botanika. Dla klasy VI*. Warsaw: WSiP, 136–140.
87 Wernerowa, Janina and Jan Żabiński. 1950. *Nauka o człowieku. Podręcznik dla kl. VII szkoły podstawowej*. Warsaw: Nasza Księgarnia, 105.
88 Rodden, 2006, 152–155.
89 Stępczak, Kazimierz. 1981. *Biologia. 4* Warsaw: WSiP, 80.
90 The complex problems of its production, distribution, consumption and culture in the People's Republic of Poland have been discussed by Krzysztof Kosiński (Kosiński, Krzysztof. 2008. *Historia pijaństwa w czasach PRL. Polityka—obyczaje—szara strefa—patologie*. Warsaw: Neriton).

4 Geography

Geography in post–World War II Polish primary schools was taught from the 4th grade. Pupils spent two years on the geography of Poland and two or three years on world geography.

The number of authors of geography textbooks was very limited. Even completely new versions of textbooks were prepared by the same people as before. New names appeared only at the beginning of the 1950s and 1980s. Some authors continued their work long after the collapse of the communist regime.

Maria Czekańska and Halina Radlicz-Ruehlowa authored primary school textbooks dealing with the geography of Poland from 1950 until 1983. Radlicz-Ruehlowa was also the author of many other textbooks (mostly for secondary schools), a film-consultant and a secondary school teacher in Warsaw. She cooperated closely with the Ministry of Education and developed teaching aids for geography lessons. For many years she was in charge of the Geography Olympiad in Poland. Interestingly, her World War II involvement in the Home Army and participation in the Warsaw Uprising did not have a negative impact on her post-war career. Czekańska was a pre-war teacher who later became involved in teacher training on the academic level at Adam Mickiewicz University in Poznań.

Most other authors also combined school teaching with academic careers in the methodology of teaching geography and propaganda tasks for the regime.

The main goals of propaganda in geography textbooks were to form pupils' scientific world view and to present the superiority of socialism over capitalism, especially in the economy.

Scientific World View

The basis for the scientific world view in geography was the theory of Copernicus. Textbooks presented its history usually by presenting Copernicus himself, discrediting the Church and condemning the "dark" Middle Ages. Photographs of the Earth from space were regarded as the ultimate proof of his theory.

Geography, just like other sciences, was supposed to convince children of the power of man in his struggle with nature. People, according to the textbooks, not only studied the entire globe, but also used the resources of the Earth and transformed the planet for their own purposes. For example, they prevented the

64 *Geography*

expansion of deserts by planting greenery along dunes and protecting them from wind. "Oases—centers of life in the desert—have been created by man and his great effort of persistent work that uses the most recent achievements of science in the unyielding struggle with nature".[1] Thanks to this progress people could not only protect themselves from natural disasters, but they could also engage in an active struggle with nature. "Modern man changes nature according to his needs, but under the socialist system and planned economy, he overcomes all difficulties with ever-increasing efficiency", read one of the textbooks.[2] The environment was not dangerous anymore as it had been "subjugated and mastered".[3] Producing and using electricity often served as an example of such "subjugation".

Economic Issues (Polytechnization)

Economic issues occupied a lot of space in geography textbooks. It is quite obvious that economic processes are a part of the description of geographic regions or countries. However, the amount of economic data and the way it was presented in the textbooks of the People's Republic of Poland leave no doubt about the political motivations of the authors.

Poland

Poland was presented as a state—not just a geographical area—with a specific political system. The authors convinced the readers that the political and economic reforms in post–World War II Poland were fully justified and beneficial to the country. It often started with the agrarian reform introduced in 1944 which gave land to so many individual farmers. Already in 1948 the collectivization of industry was promoted together with the nationalization of trade (which meant eliminating the private sector) and the introduction of a planned economy. Whole chapters in the 1950s were devoted to detailed descriptions of various types of collective farms or to the concepts of economic plans of the government. The government was generally presented as the initiator and manager of all positive changes. It made decisions about new investments while caring for the harmonious development of all parts of the country and counteracting the disproportions caused by the chaos of the unplanned capitalist economy of the pre-war period. The government made special efforts to better use natural resources, which were being searched for with far greater intensity than ever before. The government was the protector of the working people.

Details of Polish **industry** were given. Descriptions of coal mines, steelworks, and sugar and textile factories included information on technological processes: how coal was mined; how steel, charcoal or cement was produced; how thread was spun and textiles woven. The mechanization and electrification of factories and farms were stressed as aspects of general technological progress.

The investments of the **Six Year Plan** were presented in great detail in the early 1950s. Strategic concepts of the Plan were characterized, including such elements as the step-by-step elimination of capitalists from the Polish economy.

Planned production achievements were cited, such as "11,000 tractors, 25,000 lorries, 12,000 automobiles" to be produced annually, the electrification of 10,000 villages, and extraction of over 100 million tons of coal compared to the 80 million mined previously.[4] Agricultural production was supposed to grow by 50% over 1949 levels. The number and variety of new investments, which were enumerated in great detail, must have given the impression that things were being built everywhere in Poland.

International relations. It was stressed that Poland was enjoying peace and an absence of conflict with her neighbors for the first time in history. The traditions of Polish-Czech cooperation dated back to prehistoric times. Later, the brave Hussite warriors helped the Polish king Władysław Jagiełło during his struggles with the Teutonic Knights in Pomerania. Poland served as a shelter for Czech refugees in the 17th century. The biography of Comenius, one such refugee, was presented. The Soviet Union was regarded as an unappreciated neighbor, the liberator of Poland and the guarantor of her new post–World War II borders. Germans in the immediate post-war period were expected to be ready to take revenge for their defeat. After the GDR was created in 1950, the textbooks assured pupils that "a democratic Germany" did not question the "border of peace" on the Odra and Nysa rivers. Soviet assistance in the reconstruction of Poland together with its political system built the basis for neighborly relations between the two countries.

The new post–World War II borders of Poland were presented as sustainable and just. The role of the Soviet Union and the Red Army in their establishment was reiterated. The new western border and access to the Baltic sea were presented in detail and with emotion, while the eastern border was hardly mentioned. The repatriation of Poles from the Soviet Union was only mentioned in the 1940s.

The long **sea coast** that Poland acquired after World War II was presented from an economic perspective. The government supported Polish fisheries which were organized into cooperatives and state-owned companies to facilitate their further development. The Polish commercial fleet was expanded and sailors were trained at the Maritime Academy. In the 1970s textbooks devoted more space to Polish shipyards. They stressed that neither before the war nor even as late as the mid-1950s had Poland produced any ships. The development of this branch of industry was one of the top achievements of the People's Republic of Poland. Pictures of vessels in various stages of construction, sometimes in particular shipyards, accompanied the texts.

Polish ports were also presented. In the years immediately following the war, the majority of attention was paid to their destruction and rapid reconstruction, which was possible thanks to joint Polish and Soviet efforts. The growth of the ports reflected the economic development of the whole country.

The characteristics of the port cities are worth mentioning.

Szczecin was presented as the former Slavic settlement of Szczytno which later came under German possession and returned to Poland only after the war, becoming a "port of the entire Slavic region",[5] since it was also used by Czechoslovakia.

66   *Geography*

In the description of the city, traces of the Piast times (from the Middle Ages) were highlighted, which testified to the city's historical connections with Poland. The port, shipyard and ironworks in nearby Stołczyn were also mentioned.

Gdańsk's return to post–World War II Poland was also described. The textbooks stressed that it had enjoyed its best times under Jagiellonian rule in Poland (during the 15th and 16th centuries). Its pre-war status as a Free City was also discussed, followed by the destruction of the war and post-war reconstruction. The rest of the city's history (including its German heritage) was neglected. In the 1970s and 1980s the shipyards, the Northern Harbor and the newly opened refinery were also mentioned.

The past of Gdynia was presented much more briefly. In the 1940s and early 1950s the textbooks stated that it was an investment of the interwar period, undertaken because of the unjust decisions of the Treaty of Versailles that did not give Poland any significant harbor along the narrow sea strip it owned. From the mid-1950s only the post-war development of the "Tri-City" (Gdańsk, Gdynia and Sopot) was presented. Nothing positive could be said about the Second Polish Republic (1918–1939). Information on the construction of the port in Gdynia in the interwar years returned only in 1988.

Tourist attractions along the Baltic Sea enjoyed much less attention than historical and economic issues. Even when the Baltic Sea coast was presented as a place to spend summer holidays, textbooks pointed out that it was "the weavers of Łódź, the miners of Silesia and workers from all over Poland"[6] who went to rest at the seaside.

Kashubians (the indigenous population of Pomerania) were presented as proof of the Slavic history of the region and justification for Polish claims on that territory. In the 1940s they were regarded as the descendants of the medieval Pomeranians. Their attachment to Catholicism was praised. Later, a textbook by Maria Czekańska presented them as "the descendants of an old Polish tribe" and characterized their language as a bit different from Polish, but resembling the language of the old Baltic Slavs.[7] That sentence survived all textbook revisions undertaken from 1950 through 1980. Other authors stressed the attachment of Kashubians to the land and to Poland, as well as their resistance against Germanization.

The inhabitants of the lake region of Warmia and Masuria were treated in a similar way. Attempts at Germanization, especially in the 19th and 20th centuries, only increased their attachment to Poland and Polishness. The authors usually regretted the region's poor industrialization and assured readers that the new government was working on its economic development. "The landscape of Masuria will be enriched with smoke-producing chimneys and factory buildings", promised one of the textbooks of the 1950s.[8] In the following decades the tire factory in Olsztyn was mentioned. Assistance from the government for local fishing businesses and agriculture was given appreciation.

The third ethnic group loyal to Poland despite hundreds years of separation from the core Polish territory were **Silesians**. Their bravery, which manifested itself during the Silesian uprisings in the 1920s, was not the most important feature of the inhabitants of those lands, however. It was their diligence which was most highly praised. According to a 1949 textbook, the people of Silesia could "serve the whole country as a model of diligent, brave and heroic work".[9] Twenty years later another textbook pointed out the fact that the first workers' strike in Silesia took place under German domination, and that workers organized May 1st demonstrations in Silesia.[10] The post-war labor competition in Poland started in the Silesian coal mine Zabrze-East.

Silesian **workers** represented the professional groups given the most respect in propaganda: miners and metallurgists. Mining and metallurgy were presented as the driving forces of the Polish economy. "Upper Silesia is the most important region for the Polish economy. [. . .] Coal is our most important natural resource and the foundation of the industrialization of our country".[11] The uses of coal and steel were enumerated. The dynamic growth of both branches in post-war Poland was described and technological progress stressed. Texts were illustrated with schematic images of mines and furnaces, along with numerous photographs of miners and metallurgists at work. Textbooks on the one hand persuaded young readers how difficult their work was ("Miners and metallurgists do the most important and the most dangerous jobs, which all of us benefit from".[12]), but on the other hand argued that their living and working conditions considerably improved under socialism. Workers enjoyed special benefits, lived in nicer and more comfortable homes and enjoyed summer holidays.

The geography of **Silesia** seemed to be less important than its economy. As a 1948 textbook read: "We will not look for beautiful views during our journey, but we will get to know the rhythm of work in Silesia, work that increases the wealth and power of our country".[13] The industrial landscape transformed by man fascinated the authors. "Humans broke into the black abyss, marked the ground with a multitude of mining pits, and covered its surface with endless heaps of coal and slag".[14] Only after some time was the negative impact of those changes on both the environment and people noticed. Yet even then it turned out that the socialist government had already taken care to minimize the negative impact of industrialization. The remnants of the "old predatory economy"[15] were removed, sewage treatment plants constructed, filters placed on chimneys and new trees planted. The Park of Culture and Rest in Chorzów served as a flagship example of the state's care.

As for Silesian cities, two of them were usually mentioned: Katowice (or Stalinogród—the city of Stalin—between 1953 and 1956, "that was offered this honorable name on March 7, 1953, to commemorate the Great Leader and Teacher of the working masses, Joseph Stalin"[16]) and Nowe Tychy, one of two cities built from the scratch in the People's Republic of Poland.

Lower Silesia remained in the shadow of Upper Silesia. As in the case of the Baltic cities, the textbooks presented both the Polish past of this territory and its economic development. The first place of note in Wrocław was the PaFaWag Railway Wagons Factory, followed by the Town Hall and the university. In Opole the cement plant—one of the investments of the Six Year Plan—was situated near the castle of the Silesian Piasts and a nearby Slavic settlement. In the 1970s and 1980s Legnica appeared as part of the newly established Copper Mining Basin.

68   *Geography*

Other achievements presented in the last years of the People's Republic of Poland included the oil refineries in Płock and Gdańsk, the salt mines near Inowrocław and the power plant in Bełchatów.

Earlier textbooks concentrated on the Six Year Plan and its investments, especially **Nowa Huta**, presented as the top achievement of the plan. Geography textbooks played their role in stressing the enthusiasm of the builders, many of whom were young people coming from all over Poland. Soviet assistance was also mentioned. The huge size of the steelworks and its production capacity were said to be truly impressive.

The modernization and expansion of old industrial centers was also presented. **Łódź**, which was portrayed as a rather ugly industrial city famous for its textile factories immediately after the war, later benefited from the investments of the socialist government: the extremely long pipeline that brought water from the Pilica river, new residential districts that replaced the demolished slums, and new institutions of higher education that were said to help transform this factory city into a cultural center.

Warsaw, too, benefited from post-war reconstruction. It was presented in textbooks of all subjects. Geography once again told the story of its liberation by the Red Army and the Polish People's Army, the extent of wartime destruction and the enthusiasm of the Poles who immediately started rebuilding their capital city. Thanks to the Office of Reconstruction, the most significant historical monuments were restored, while many parts of the city were created anew to give workers a new, beautiful, spacious, friendly city. The East-West Route, the Palace of Culture and Science and the Marszałkowska Residential District were the newly created points of interest that the textbooks presented in the process of construction and after completion. In the 1970s the Central Railway Station was added to the list. The headquarters of the Polish United Workers' Party, the Belvedere Palace (the residence of President Bierut in the 1950s) and the Parliament building represented the administrative functions of Warsaw, while its economic role was illustrated by the automobile factory in Żerań, the Marcin Kasprzak radio factory and the Warsaw Steelworks.

Political influences on the presentation of other places in Poland can also be observed.

Lublin was regarded as the first Polish city "liberated" by the Soviet Army during World War II and the first post-war capital of Poland—the headquarters of the Polish Committee of National Liberation. A description (or rather praise) of the July Manifesto issued by this provisional government followed. The happiness of the Lublin inhabitants welcoming their "liberators" was described. The post-war development of the city and region was possible—according to the textbooks—thanks to the policies of the People's Republic of Poland which supported agriculture (with machines and chemical fertilizers), the food industry, cement factories and automotive factories that produced trucks. The new coal mining basin was detailed in the 1970s and 1980s, but it eventually turned out to be too poor to bring a profit (but this was not mentioned in the books).

Poznań was introduced as the home of the Cegielski machine works, usually presented in at least one photograph in each textbook. The Poznań International

Fair was also mentioned as a place where the economic achievements of Poland were presented. The entire region enjoyed a high level of agricultural production, mostly by individual farmers, but this latter fact was not emphasized so much. According to textbooks, individual farms profited thanks to the production cooperatives and state-own farms that provided machines, fertilizers, seeds and fodder.

Descriptions of the **Tatra Mountains** usually concentrated on their alpine landscape, but all of the textbooks made a point of mentioning Poronin, a Tatra village where Vladimir Lenin had spent some time before the Soviet revolution. They invariably included a few kind sentences about Lenin himself.

Another hero of the Polish past connected with the mountains was Kostka Napierski of the sub-Carpathian city of Nowy Targ. He was a leader of the peasant uprising of 1651 that was cultivated by communist historiography in Poland as an example of the revolutionary struggle against the Polish monarchy.

Coming back to the Tatra Mountains, the textbooks mentioned state assistance for highlanders. Shepherds received spacious, new pastures in the Bieszczady Mountains in the southeast of Poland, together with transportation for themselves and for their sheep and the professional advice of qualified breeders. The state also organized the distribution of regional products manufactured by local artists working in the cooperatives. Last but not least, the authorities chose the Tatra Mountains as a place of rest and relaxation for workers and their families.

The **Świętokrzyskie Mountains** in central Poland were presented as the cradle of Polish mining and metallurgy. Archeological excavations were mentioned in order to prove this theory. Lime quarries were also located there after World War II. "In the past a quarry was a symbol of hard manual work; today the work is fully mechanized, but it is still not easy", read a textbook from the 1980s.[17]

Plans to regulate the **Vistula River** were presented continually from the 1950s until the 1980s. The project was expected to be yet another achievement of the socialist economy, but it never actually materialized.

Thus the economic achievements of post-war Poland dominated the presentation of the country's natural environment. Students were expected not only to know about them, but also to be proud of them. Quite often the entire final chapter or two dealt exclusively with the post-war economic development of Poland, its current situation and plans for the future.

John Rodden's comments on geography teaching in East Germany, that it was "less concerned with the study of the earth than with the revolutionary advance of socialism upon it",[18] could be easily used to describe school geography in post–World War II Poland.

The World

The Soviet Union

The world of the Polish geography textbooks started with the Soviet Union, whether a political or physical map was being discussed. The USSR was presented in only the most positive light. It was the largest country in the world and had a large number of geographical features which were the largest in the world

70   *Geography*

as well: seas, lakes, natural resources. To cite Rodden again, "That the USSR [. . .] is the 'biggest' country in the world geographically leaves the implication of its greatness in other areas of importance".[19] Human achievements in the Soviet Union were also the largest and the best in the world, especially those from the post-revolutionary period. Hydroelectric power plants and railways were particularly promoted. The Dnieper Hydroelectric Station (called Dneproges) was said to produce more energy than Niagara Falls. Textbooks claimed that it had been built in 1927, while in fact that year the construction work was only begun. The Trans-Siberian and BAM (Baikal-Amur Mainline) railways were impressive because of their length and the severe climate of the territories where they were built. They testified to the omnipotence of the "Soviet man" who could not be discouraged by any circumstances.

According to a 1952 textbook for the 7th grade,[20] which remained mostly unchanged until the mid-1960s: "the coastline of the Soviet Union is the longest in the whole of Europe", Murmansk "is the largest city on Earth inside the Arctic Circle", and "The herring fisheries on the Okhotsk Sea and the Sea of Japan are larger than anywhere on the Pacific Ocean". Other mentions of "best" things in the textbook included: the Caspian Depression ("one of the deepest depressions on the Planet" and "the broadest depression on Earth"); "The Volga river basin, one of the largest on Earth, is inhabited by 50 million people"; "Beyond the Ural Mountains lies the vastest plain on Earth"; the Siberian rivers are "some of the longest on Earth"; "The peak of Stalin, the highest point of the Soviet Union, and at the same time one of the highest peaks on Earth"; "According to the calculations of Soviet water engineers, the 1500 largest rivers of the Soviet Union have four times more energy than the rivers of the United States of America"; "No country on Earth has as large a forested area as the Soviet Union"; "In the production of cotton the Soviet Union surpasses even India and occupies second position in the world, just behind the United States"; "No country has as many tractors as the Soviet Union. Even the United States, where agriculture has been using machines for a long time, does not match the Soviet Union in this regard"; "The Soviet coal resources surpass the resources of Poland and England eightfold. The petroleum resources of the Soviet Union are larger than those of all other countries on Earth"; "The Ural Mountains alone could provide the entire world with iron ore. In the rocks of the USSR there is one half of the world's supply of iron".

The litany continued with other natural resources, ports, rivers, power plants, cities, furnaces, canals, railways and so on, concluding with general remarks that "The Soviet Union is the largest country that has ever existed in history. It comprises one-sixth of all inhabited land. [. . .] No other nation on Earth has joined such vast geographical areas in one unbroken state as Russia has. When Napoleon conquered half of Europe at the beginning of the 19th century, only the Russians defeated him and crushed his armies". The Soviet Union was mentioned on sixty pages (17.5%) of the entire book. This frequency later declined, but still remained quite high: in 1962 thirty-two pages (11.7%) and in 1976 forty-two (12.8%).

The Soviet economy was constantly compared to the tsarist one before it. Progress was observed and its management was praised. The country was flourishing. The electrification of the country, discoveries of new natural resources, development of vast areas of Siberia and cultural progress of its inhabitants,[21] new industrial centers beyond the Arctic Circle and the Urals, the expansion of areas where new crops could be cultivated, including cotton, and the irrigation of the steppes of Ukraine were all presented as Soviet achievements. In the early 1950s there were plans to reverse the Siberian rivers, to construct gigantic canals and to irrigate the Turan Lowlands, but they were discontinued after Stalin's death.

Any Soviet scientific and technical achievements that could be somehow related to geography were described. Soviet polar exploration was presented as planned and regular. The Soviet Union had permanent meteorological and research stations conducting systematic observations. As a result, the Soviet part of the Arctic was known far better than the American one.

Soviet spaceflights were presented in detail, with the names and photographs of cosmonauts.

Of all the Soviet cities, Moscow enjoyed the most special attention. Its broad streets and new living quarters were described. Lenin's Mausoleum at Red Square was the site of the military parades and May 1st demonstrations. Leningrad was the home city of the "Great October Socialist Revolution", always highly appreciated. The military blockade of Leningrad during World War II was also mentioned. Baku was presented as a petroleum processing center with impressive drilling rigs along the Caspian Sea. The new cities founded under Soviet rule were enumerated: Magnitogorsk, Karaganda, Komsomolsk, Kemerovo, Novokuznetsk, Magadan, Igarka, Kirovsk, Vorkuta, Bratsk. It was never mentioned that most of them were constructed by the forced labor of Gulag prisoners, nor that for many parents and grandparents of Polish children their names evoked traumatic wartime memories.

Post–World War II reconstruction followed the remarkable time of Soviet heroism and losses during the war. The Soviet Union was back on track with its intensive development.

The international role of the Soviet Union was also stressed. The USSR presided over the "camp of peace", assisted other countries in the family of "people's democracies" and the developing world. It looked after all those struggling against colonial oppression and capitalist exploitation. Polish-Soviet friendship and Soviet aid to Poland enjoyed special attention.

The Soviet Bloc

The Soviet Union was to be followed by other countries of the Soviet bloc in all spheres: the economic, social and political. Socialist forms of property and management were presented as superior to capitalist forms. They guaranteed social justice. There was no exploitation in the Soviet Union, according to the geography textbooks. State-owned factories never worked for their own profit, but instead served the whole country. The grand kolkhozes and sovkhozes facilitated

72   Geography

mechanization and implemented the most recent scientific achievements. All Soviet ethnic groups were said to be equal and cooperating with one another. Yet at the same time, the textbooks stressed that the Russians contributed the most to the victory of the revolution and to the development of the country. The Soviet constitution was presented as a model of democratic law.

In Polish textbooks, just as in East German ones, the world was divided along political, not geographical lines.[22] Socialist and capitalist countries were presented in separate sections. And as in the GDR, the countries of the Soviet bloc (the so-called people's democracies) were treated with the utmost enthusiasm (though gradually in less and less detail). The European allies of the Soviet Union attracted the most attention. The pattern for their presentation included comparison of post-war growth under socialism with pre-war difficulties and identifying the sources of progress: the collectivization of agriculture, nationalization of industry, independence from foreign capital, economic planning and large-scale industrialization.

Socialist countries were compared to capitalist ones according to arbitrarily chosen criteria that favored the Soviet bloc. If the results generated by a socialist country were unsatisfactory, the capitalist countries could still be to blame. For example, a 1984 textbook remarked that the socialist countries had a rather small and diminishing share of world trade, but explained that it was due to the difficulties imposed by the highly developed capitalist states, plus higher production costs, and sometimes by the lower quality of socialist products. According to a book published three years later, this share was still not very high, but was systematically growing.

The collectivization of agriculture was presented as a condition of its growth and development. Bulgaria was shown as a model to follow: "Instead of the 800 collective farms that had been planned, 1100 emerged after two years; they encompassed 300,000 hectares of land".[23] On the other hand, Yugoslavia experienced food shortages since "the majority of the land [in Yugoslavia] belongs to private proprietors".[24]

In the 1950s the economic plans of individual socialist countries were discussed and sometimes even illustrated with statistical data, such as "according to the five-year economic plan of the Czechoslovak Republic, mineral fuel production will increase by 150% percent".[25] The five year plan in Bulgaria envisaged an approximately threefold increase in coal production compared to 1939, and ore production was supposed to grow twentyfold. Even as late as 1983, a textbook proudly stated that "the production of energy [in Czechoslovakia] has grown seven times when compared to the pre-war era".[26] In 1987, however, it was admitted that "the economic development of socialist countries was not as harmonious as it had been planned. Periodically various economic difficulties appeared [. . .] which were overcome thanks to the assistance and cooperation of the countries of the socialist community".[27]

Examples of the cooperation between socialist countries included the pipeline "Friendship", first mentioned in 1965, the Polish-Czechoslovakian work on sulfur excavations in Tarnobrzeg and copper in the Legnica-Głogów region, and other similar ventures.

Particular places, or rather factories, from socialist countries were described, such as the shoe factory in Gottwaldov in Czechoslovakia where a quarter million pairs of shoes were produced every day, according to a 1952 textbook.[28] The book did not mention that Gottwaldov was the name given by the communist regime to the town of Zlin in Moravia to commemorate the party leader Klement Gottwald, nor that it had been developed in the pre-war years by Tomas Bata, the founder of the Bata shoe company. The steelworks of Dunaujvaros and the aluminum smelter in Szekesfehervar were points of interest in Hungary. Metal works in Romania (Galati) and Bulgaria (Kremikovtzi, constructed in the 1960s), power plants in Bulgaria (Maritsa-Vostok) and Romania/Yugoslavia (Djerdap), the Bulgarian oil refinery in Burgas and the carpet factory in Tolbukhin (Tolbukhin was the name given to Dobrich in 1949–1993, after the Soviet marshal who fought in Bulgaria during World War II—the old name of the city was not mentioned in the textbooks) were discussed as well.

Immediately after the war and in the 1980s Yugoslavia was presented as a democratic country. Textbooks praised the partisan struggles of Joseph Tito's army during World War II. After the conflict between Tito and Stalin, at the beginning of the 1950s Yugoslavia was grouped with the capitalist countries while Tito was completely condemned: "Yugoslavia was liberated from German occupation by the Soviet Army. Nevertheless, the reactionary government of Yugoslavia [of which Tito was in charge] betrayed the socialist camp, joined in Anglo-American imperialism and totally succumbed to it".[29] The textbooks then concentrated on the country's economic problems and accused foreign capitalists of engaging in its exploitation.

After Stalin's death, Yugoslavia returned in 1955 to the "socialist" parts of the textbooks and remained there until the collapse of the communist regime. However, the books always stressed that it did not belong to any military alliance (i.e. the Warsaw Pact), and keeping private property led to economic difficulties— which were never mentioned in case of the other countries of the Soviet bloc.

The socialist countries could be found also outside Europe. **China** was presented as the second largest socialist nation. The Chinese communists were praised for the progress in agriculture (larger crops were distributed in the fairer way) and in industry which did not depend on the Western and Japanese capital any more. The most detailed information concerned the flood prevention policy of the Chinese government: river-engineering with impressive dams and water reservoirs with power-plants. In the 1980s one of the textbooks noticed, however, that the Chinese people "lived in very modest conditions and were paid for their work with food rations and small amount of money".[30]

Mongolia was also said to be liberated from the foreign capital, to have the world's largest proportion of cattle per inhabitant, developing food industry, modern housing and culture.

Positive socio-political reforms accompanied with economic and cultural development dominated in the textbooks' descriptions of **North Korea, Vietnam and Laos**. At the beginning of the 1950s geography textbooks could not resist presenting the Korean war. The appropriate chapter was expanded and updated

74 *Geography*

every year. It looked as if the war did not disturb the dynamic economic growth, neither in industry nor in agriculture.

> The planned economy was launched. Thousands of schools and universities were opened. The Soviet Union offers democratic Korea a huge help in organizing economic and cultural life. South Korea under the rule of the American imperialists is totally different. The farmer's position is no better than under the Japanese occupation. The industry is being transferred to the hands of Americans who transform Korea into a base of their invasive politics. Lots of people have no job nor a piece of bread.[31]

Even as late as in the 1980s the constant industrialization of North Korea was mentioned.

The description of Vietnam in the 1950s concentrated on its anti-colonial struggle with France. The textbooks called the French intervention "the dirty war" and noticed the protests of the French working class. After the country was divided into two parts, the northern Vietnam was said to implement reforms and enjoy progress, while the southern part had an anti-democratic pro-American government and "the struggle for social and national liberation continues and intensifies".[32] Surprisingly, in the 1960s and 1970s, American involvement in Vietnam did not enjoy as much attention.[33] In the 1970s North Vietnam was still developing both its industry and agriculture. In the 1980s it was only briefly given the label of a socialist country and mentioned as part of the Comecon. A 1987 textbook admitted that "the socialist countries of Vietnam, Laos and especially Kampuchea are in a difficult situation, devastated by prolonged wars".[34]

If schoolchildren trusted their geography textbooks, they would come to the conclusion that the development of Japan did not progress as smoothly as the other Asian countries. In the 1950s narratives concentrated on Japanese imperialism of the pre–World War II and World War II period. At the same time, they sympathized with the Japanese people, who had suffered from American nuclear attacks and regretted that the post-war American occupation had made Japan a military base for US expansion towards the Soviet Union and the Far East. A 1963 textbook commented on the Japanese economy: "Labor in Japan is poorly remunerated. Workers live in poverty. Factory owners lower their prices at the expense of workers' salaries. They subsequently sell cheap products in other countries and make huge profits on them".[35] As time passed, the textbooks observed the development of Japanese industry, but they always stressed its unfair roots: lower prices were achieved at the expense of both Japanese and foreign workers (Japanese products were cheaper than those of other countries). Eventually, in the mid-1970s the text factually stated that Japanese industry was owned by "big capitalists" and developed mass production of a broad range of products with cheap labor.

The textbooks praised the post–World War II changes in **India**. They usually described the British exploitation of India, appreciated its independence and sympathized with the problems of the poor Indian population who suffered hunger and diseases. Great Britain was accused of ignoring these issues while the Soviet

Union and China provided help. The positive reforms of the Indian government were enumerated: abolishing the caste system, introducing planned economy, industrial investments with the help of the socialist countries, including Poland. The books admitted that the Indian agriculture still could not fulfill the needs of population but the country seemed to be on its way to the "people's democracy".

Algeria, too, was said to "have entered a non-capitalist way of development".[36] The socialist reforms in the country's industry and agriculture were mentioned.

Cuba was a bridgehead of socialism in America. The textbooks concentrated on the development of the island after the 1959 revolution, on Cuba's independence from the United States (unique in the region), improving living conditions and wonderful housing projects. Other American countries (Argentina, Brazil, Venezuela, Mexico, Canada) were regarded to be exploited by the United States and dependent on the American economy with its periodical fluctuations. The textbooks could not stand American profits from the Panama Canal.

The way the **canals** were presented in the geography textbooks deserves special attention. It depended on whom they were administered by. "The Suez Canal from the very beginning served the interests of the British Empire. [. . .] Great Britain uses this connection to exploit the richest colonial areas of Africa and Asia".[37] The Panama Canal was "a military base and a starting point of American imperialism in Central and South America".[38] "Its construction had come at a price of lives and the health of thousands of people who had died in the lethal climate at the extremely hard work".[39] Nationalization of both canals was welcomed. The Soviet canals, on the other hand, evoked most positive emotions. They facilitated communication and agriculture, and served as a proof of the human power. The sacrifices and difficulties were noticed, but the victims or forced labor were not mentioned at all. The sentence "160,000 farmers dug 270 kilometers of canal in 45 days"[40] was intended to testify to their devotion to the construction of communism, but not to them being exploited. One Stalinist textbook reported on "the most modern machines" used in the construction of the White Sea–Baltic Canal, which made it possible to overcome the extremely difficult natural conditions: "hard rocks of the subsoil had to be dug out, and the route went partially through mud and marshland".[41]

The Western Countries

As for the presentation of the **United States of America**, it was given extensive attention in many areas. However, the disadvantages of the American economy were highlighted at every turn. They originated from the very nature of capitalism. The country experienced periodic crises. The economy served the needs of giant monopolies, but not the well-being of the state or its citizens. Long-lasting unplanned exploitation led to the exhaustion of natural resources, starting with forests and ending with petroleum (which the United States had to import). In 1984 the economic situation of the United States seemed generally poor. According to one geography textbook, the country's development lagged behind that of socialist and even some capitalist countries, and as a result "the

76   Geography

share of this country in global industrial production has been decreasing since the mid-1950s".[42]

American industry and large cities had devastating effects on the natural environment. "What monstrous amounts of pollution New York, Chicago and Los Angeles must produce each year!"[43] one textbook exclaimed. The skyscrapers were characterized as "overwhelming".[44] Textbooks complained that their lower floors had to use artificial lighting and large numbers of cars often jammed the streets. The tone of descriptions of the same phenomena in Moscow was completely different: "on the wide and clean streets of Moscow there is much traffic at all hours of the day. Thousands of cars move along smooth streets while fast buses connect the city's districts".[45] The textbooks reminded pupils that in American cities, colorful and lavishly illuminated rich neighborhoods were located directly next to vast districts inhabited by a poor and mostly black population.

The United States was permanently accused of discrimination against blacks. American ethnic policy was juxtaposed with the friendly and peaceful coexistence of the many nations of the Soviet Union.

The international policies of the United States were also targeted with negative comments. The United States was in charge of the imperialist camp, actively participated in neocolonialism, organized various military pacts and had numerous military bases all over the world, not only in neighboring countries totally dominated by the United States. For example, Iceland in the Stalinist period was seen almost exclusively as an American **military** base. The European capitalist countries acted under American direction.

Presenting capitalist countries in a negative light corresponded with the guidance of the school curriculum of the Stalinist times. It read:

> On the basis of the known economic and political systems of certain countries, a pupil comes to an understanding of the grounds for the division of the world into two opposing political systems: the camp of peace and progress, and the camp of war and predatory colonial politics.[46]

Problems, difficulties and injustice were emphasized in the capitalist countries, while their achievements were presented in a very factual manner, with none of the enthusiasm typical for the successes of the communist bloc. The cooperation of Western Europe was nothing like the friendship of the Soviet bloc. It did not bring any positive results, but only covered contradictory interests intrinsic in the very nature of capitalism. Their economic processes remained uncoordinated.

Scandinavian countries enjoyed relatively positive comments. Textbooks concentrated on their natural landscapes. However, in the history of Finland the two wars with the Soviet Union were presented as a result of the politics of local bourgeoisie that had negative consequences for the country.

Denmark was famous for the high level of its agriculture. However, it was not immune to economic crises. The differences between Danish agricultural cooperatives and socialist ones were discussed in the 1950s. In Denmark the cooperatives "worked according to capitalist principles, were based on the exploitation of employees and the profits did not belong to the entire working collective".[47]

Economic crises, deficits in the labor force caused by low birth rates and the defective structure of agriculture (landlords who lived from the exploitation of farmers who possessed no or little land) were said to have a negative impact on the economy of **France**, which—in spite of this—was generally in sound condition. In the Stalinist years its colonial policy in Africa and Indochina received very critical reviews.

Belgium, the Netherlands and Great Britain were also accused of exploiting colonies. Textbooks generally supported all forms of resistance against the capitalist countries, including the liberation wars in colonies. The cruelties of colonists from the past and present were described, along with the devastation of the environment and the reluctance to develop the colonized countries.

Great Britain was assessed particularly negatively. British imperialism, the worst examples of which consisted in policies concerning India and the Middle East, was severely criticized. The nationalization of industry (including petroleum resources) in Iran and Saudi Arabia were most welcome. Geography textbooks cited the (hundred-year-old) works of Karl Marx on the situation of the British working class that showed the bloody origins of the country's wealth. The authors concentrated, however, on the symptoms of decay of the empire which were visible already during the war, when Great Britain ultimately proved incapable of resisting Germany, and had it not been for Soviet aid would have suffered the fate of France. It was during the war that British economic power started giving way to the United States and other countries. The textbooks reminded pupils that Great Britain was not self-sufficient. It had to import not only food but also raw materials for industry. British industrial growth had devastated the natural environment.

Again, the manner in which the industrial environment was presented depended on the country (and political system) being discussed. In Britain, according to textbooks from 1963 to 1980,

> Wherever you look—there is a forest of chimneys, the extraction towers of mines, enormous furnaces, huge slag heaps [. . .] factory buildings, grey skies veiled with smog. The space is covered with roads, streets and railroads in all directions. Along the dirty waters of rivers and canals, ships carry coal, raw materials and products from factories.[48]

The same textbook also described the Soviet Donetsk coal basin:

> The coal mines, easy to recognize thanks to their extraction towers, steelworks and factories, huge factory buildings, storages, mounds of various rocks and slag heaps. All this is dominated by numerous tall chimneys, enormous furnaces belching fire, bulky boilers, thousands of poles and high-voltage wires—and grey skies veiled with smoke. The entire Basin is covered in all

78   Geography

directions by roads, streets and railways. Work goes on everywhere, and the nights are illuminated with thousands of lights.[49]

Western Germany was severely criticized. Its industrial centers were presented as the former sources of military power of the Third Reich (which was not mentioned in the case of the GDR). The Federal Republic of Germany (FRG) was accused of revisionism, failure to deal with its fascist past and dependence on Anglo-American imperialism. After 1970 and the border treaty between Poland and the FRG, the geography textbooks noted the change of West Germany's attitude towards Poland's western border, but the previous German position was also presented. At the end of the 1980s the problematic demographic structure of West Germany was mentioned, while the concentration of capital, the influx of foreign capital and the lack of self-sufficiency were regarded as the main problems facing the country. One of the few positive aspects of that country was the fact that Karl Marx was born there, which was mentioned in the caption of the photo of Trier.

Spain and Portugal were presented as fascist countries, while in the period immediately after the war as just "military dictatorships". Repressions committed by their regimes were criticized, while economic backwardness and dependence on foreign capital were stressed. These were mentioned alongside the struggles of the people of these countries to abolish the ruling dictatorships that eventually succeeded in 1974.

Textbooks sympathized with **the Greeks**, who were regarded as involved by Western imperialists in a civil war. Communist partisans enjoyed the full support of textbook authors.

Italy was portrayed in textbooks as a poor country struggling with economic difficulties, with very few natural resources and underdeveloped agriculture. High unemployment rates led people to emigrate. All of this was due to capitalism and economic dependence on the United States.

***

The world as presented in geography textbooks was thus bipolar, black and white. It was an arena of battle between capitalism and socialism. According to Marxist theory, the former was just about to perish, while the latter was on the verge of triumph. Capitalism seemed to be losing ground in developing countries, colonialism was fading away, while newly created states found allies in the Soviet Union and other countries of the Soviet bloc. Capitalism was also crushed from inside. To cite one of the textbooks:

> in capitalist countries there are tens of millions of working people who, together with the Soviet Union and other countries of the Soviet bloc, are combating imperialism. The working class everywhere aims at abolishing capitalism and preserving peace around the entire world.[50]

Socialist countries were developing by following the same pattern: a planned economy, the collectivization of agriculture, investments in heavy industry and

Geography   79

the increasing prosperity of the working class. Cooperation between the socialist countries was emphasized, along with their peace-loving policies.

Textbooks from the 1950s gave the most sharply contrasting presentations of the two competing blocs and the most detailed analysis of economic issues. Later on, more and more space was devoted to the natural environment, while the economy enjoyed somewhat less attention; however, the topic did not entirely disappear. The style of the narrative always depended on the political system of the country where particular issues appeared.

Notes

1 Czekańska, Maria and Halina Radlicz-Ruehlowa. 1950. *Wiadomości z geografii. Dla klasy V szkoły podstawowej.* Warsaw: PZWS, 192.
2 Czekańska, Maria. 1951. *Geografia Polski. Klasa VI.* Warsaw: PZWS, 86–87.
3 Ibid.
4 E.g. Kondracki, Jerzy and Wiesława Richling-Kondracka. 1951. *Geografia Polski. Dla klasy VI. Cz. II szczegółowa. Gospodarka i ludność.* Warsaw: PZWS, 78.
5 Wuttke, Gustaw. 1949. *Poznaj swój kraj. Podręcznik geografii dla klasy IV szkoły podstawowej.* Warsaw: PZWS, 230.
6 Brzozowska, Felicja and Maria Kanikowska. 1963. *Geografia. Dla klasy IV.* Warsaw: PZWS, 126.
7 Czekańska, Maria. 1951. *Geografia Polski. Klasa VI.* Warsaw: PZWS, 257.
8 Wuttke, Gustaw. 1949. *Poznaj swój kraj. Podręcznik geografii dla klasy IV szkoły podstawowej.* Warsaw: PZWS, 182.
9 Ibid, 166.
10 Brzozowska, Felicja and Maria Kanikowska. 1969. *Geografia. Dla kl. IV.* Warsaw: PZWS, 111.
11 Czekańska, Maria. 1980. *Geografia. Klasa 6.* Warsaw: WSiP, 153.
12 Wuttke, Gustaw. 1949. *Poznaj swój kraj. Podręcznik geografii dla klasy IV szkoły podstawowej.* Warsaw: PZWS, 160.
13 Radliński, Tadeusz and Jan Zaćwilichowski. 1948. *Nasz kraj i jego przyroda. Podręcznik dla klasy IV szkoły podstawowej.* Kraków: Księgarnia Stefana Kamińskiego i Tadeusza Radlińskiego, 37.
14 Czekańska, Maria. 1951. *Geografia Polski. Klasa VI.* Warsaw: PZWS, 189.
15 Brzozowska, Felicja and Maria Kanikowska. 1963. *Geografia. Dla klasy IV.* Warsaw: PZWS, 92.
16 Czekańska, Maria. 1953. *Geografia Polski. Dla klasy VI.* Warsaw: PZWS, 176.
17 Kądziołka, Jan. 1981. *Geografia. 4. Krajobrazy Polski.* Warsaw: WSiP, 51.
18 Rodden, 2006, 70.
19 Ibid., 75.
20 Staszewski, Józef. 1952. *Geografia. Klasa VII.* Warsaw: PZWS, 7–12, 14, 15, 20, 29–30, 32, 34, 35, 37–41, 43–48, 51, 54–57.
21 The 1950 textbook for the 5th grade (Czekańska, Maria and Halina Radlicz-Ruehlowa. 1950. *Wiadomości z geografii. Dla klasy V szkoły podstawowej.* Warsaw: PZWS, 175) mentioned the *kolkhozes* in the northern regions of Siberia where reindeer were grown and fish caught, as well as fur production centers. Fish-processing factories at the Barents Sea were mentioned. Schools and libraries, hospitals, and clinics were founded in the Nenets settlements. According to the textbooks the Nenets were not nomads of the poor tundra anymore, but instead they provided the Soviet economy with thousands of tons of precious fish and furs. Their living standards were constantly improving. Representatives of their younger generations could be found at institutions of higher education in Leningrad and Moscow. Only in 1961 did the textbook add that

80 Geography

the Norwegian and Danish governments also took care of the indigenous populations of the northern regions of their countries.

22 Rodden, 2006, 75.

23 Staszewski, Józef. 1950. *Geografia. Klasa VII. Na rok szkolny 1950/51*. Warsaw: PZWS, 65–66.

24 Czekańska, Maria and Halina Radlicz-Ruehlowa. 1965. *Geografia świata. Klasa VII*. Warsaw: PZWS, 121.

25 Staszewski, Józef. 1952. *Geografia. Klasa VII*. Warsaw: PZWS, 66.

26 Czekańska, Maria and Halina Radlicz-Ruehlowa. 1983. *Geografia 6. Europa. Azja*. Warsaw: WSiP, 83.

27 Golec, Barbara, Marianna Nowak and Ewa Przesmycka. 1987. *Geografia. Europa. Azja. Podręcznik dla klasy 7 szkoły podstawowej*. Warsaw: WSiP, 189–190.

28 Staszewski, Józef. 1952. *Geografia. Klasa VII*. Warsaw: PZWS, 68.

29 Ibid., 171.

30 Piskorz, Sławomir and Stanisław Zając. 1982. *Geografia. 5. Krajobrazy ziemi*. Warsaw: WSiP, 90.

31 Staszewski, Józef. 1953. *Geografia. Klasa VII*. Warsaw: PZWS, 228.

32 Czekańska, Maria and Halina Radlicz-Ruehlowa. 1965. *Geografia świata. Klasa VII*. Warsaw: PZWS, 233.

33 Unlike in the GDR; see Rodden, 2006, 79.

34 Golec, Barbara, Marianna Nowak and Ewa Przesmycka. 1987. *Geografia. Europa. Azja. Podręcznik dla klasy 7 szkoły podstawowej*. Warsaw: WSiP, 67.

35 Czekańska, Maria and Halina Radlicz-Ruehlowa. 1963. *Geografia. Dla klasy V*. Warsaw: PZWS, 122.

36 Mordawski, Jan. 1986. *Geografia. Ameryka, Afryka, Australia i Oceania. Podręcznik dla klasy 6 szkoły podstawowej*. Warsaw: WSiP, 139.

37 Czekańska, Maria and Halina Radlicz-Ruehlowa.1950. *Wiadomości z geografii. Dla klasy V szkoły podstawowej*. Warsaw: PZWS, 141.

38 Staszewski, Józef. 1952. *Geografia. Klasa VII*. Warsaw: PZWS, 323.

39 Czekańska, Maria and Halina Radlicz-Ruehlowa. 1950. *Wiadomości z geografii. Dla klasy V szkoły podstawowej*. Warsaw: PZWS, 141.

40 Staszewski, Józef. 1953. *Geografia. Klasa VII*. Warsaw: PZWS, 26.

41 Czekańska, Maria and Halina Radlicz-Ruehlowa. 1951. *Wiadomości z geografii. Dla klasy V szkoły podstawowej*. Warsaw: PZWS, 141.

42 Mordawski, Jan. 1984. *Geografia 7. Afryka, Ameryka, Australia. Podręcznik dla klasy 7 szkoły podstawowej*. Warsaw: WSiP, 80.

43 Ibid., 169.

44 Czekańska, Maria and Halina Radlicz-Ruehlowa. 1963. *Geografia. Dla klasy V*. Warsaw: PZWS, 88.

45 Ibid., 217.

46 Ministerstwo Oświaty. 1949. *Program nauki w 11-letniej szkole ogólnokształcącej. Projekt. Geografia*. Warsaw: PZWS, 72.

47 Staszewski, Józef. 1952. *Geografia. Klasa VII*. Warsaw: PZWS, 140–141.

48 Czekańska, Maria and Halina Radlicz-Ruehlowa. 1963. *Geografia. Dla klasy V*. Warsaw: PZWS, 207–208 (and the following editions, until 1980: Czekańska, Maria and Halina Radlicz-Ruehlowa. 1980. *Geografia. Dla klasy V*. Warsaw: WSiP, 68).

49 Czekańska, Maria and Halina Radlicz-Ruehlowa. 1980. *Geografia. Dla klasy V*. Warsaw: WSiP, 64.

50 Staszewski, Józef. 1952. *Geografia. Klasa VII*. Warsaw: PZWS, 198.

5 Polish Language Instruction

Polish language textbooks were the most numerous and voluminous of all primary school textbooks, because the subject was taught in all grades and during the highest number of lessons. The authors, as in the case of other disciplines, were either academics, teachers or ministerial officials, or, specifically for this subject, writers. There were two kinds of textbooks: readers and grammars. The former included selection of poems, short stories, excerpts from novels and other texts usually accompanied with some guiding questions, comments and exercises for content analysis (including suggestions for essay topics), while the latter introduced the principles of the Polish grammar usually in the form of a short theoretical explanation of a certain issue accompanied with a set of practical exercises. Grammar books usually also included spelling exercises. Sometimes readers and grammar exercises were combined in one book for a certain grade, while other times a third book was added dealing with writing composition, or grammar and spelling were divided into separate volumes. All of them included propaganda, but the readers were the longest so most propaganda issues were developed there.

Readers were supposed to be a tool not so much of literary or cultural education as of indoctrination. Before the 1980s they did not contain too many excerpts from classical literature, but rather poor quality texts written specifically for use at school. In the 1950s the testimonies of working foremen were included, alongside revolutionary songs, and citations from the speeches and writings of Communist Party leaders or revolutionary activists (such as Stalin or Bierut, or Prime Minister Cyrankiewicz). Excerpts were reprinted from communist newspapers, from *A Propagandist's Handbook*, *The Library of Working Foremen* or from the collection *May 1st—60 Years of the Holiday of International Solidarity*. Some texts about President Bierut were authorized by his office. There was a poem written by a 14-year-old activist of the Union of Polish Youth that combined poetry with communist newspeak to tell about the young activists' help for Polish farmers. Władysław Broniewski, a well-known poet, wrote a poem called *Trade Unions* to commemorate the 2nd Congress of the Trade Unions in June 1949, and another one, *Zabrze*, about the coal mine Zabrze-East that called on all Polish workers to celebrate the Congress of the Polish United Workers Party by fulfilling production plans ahead of schedule. Classical revolutionary songs were also published

82   *Polish Language Instruction*

in the textbooks, such as the *International*, the *Red Banner* and the anthem of the World Federation of Democratic Youth.

Texts written specifically for the textbooks were usually of a propagandist character, had a banal plot and striking didacticism. Even the communist authorities were aware of this situation, but the curricula demanded texts dealing with so-called contemporary issues, while children's literature in the People's Republic of Poland did not have them. Publishers had little choice and used whatever was available regardless of its artistic value. Only readers from the end of the 1950s and the beginning of the 1960s for the 6th and 7th grades, and from the late 1980s, abandoned these kinds of texts.

Even in the case of classical texts, fragments were selected that corresponded with the propaganda needs of the regime, for example those dealing with the hardships of the lower social classes of old Poland or with Polish-Russian solidarity and cooperation. In the 1940s Polish-German conflicts were also highlighted. On the other hand, any references to Christianity were deliberately omitted,[1] which severely distorted the image of Polish literature. Textbooks from the late 1980s included many more literary works, including some by contemporary writers. The social background of the authors was an important point in the biographies presented in the textbooks.

Not only texts, but also questions and pupils' tasks conveyed propaganda. They directed the interpretation of the readings. In the 7-year school they suggested, for example, comparison of the reality of the stories with that of the People's Republic of Poland. A story about a poor Japanese boy who had to earn his living himself ended with a series of questions: "Is it allowed in our country today to hire 12-year-old children? When was it allowed? Why do capitalists hire small children? What is the difference between children's fate in a socialist (USSR) country and in countries ruled by landlords or capitalists? What countries do you know that fight against the countries where the working people are exploited? Should a Polish child be proud of his life in the People's Poland and why?"[2]

Questions and tasks were also asked which had no relation to the literary texts or to the Polish language, such as: "Collect information on revolutionary activists from your region",[3] "Tell what workers contemporary industry needs today. Why?"[4]; "Make a list of the characters from the readings you read who deserve the title: Heroes of Work",[5] "Who is the founder of scientific socialism?",[6] "How does the people's state care for the health of its citizens? What healthcare have you used already?",[7] "On the basis of radio news and television reports, tell what the attitude of the Party and Government toward the miners is",[8] and so on.

Grammar textbooks had almost unlimited opportunities for indoctrination. Every text combines grammatical, spelling and stylistic themes, so propaganda ones were used wherever possible. Sentences to analyze could deal with the Red Army or with production cooperatives. Pupils were asked to develop sentences from "A farmer is ploughing" to "A farmer is ploughing a field with his district's tractor",[9] or "Little Janek is marching in a parade" to "Nice little Janek is cheerfully marching with his mother in the May 1st parade".[10] They could also decipher acronyms such as PZPR which stood for the Polish United Workers' Party (*Polska Zjednoczona Partia Robotnicza*), and use them in three sentences.[11] They practiced numerals on the achievements of the Six Year Plan or on the profits of a production cooperative, conjugated verbs such as "to march" and "to speak", declined the nouns "a citizen" and "a leader", and put the names of prominent figures of the People's Republic of Poland or words related to certain professions in alphabetical order.

Children were asked to write speeches or reports from celebrations, for example, on the occasion of May 1st or an excursion to a factory. They also wrote letters to miners or announcements on the collection of waste paper, described a cooperative shop or the decoration of a hall for the celebration of Lenin's birthday. They were supposed to prepare materials for a bulletin board about "The cultural and scientific cooperation of Poland with the Soviet Union"[12] and to write a short note on the October Revolution ("when did it break out, who was its leader, what party was in charge, what changes did the revolution bring, why do we celebrate so solemnly in Poland the anniversary of its outbreak?"[13]).

In order to expand vocabulary, words were introduced such as "rationalizer", "means of production" and "mechanization". Other words had very peculiar explanations, for example, a businessman was "a man of interests, a speculator".[14]

Many exercises were obviously propagandist but at least dealt with some real linguistic issues. Some of them did not have even that. There was, for example: "Copy the text and underline the name and surname of the President: The President// There is a portrait on the wall. It is a portrait of Mr. President. Mr. President is looking at the children. He is looking and smiling. Mr. President's name is Bolesław Bierut. Mr. President loves children. He watches how the children are working".[15]

The grammar textbooks of the 1960s were full of individual words and phrases about types of work, workers, scouts and soldiers that together did not form any meaningful images or stories, but made a general impression of the omnipresence of the topics they dealt with. The topics did not significantly differ from those covered in the readers. Therefore, all types of the Polish language instruction textbooks will be analyzed together.

Before entering into a detailed analysis it should be noted that these textbooks preferred general issues concerning Poland, the Soviet Union and even the world over the everyday problems familiar to children, serious texts over entertaining ones, the real world over fantasy,[16] the world of adults over the world of children. Children tended rather to imitate grown-ups than enjoy their own childhood. Textbooks had a special interest in the past, especially in social struggles and World War II, which was presented as the main turning point in the history of Poland.

The Past

Polish language classes also served as an introductory history course in the initial grades. In the following years of education they presented the past in a less scientific, but more emotional and imaginative manner.

In the 1940s the history of Polish-German and Slavic-German conflicts was given particular attention. One of the grammar textbooks cited critical remarks by Tacitus about Germans, with no mention that they came from the 1st century.[17]

84   *Polish Language Instruction*

Instances of conflicts were presented from the very beginning of the Polish state until World War II as if they were all incarnations of the same perpetual hatred. This is how the battle of Grunwald of 1410 (when the Teutonic knights were defeated by Polish-Lithuanian forces) was presented in 1948:

> Two battles are particularly important for Poland: of Grunwald in 1410 and of Berlin in 1945. In these two battles German aggression was crushed. We can be proud of these two battles also because of the victory of the whole Slavic world over its eternal enemy.[18]

But also in 1977 a textbook referred to the 1976 ceremony during the unveiling of a monument of the battle of Grunwald "symbolizing both the 'old Grunwald', an achievement of Polish arms and the arms of the united Slavs and the 'new Grunwald,' i.e. breaking Hitler's power".[19]

The eternal Slavic brotherhood was presented in detail. It was said to have been manifested first and foremost in the common fight against the German onslaught. Its origins were explained in the legend of Lech, Czech and Rus[20]—the story of three brothers who walked out of their Slavic homeland and sought new homes. Rus settled down in the East, Czech in the South, and it took Lech a long time before he found an appropriate place under a tree where a white eagle had made its nest.

The Lusatians were mentioned in the 1940s as a Slavic people who survived despite German influence that lasted for ages. The textbooks expressed hope for their autonomy.

The establishment of the German Democratic Republic in 1949 ended the openly anti-German period in textbook narratives. The Polish-German border was from that moment called the "border of peace", and the Odra River became the "river of peace".

In the 1950s ethnic problems became less important, while social ones gained in significance. Textbooks focused on the hardships of life and the exploitation of common people, starting in ancient Egypt. A papyrus about the cruel tax collectors was cited together with fragments from *Pharaoh* by Bolesław Prus, a famous 19th century Polish writer.

In the Middle Ages and in nobility-ruled Poland, the situation of the peasant population was said to have systematically deteriorated. It remained a serious social problem throughout the 19th century and even in interwar Poland, as well as in non-socialist states after World War II. Textbooks presented stories about poor peasants who worked hard in the fields of their landlords and who nevertheless could afford next to nothing, who had no one to complain to and whom no one offered help. Children suffered most since their parents had no time to take care of them. They could not learn (and even if they went to school they would not learn anything useful there and were often beaten), nor fulfill any of their dreams, but only worked from their youngest years. The living conditions of workers and their children were presented in a similar manner.

However, examples of the workers' struggle for their rights appear more often than examples of the struggle for peasants' rights. This started with the saboteurs,

Polish Language Instruction   85

and ended with revolutions. The Paris Commune was one of the most popular events. Polish language textbooks paid special attention to its Polish participants and to the death of Jarosław Dąbrowski. Polish contributions to the Russian revolution of 1905 were also mentioned, and other revolutionary events, such as demonstrations (especially on May 1st), rallies and strikes were covered. The texts emphasized the solidarity of common people, often poor and persecuted.

The October Revolution was often linked with Lenin. Textbooks also showed a few other episodes from his life. They usually came from Polish translations of texts by the Soviet writers: about Volodya Ulyanov—a good pupil, Lenin in Siberia, Lenin's meetings with workers, Lenin during the revolution, Lenin taking part in a *subbotnik*. They were supplemented with warm testimonies from Poles who met Lenin in Poronin in the Tatra Mountains and stories and poems about his contacts with Poland and Polish issues. Writings that praised Lenin's talents, diligence, modesty and charisma were published.

The positive impact of the October Revolution on ordinary peoples' lives was stressed. The negative aspects of the revolutionary terror were not mentioned. Polish influences on the Revolution were highlighted. Stories of Dzerzhinsky were most popular in the 1950s.[21] They presented his life in conspiracy in Warsaw where he helped his fellow inmates maintain their physical and mental strength, carried an ill roommate for a walk on his own back, stayed in touch with other prisoners and with the outer world. He was presented not as a leader of the revolutionary terror, nor the founder of the infamous Cheka, but as an intelligent, unconventional man, sensitive to injustice and noble-minded.

In grammar textbooks there were plenty of sentences about the significance of the October Revolution and celebrations of its anniversaries.

The October Revolution was regarded as the culmination of the workers' struggle for their rights and as practical evidence of Marxist theory. The theory, its founders and their predecessors were also portrayed in textbooks. Voltaire and the Encyclopedists, the utopian socialists (regarded as respectable though naïve people) and the machine-destroyers all preceded Marx and Engels. Marxist theory was not explained in Polish language textbooks. They rather concentrated on forming schoolchildren's positive attitude towards Marx, but not as much towards Engels. There were more texts by Engels in the textbooks than about him, while Marx was presented in the memoirs of his wife, son-in-law (Pierre Lafargue) and a friend (Karl Liebknecht). They showed him with his family and told about his beloved daughters whom he used to tell fairy tales for hours, about his maid whom he treated kindly (the books did admit that the promoter of equality and the enemy of exploitation had a maid), about his hard work. Only health problems forced him to follow (but only partially) his doctor's advice to limit his activities.

Among the Polish democrats, Thaddeus Kościuszko was mentioned as one who first fought in America for the freedom of the United States and bequeathed all his land to the blacks who worked there. Then he returned to Poland and took the leadership of the insurrection of 1794 which, as the textbooks stressed, put a lot of emphasis on reforms to improve the situation of the peasants. The

86   *Polish Language Instruction*

textbooks often cited a passage from *The Insurrection* by the Polish Nobel Prize winner, Władysław Reymont, where Kościuszko refused to let a landlord take back one of his subjects who had escaped to join the insurgent army.

Cooperation between Polish and Soviet revolutionaries dated back to the famous Polish Romantic poet Adam Mickiewicz and his friendship with the Russian poet Alexander Pushkin. One of the central figures of the anti-Russian January Uprising of 1863 in the textbooks was Andriy Potebnya, an officer of the Russian army who joined the insurgents and was killed in action. The textbooks suggested that he was not the only Russian officer who supported the Poles.

Episodes from the biography of Ludwik Waryński, a leader of the first Polish socialist party, "Proletariat", were published until the 1970s. They presented the Polish socialist conspiracy. All pupils, from the years immediately following the war until the collapse of the communist regime, could learn a poem by Władysław Broniewski mourning the death of Waryński.

Interwar Poland was presented as a time of massive disillusionment for ordinary people. The promises of agrarian reform went unfulfilled, while the exploitation of the workers continued. They had to work almost for free, and protests resulted in repressions. The books told the stories of the workers' children, especially of Jewish or Roma background, who lived in extreme poverty. Only a few of them were provided day care. Left-wing social activists of that time were presented to pupils, especially in the 1950s while to a lesser extent later on.

Thus, the authorities of interwar Poland were portrayed as continuators of the policies of the partitioning powers, and the common people were said to have come to the conclusion that a total change of the political system was the only way to improve their lives. Only the People's Republic of Poland could fulfill their expectations.

World War II was presented as a prelude to the People's Republic of Poland. There were numerous stories and poems about this period in textbooks. In the 1940s they concentrated predominantly on the war's destruction, the martyrdom of the Polish nation, fear experienced by children during the war, the fate of their families, the death of their dearest ones—which is quite understandable when taking into consideration the raw memories of both the authors of textbooks and pupils. The heroism of children was also highlighted. Texts often had a strong anti-German bias.

As time passed, more attention was paid to the struggle with the occupier (only the German one), particularly by the People's Army and other pro-communist groups. The readings favored left-wing parties and organizations in the portrayal of the Polish Resistance. Their names were presented as well as the biographies of their activists, old and young. They appeared in the memoirs of their companions, as well as of people who met them just once, but portrayed them as brave and good-hearted people who understood the nature of conspiracy.

In the Stalinist years the talents of Bolesław Bierut were illustrated in the story of a clandestine meeting on New Year's Eve of 1943 when the State National Council was established under cover of a New Year's ball. Textbooks of the 1960s described the activities of the pro-communist People's Guard and People's Army in the Warsaw Café Club and in the battle of Rąblów. There are hardly any texts about the Home Army, which in reality dominated the Polish Resistance (the Home Army was estimated at 400,000 soldiers in 1943 while the People's Army at no more than 100,000, though some historians put its number as low as under 10,000 before 1944). Even in the very few readings that dealt with the Warsaw Uprising (which was the flagship action of the Home Army) attention was placed more on its communist participants. Fragments from *Stones for the Rampart* (*Kamienie na szaniec*), a novel about the Polish Scouts during World War II written in 1943, were not published until 1960[22] and in the 1970s the excerpts in the textbook concentrated on anti-German actions without mentioning who had organized them.[23]

In narratives about World War II the Soviet Union was presented as the leader of the anti-German coalition. The heroism of its citizens was admired alongside their disdain for the occupants, and in the 1950s the role of Stalin was emphasized. German cruelty against the Soviets seems to be described even more extensively than in the case of German attitudes towards Poles. Stories presented civilians, especially young people and even children, who worked in the factories in the far north of Russia in order to equip the Soviet army at the front. They were said to have performed outstandingly well thanks to the methods of the Stakhanov movement and labor competition. Translations of classic Soviet war literature were reprinted, such as *The Young Guard* by Alexander Fadeev and *Timur and His Squad* by Arkady Gaydar.

Some stories, especially from the first decade of the People's Poland, also presented Poles working during the war in the Soviet Union. They did not mention how the Poles had arrived to the USSR (apparently they had been resettled from the Soviet-occupied eastern territories of Poland in 1940 and 1941, before the German invasion on the Soviet Union). The persecution of Poles was not mentioned, nor were the Polish victims of the Soviet Gulags or deportations. The Polish people seemed to be happy living and working in Soviet factories and kolkhozes, and made friends with the local population. The adults had secure jobs while the children went to school and daycare. Even after the war they had good memories of those times.[24]

Friendship between Polish and Soviet soldiers also survived the war. Textbooks presented thousands of volunteers in the pro-Soviet Kościuszko Division that was formed in the Soviet Union (but did not mention the Anders Army that had been created earlier and evacuated to Iran in 1942 as a result of the conflict between the Polish government in exile in London and Stalin). They praised the ideological training that the soldiers received before going to the front. The first battle of the Kościuszko Division, near the Belarussian village of Lenino in October 1943, was described in separate readings and mentioned in exercises (without questioning the rationale for using Polish soldiers, a quarter of whom lost their lives in the fight).

Chełm and Lublin, where the pro-Soviet provisional government was announced by communists in July 1944, were presented as the first two Polish cities liberated from German occupation. In fact, they were the first two cities

88   Polish Language Instruction

behind the Curzon line—the Polish-Soviet border approved by Stalin, but about two hundred kilometers west of the pre-war border. Textbooks stressed the enthusiasm of the population in the liberated places. Everybody was said to welcome the Polish and Soviet soldiers. The People's Army managed to help the farmers with the harvest before continuing along the combat trail. Cooperation between the army and the civilian population was emphasized. No conflicts were mentioned (though the reality was much more complicated).

The liberation of Warsaw on January 17th, 1945, was the next stage of the war in Polish textbooks. In the testimonies cited in the textbooks the eyewitnesses expressed their happiness, but also concern about the level of destruction of the city. The anniversary of that day was commemorated even in the 1980s. Children from the textbooks took part in military parades on this occasion, organized school events, and listened to radio programs and eyewitnesses' accounts.

The liberation of Silesia and Pomerania and the battle near Bautzen were presented only in the 1940s, but stories about the Polish army reaching the Baltic Sea and Berlin were published even in the 1980s. The 4th grade reader from the 1960s portrayed the Soviet colonel Vasyl Skopenko, who fell in love with the monuments of the city of Sandomierz, and thanks to his special maneuver Sandomierz was liberated with no destruction. Skopenko was killed in Wrocław, but was buried in Sandomierz according to his will.[25]

Only in the 1940s did the Polish soldiers supporting the Western allies appear in the readings (in the battles of Monte Cassino, Narvik and Tobruk). So did the Polish Displaced Persons returning home from the West. Later, their biographies were completely ignored (I have found only two textbooks that briefly mentioned such episodes in biographies otherwise not focused on the war[26]).

Karol Świerczewski and Konstantin Rokossovsky dominated the World War I Polish pantheon. Rokossovsky, a Marshal of the Soviet Union and of Polish origin, disappeared after 1956, while Świerczewski survived until the last years of the communist regime. Stories of their pre–World War I childhoods in working-class families were published, followed by their experiences in the Red Army in the interwar period. Świerczewski was presented during the Spanish Civil War[27] when he took special care of his soldiers and asked Polish volunteers about details of places in Warsaw that he remembered very well. During World War II he swam across the Vistula River near Warsaw without regard for German fire. His death at the hands of Ukrainian partisans in 1947 was described with pathos.

Another historical motive from Polish language textbooks was the history of scientific and technological progress. The readings emphasized the difficulties experienced by scholars from the past who had attempted to question the theories approved by the Church. The biography of Nicolaus Copernicus took note of his positive attitude towards lower social strata and his social engagement. Marie Curie was praised for rejecting an opportunity to make a profit from the patent of radium. The story of Walerian Łukasiewicz, inventor of a kerosene lamp, stressed that he had provided very good working conditions for the employees of his mines. Some stories had the obvious intention of proving the omnipotence of science and of the human mind. Some fantastic research projects were described, especially in medicine, energy and other areas. They corresponded with the content of science

Polish Language Instruction   89

textbooks. On the other hand, just as in those textbooks, the Church was regarded as a supporter of reactionaries, backwardness in science and social inequality.

The Image of the People's Poland

The People's Republic of Poland was claimed to be the fulfilment of the dreams of many generations of Poles and the culmination of years of struggle for national and social liberation. Prominent pre-war figures who praised the post-war reforms and urged others to join them were cited. Grandmothers at the turn of the 1950s envied their children's happiness and future. Support for the new system was epitomized in the return of pre-war Polish emigrant miners from France and farmers from Canada. Textbooks discussed their motivation: to work for their own country, not for a foreign one. Appeals to return addressed to those who were having trouble making a decision were also to be found in the books.

From the very beginning until the very end of the communist regime, textbooks discussed the post-war Polish borders. The territories lost to the Soviet Union were ignored, but the land acquired in the north and west was presented in great detail. The new borders were regarded as just and sustainable. The historical and economic rights of the so-called recovered territories were presented. Monuments of the Polish past were emphasized. The opinions of Polish writers longing for Polish Silesia and Pomerania were cited, starting with the medieval chronicler Jan Długosz, up to 19th and 20th century poets such as Jan Kasprowicz and Maria Konopnicka. The hammering of Polish border posts along the Polish-German border after World War II was compared to a similar action by Boleslaus the Brave, the king of Poland, in the 11th century. Stories of the Polish post-war settlement of the "recovered territories" were particularly popular in the 1940s. Whole families and individual workers moved there. They wrote letters to their families and friends, including former schoolmates. School groups visited Silesia and Pomerania. Scouting camps and workers' vacations were organized there.

The books of the 1940s emphasized achievements in the economic development of these lands: the reconstruction of their ports, the drainage of the Żuławy Wiślane at the alluvial delta of the Vistula river, the start-up of the railway car factory in Wrocław (PaFaWag, which became a model socialist factory with its social infrastructure of factory shops, nursery, kindergarten and day care). Even many years after the war, readings described anonymous factories reconstructed after the war thanks to the joint efforts of the workers. The exhibition of the Recovered Territories in Wrocław in 1948 was mentioned in at least three textbooks published between 1948 and 1950. Only in 1946 and 1948 (i.e. before the "ideological offensive" in education) were any problems with the integration of the Recovered Territories with the rest of the country mentioned.

Warsaw was the city most frequently found in school textbooks. Its administrative functions were stressed. The first [!] grade grammar book from 1950 had the following text:

> Warsaw is the capital city of Poland. The Sejm [parliament] composed of members from all over the country convenes there. The government,

90 Polish Language Instruction

consisting of ministers, works there. The President of the Republic of Poland, Bolesław Bierut, and the Marshal of Poland, Konstanty Rokossowski, live in Warsaw.[28]

The war-time destruction of the city and its swift reconstruction must have impressed the readers especially in the early 1950s when it was topical news, but poems reminded people of those feelings many years later as well. Textbooks stated that the reconstruction was possible thanks to the engagement of residents, the clever decisions of the "people's" authorities (in particular, the decision to bring the capital city back to Warsaw despite its total destruction) and the help of all of society, both adults and children. Everybody collected money, scouts collected waste paper and glass, volunteers—and among them the activists of the paramilitary "Service to Poland" formation—came to Warsaw to work, and even kindergarten children tidied the gardens. The new constructions, designed in the Office of the Construction of the Capital, also evoked pride. Two newly built structures, the Śląsko-Dąbrowski and Poniatowskiego bridges, were presented as gifts by laborers from Silesia who worked day and night to give them as soon as possible to the people of Warsaw. The new residential districts of MDM and Mariensztat offered workers appropriate living conditions. The construction of the East-West route (with the famous escalator donated by the Soviet Union) was visited even by President Bierut. The Palace of Culture and Science, which was the tallest building in the city and which dominated the skyline, was a gift of the Soviet nation. Even as late as in the 1980s, textbooks compared the post-war beauty of Warsaw with pre-war pictures of the city. Plans to construct a subway in Warsaw were presented from time to time, starting from the 1950s, but they materialized only after the collapse of the communist regime.

The reconstruction of the whole country was also presented. Some texts openly claimed that during the war it is a civic duty to fight, while in peace time it is a civic duty to work. Textbooks argued that such reconstruction was possible only in a socialist country with engaged workers who were taken care of by the government, and with wise authorities on all levels who guaranteed the good organization of the work.

The socialist economy was by design based on planning. Polish language textbooks joined the campaign that propagated the superiority of the planned economy over the unplanned capitalist system based on competition. They argued that only when profits go to a common treasury and not into the private pockets of capitalists is it possible to conduct big investments and transform the country from an agrarian one into an industrialized country with productive mechanized agriculture. A poem of the day by Jan Brzechwa, the famous children's poet, was titled *You Cannot Get by Without a Plan* (*Bez planu sobie nie poradzisz*). At the same time, textbooks showed how difficult large-scale planning was. The Three and Six Year Plans (of 1947–1949 and 1950–1955, respectively) were presented in the greatest detail. All the achievements of the first years of the People's Poland were attributed to these plans. The grammar textbooks of 1949 and 1950

Polish Language Instruction   91

cited the speeches of Bierut and Minister of Economy, Hilary Minc, promoting the Six Year Plan.

Industry

The nationalization of industry was decreed by the communist government in 1945. Textbooks promoted its positive results: the independence of Poland from foreign capital, the improvement of the situation of workers now formally regarded as co-owners of the factories, the more active participation of workers in factory management, especially through trade unions and factory councils. In fact, the factories became state-owned and the councils and trade unions were used as a means of transmitting the regime's decisions and demands to the workers, not vice versa. They were said to take care of employees, follow safety rules, guarantee workers' rest and relaxation during and after work, organize canteens, factory gardens, common rooms, libraries and vacation funds. Healthcare was provided to workers and their families. The textbooks praised new, bright apartments with running water, sewage, electricity, gas and even radio offered by the communist authorities, incomparable to the pre-war living conditions of the working class.

For their part, the workers from the readings tried to do their best to fulfill the plan on schedule or even ahead of time. Dozens of the stories and poems were devoted to work. All the textbook workers were laborious, disciplined and engaged in their professional lives. Individual sentences as well as whole stories presented workers rushing to factories in the morning or working at night. Work foremen were particularly popular in the 1950s but appeared also much later in both fictitious and real stories of concrete or anonymous persons. They told their life stories and how they achieved their status—usually it seemed to be nothing complicated: one should have simply fulfilled his/her duties and showed some wit and ingenuity, called "rationalization" in the vocabulary of the regime. Miners, bricklayers and female textile workers, often given names, dominated the foremen in the school textbooks of the 1950s. Production commitments and achievements survived in the textbooks until the 1980s. A textbook from 1984 used the following sentences to illustrate some grammatical issues: "Having undertaken a production commitment the factory crew fulfilled it faithfully" and "Our state-owned farm had great production achievements last year".[29]

Readings presented technologies used by various professions, together with the associated vocabulary, such as the names of devices used in construction projects or the parts of an excavator. They praised the capabilities of agricultural machines. Tractors were treated with special reverence. The technologies of coal excavation, transportation and use were described. Accidents in the coal mines also appeared, but not too frequently. Stories told how various goods were produced, such as textiles, sugar and candies, ships, steel products, glass, shoes, paper, books and newspapers, and vehicles, how a pipeline works, and how work is organized in a port. Such readings were not only consistent with the notion of polytechnization of education, but were also intended to evoke esteem for the

92 Polish Language Instruction

workers and their toil as well as to persuade the children that they should take care of the things they use.

The People's Republic of Poland not only rebuilt old factories, but also built lots of new ones. The textbooks were eager to present them. Already in the reading primer (*Elementarz*) a certain young Kazik left his school to move to Nowa Huta, a newly constructed steel mill and housing estate near Cracow.[30] The reading survived even the communist regime. Other children moved there with their parents, who were either construction workers or metallurgists in Nowa Huta. In the 1950s the textbooks mentioned the initial antipathy of the local population towards the builders of the steel mill and the endurance of the workers who did not give up and continued their work. Later, solely achievements were shown.

The oil refinery in Płock and the dam on the Vistula River in Włocławek were promoted in the 1970s, but apparently not as earnestly as the Stalinist investments of the 1950s. In post-Stalinist textbooks the production of chemical fertilizers in Police was welcomed, as were the steel mills in Katowice and in Częstochowa, the power plant in Turoszów, the sulfur basin of Tarnobrzeg and the copper mines and works in the Legnica-Głogów region. The modernization and expansion of old factories in Silesia and Łódź was mentioned both in the 1950s and later. The economic role of the Odra River was presented alongside the development of the automobile industry and the automation of production processes. Even literary texts included a series of great numbers to illustrate the volume of investments and production, to stress the modernity of the endeavors and the wisdom and enthusiasm of their designers and workers. Grammar exercises provided the geographical details of investments or asked students to figure them out: "Enumerate all the grand and modern industrial works in Poland that you know. To what and to whom do we owe their creation?"[31]

Agriculture

Life in the countryside enjoyed considerable attention from Polish language textbooks. Usually the textbooks concentrated on the most topical issues.

Agrarian reform was promoted in the first post-war years as the fulfilment of the eternal dreams and aspirations of peasants and as the implementation of historical justice. Textbooks mentioned the material position of the farmers that had improved considerably thanks to the reform. Farmers enjoyed working on their own property. The readings and exercises presented the houses and palaces of the former landlords transformed into schools, health centers, the headquarters of state-owned farms or other institutions. Children from the textbooks were often surprised, but at the same time happy that spacious buildings with vast gardens which had served just a few people before the war had now become widely available after the reform.

The Six Year Plan in agriculture meant the well-being of farmers from the cooperative villages. The textbooks argued that there were no rich farmers who would exploit the poor any more, and that the vast common fields were easier to farm with agricultural machines. The Union of Farmers' Mutual Aid (*Związek Samopomocy Chłopskiej*) provided machines and instructors who helped farmers. The

Polish Language Instruction 93

collective farms had clean villages with day care, cooperative shops, healthcare centers, libraries and sometimes even kindergartens. Nurseries were organized at a minimum during the harvest time. Stories of the members of a cooperative farm who received new apartments with electricity and radio were published. On the other hand, books from 1946–1952 presented the decision-making process of the farmers before joining the cooperative. They attended special meetings, asked friends and relatives from other villages where the cooperatives had already been established (and who were very positive about it) and eventually always joined. There were very few readings that presented the difficulties experienced by the newly established collective farms. They were caused by the so-called kulaks and pests who set fire to the barns of collective farms' members, placed rats there or devastated machines.

The state-owned farms dominated textbooks beginning in the 1960s, even after the authorities had abandoned the idea of the mass collectivization of agriculture in Poland. Even then, just as in the textbooks for other subjects, collective forms of economy were promoted and the active role of the government appreciated. Children in the textbooks loved to watch the tractors at work on the fields of the state-owned farms or being repaired in the State Machinery Centers.

The achievements of the state-owned farms were always highlighted. In the 1970s the farm in Osowa Sień which specialized in the breeding of dairy cows was presented as a model example. Its proud history was covered in the reports of Alojzy Sroga.[32]

Trade

In the first ten years of the People's Poland, textbooks actively participated in the propaganda campaign against private property in trade. The so-called battle for trade promoted cooperative and state-owned shops as clean, neat and following the rules of hygiene (unlike the privately owned ones), with kind and honest shop assistants, and an abundance of cheap goods. In the case of cooperative shops in the countryside, the textbooks stressed that their profits went to all the members of a cooperative, not to just one proprietor, and that the farmers did not have to go to town so often because they could buy all the necessary products in the village. At the same time, in the cities the department stores were said to impress people with their size (they occupied multi-story buildings), the wide assortment of goods for sale (sometimes the children from textbook stories were not able to see everything during one visit and promised to come again), low prices and long opening hours, including Sundays. Until the end of the 1970s the word "shop" disappeared from the Polish language textbooks and customers were visiting "cooperatives", not "shops".

Social Property

Social property was highly appreciated in the socialist economy. The first post-war textbooks showed how it was created, for example, at schools where pupils set up school and class libraries, gardens or cooperatives that sold food and

94   *Polish Language Instruction*

stationery. They were assisted by parents who provided schools with the necessary equipment, such as furniture. Even animals in the textbook readings established cooperatives. The textbooks argued that the wealthiest children had the biggest problems in sharing their property with others.

The pre-war cooperative movement was briefly presented and communal work such as the restoration of a bridge or road construction appeared in the readings from time to time.

State-owned property was also interpreted as "ours". The property of the state-owned factories and agricultural cooperatives was allegedly taken care of better after it had ceased to belong to its former owners and became the collective property of all, that is, of everybody. The children from one of the readings were happy to see the changing sign at the factory entrance in their town reflecting its "nationalization".

Textbooks tried to educate children to respect collective property both at school and in general. There was a reading in several books from the 1940s until the 1950s where one young boy named Jurek broke a tree on his playground in order to get a twig that he needed to pretend he was a horse rider. His companion exclaimed: "'You broke the tree! You must not do that! This is a park for all children! I am not going to play with you!' Other children also moved away from Jurek".[33] According to a 1953 grammar textbook, fires were harmful because they destroyed collective property.[34] Another one, from 1964, claimed that if one does not keep things in order, he destroys his own belongings as well as collective property.[35]

The Union of Workers and Peasants

From the earliest grades, textbooks persuaded schoolchildren through stories, poems and slogans that farmers could not survive without workers and vice versa. Numerous examples and illustrations showed what goods were exported by cities to rural districts and by rural districts to cities. Books from the 1940s and 1950s covered this topic in great detail. They presented the visits of village children in the cities, and of farmers in the city shops. On Sundays, trucks brought factory workers to the villages where they helped farmers repair and maintain their machines. The enthusiasm of both sides was stressed, as well as the competence of the workers and gratitude of the farmers. The villages of the 1950s were also visited by doctors (unavailable on a regular basis) and by traveling cinemas. These propaganda stories, in fact, revealed how much the countryside of the People's Republic of Poland lagged behind the standards of the civilized world. Running water, sewage systems and gas were regarded as great achievements as late as in 1980. Telephones, cars and refrigerators were mentioned in 1971. One of the 1970s textbooks proudly announced that villagers lived in blocks of flats as in the cities and worked in the factories.[36] This in fact reflected a reality in which many farmers combined work on a farm and in a factory because one job was not enough to earn a living; they could not afford houses and therefore rented apartments, but it was nothing to be proud of.

The Progress of Civilization

The progress of civilization in the People's Republic of Poland was one of the leading topics of textbook propaganda. Polish language textbooks also made their contributions to this campaign. They told the stories of new bridges, railway viaducts, roads, river dams and other investments or compared old and new household appliances. In the first post-war decade they concentrated on the electrification of villages and connecting them to radio services. Stories described this in detail, and "electrician" became a dream profession for young people. Radio was presented in the 1950s as an object of widespread desire. Receivers were installed in houses of culture, common rooms in factories and at schools. They were also given as prizes for the best miners. The books summarized particular radio programs, mostly dealing with propaganda issues such as fulfilment of production plans, the achievements of work foremen or welcoming the schools that had just been connected. In 1965, the pupils were asked to write a report on a broadcast about Lenin.[37]

In the first post-war years, newspapers were the main source of information for textbooks' characters. Whole families sat in a room and listened to one member reading and explaining the articles. The elimination of illiteracy, regarded as one of the top achievements of the communist authorities, was said to enhance readership.

Political Issues

Polish language textbooks published strictly political texts such as excerpts from the proclamation of the Polish Workers' Party (the Communist Party), the July Manifesto of the Polish Committee of National Liberation of 1944 and the constitution of the People's Republic of Poland. They were accompanied with commentaries. The resolutions of Communist Party congresses and speeches by the participants were also cited. There were stories about the presidential elections of 1947 and the parliamentary elections of 1947 and 1952. One story presented boys who helped a farmer with a broken leg get to his polling station and vote.[38]

Books of the Stalinist times did not forget to emphasize the significance of the 1952 Constitution. The 1980 textbook for the 3rd grade explained the meaning of the Polish coat of arms: "It is a Piast eagle with no crown, as a symbol that in the People's Republic of Poland the people are in charge and not—as in the past—kings".[39]

Textbooks presented the biographies of Party and state leaders. This was the case especially in Stalinist times, when Bierut and Rokossovsky appeared in many readings and poems. Bierut enjoyed particular popularity in this regard. He was said to have earned his living from his early years, even at the expense of his health (carrying buckets of water which were too heavy for him). He worked at a construction site and as a typesetter. He was said to be a promoter of cooperatives and a workers' activist in the interwar years. He was even arrested for that reason. His leadership and conspiratorial skills were revealed during World War II

96 Polish Language Instruction

(his relations with the Soviet intelligence services were not mentioned). After the war he became president, "the First Citizen",[40] "the foremen of all foremen".[41] His presence was treated as an honor at events such as a harvest festival or completion of a construction work. He comforted the victims of natural disasters and generally spoke willingly at many different occasions. Textbooks cited his New Year's speeches and texts on the reconstruction of Warsaw, on the music of Chopin, on the perspectives of and tasks for youth and the foundations of the Six Year Plan. Stories of Bierut meeting the youngest "learning forerunners" in his residence in Warsaw appeared in the late 1940s and early 1950s. His portraits accompanied the texts or were at least described. Bierut was always friendly, smiling and in a good mood. He had time for his old friends—despite the fact that he worked extremely hard in all the textbook readings. Whenever the Belvedere palace in Warsaw was described, the books mentioned that the light in the President's office was on until very late at night.

Bierut died in 1956. His successor, Władysław Gomułka, was mentioned much less often, yet there were stories about his participation in the harvest festivals and excerpts from his speeches, and from the speeches of Prime Minister Józef Cyrankiewicz. In the 1970s this practice was discontinued and the new Party leader Edward Gierek never appeared in any Polish language textbook. The 8th grade textbook of the 1970s presented Prime Minister Piotr Jaroszewicz and the Minister of Internal Affairs Mieczysław Moczar, along with their exploits during World War II.

The army in the textbooks always enjoyed high esteem, not only on the field of battle, but also in post-war activities addressed at the civilian population, such as assisting in harvest, during the thaw and in the case of flooding. Various military formations were introduced together with military terminology. The textbooks encouraged pupils to join the army after graduation. It was regarded as a civic duty, but at the same time the beneficial influence of the army on young people was praised. It offered useful skills and helped young people become independent and self-reliant. Young soldiers from textbook readings invited their families for their swearing-in ceremonies or visited them on leave. They looked great in their uniforms. The families were always impressed with the positive changes in their brothers and sons: they learned to drive a car or tractor, to get up quickly in the morning, help at work and keep their belongings in order. Younger children were eager to follow them and enlist in the army as soon as possible.

The children in textbooks were always fascinated by the army. They enjoyed military parades and shows, always greeting soldiers who marched or drove through their town or village. They loved to listen to war stories told by veterans at home (in the earlier years by parents, then by grandparents or their friends) or at school, which usually concentrated on their cooperation with the Red Army. Individual children and whole classes joined in taking care of the so-called places of national memory: Polish and Soviet soldiers' graves, cemeteries and memorial plaques. In the 1940s this care was related to All Saints' Day, while later it was moved to the spring sections of the textbooks since April was proclaimed the National Remembrance Month.

Women

The ideal woman of Polish language textbooks of the 1950s was a working fore-woman. Later it was just "a working woman" who combined her household duties with a professional career. Professional achievements testified to the woman's position. Female tractor-drivers appeared in textbooks alongside female electricians, spinners, engineers, architects, conductors, submarine captains, dentists, tailors (in a cooperative) and teachers. Female army officers were presented only immediately after the war. In those years and also in the 1970s and 1980s "ordinary mums" were also mentioned.

Even housewives profited from the achievements of the People's Republic of Poland. One reading from 1952 presented children who cleaned the house and helped with other things to let their mother go to a Mother's Day ceremony. The conclusion of the reading did not refer to the children's love or family values, but explained that the children did not want "family troubles to prevent mum from having a social life with us and building, together with us, a new, better life in our People's Poland".[42]

Grammar examples presented the Women's League and the struggle for women's suffrage.

Mother's Day (celebrated in Poland on May 26th) was gradually replaced by International Women's Day, celebrated on March 8th. Textbooks published a selection of poems for this occasion. The readings described the holiday preparations at home: children tidied the apartment and sometimes baked a cake, father bought flowers and all the family had dinner together (also at home).

Holidays

The list of holidays regularly mentioned in the textbooks included May 1st (Labor Day), July 22nd (the anniversary of the establishment of the provisional communist government in 1944, called the Holiday of the Rebirth of Poland by the official propaganda), May 9th (Victory Day in the Soviet Union and in the countries of the Soviet bloc), June 1st (International Children's Day), December 4th (Miner's Day) and November 7th (the anniversary of the October Revolution in Russia). In the 1940s, Christmas and Easter also appeared in the textbooks but were removed shortly thereafter due to their religious character. Before 1949, May 3rd was mentioned as Constitution Day commemorating the Polish constitution of 1791, but the Communists did not want to keep the pre-war non-communist traditions. Christmas was sometimes replaced with New Year, but it hardly resembled the holiday atmosphere of the Christmas readings. The texts summarized the achievements of the previous year and laid out some plans for the future. In the exercises accompanying the reading primer of the 1970s, St. Nicolas was reduced to "that old Nicholas who keeps winter under his belt. [. . .] This gift-giver Nicholas. When he loses his belt he will lose winter".[43] The harvest festival was not a religious ceremony any more. In textbook readings, the working foremen brought traditional festival wreaths and gave them to the local state or cooperative officials.

98   *Polish Language Instruction*

May 1st attracted the most attention in textbooks. They focused on the ways it was celebrated by both adults and children. Readings described the parades, city and school decorations, school events and so-called social campaigns (various forms of community works or production commitments). Such acts were presented also in connection with other communist holidays, both annual ones such as July 22nd or November 7th, and special ones such as Communist Party congresses. The history of the May 1st celebrations was also discussed, including the persecutions suffered by celebrating workers under capitalism (on the other hand, in the People's Republic of Poland, the authorities imposed punishments on those who did not attend the May 1st celebrations, but this was not was mentioned in the textbooks). The books created an impression of universal festivities, both in Poland and worldwide, and of the widespread enthusiasm of the participants. The repertoire of the poems published on this occasion was truly impressive. In each grade every pupil read (and probably learned by heart) a new one, which made a total of seven or eight per primary school graduate. Altogether there were over thirty various May 1st poems in all the textbooks published throughout the whole period of communist rule in Poland. They usually presented parades and their youngest participants, expressed the pride of workers in their achievements and the joy of nature blossoming for that occasion.

July 22nd was not as convenient as May 1st because it was celebrated during the summer holiday. Therefore, most textbooks mentioned it in their very last section. The historical readings presented the "liberation" of Lublin and proclamation of the July Manifesto in 1944. Parades and other forms of celebration on this holiday took place during the summer camps. Textbooks published poems and other materials admiring the achievements of the People's Republic of Poland to be performed on stage during such celebrations.

May 9th was associated with combatants' stories. Immediately after the war, they stressed the annihilation of German power in which the Slavic countries played a crucial role. Later, Polish-Soviet friendship dominated those tales.

Children's Day was to be associated not with joy and gifts (though sometimes the textbooks mentioned celebrations organized by the "school parents' committees" for the pupils), but rather with the struggle for children's rights in the countries where children were exploited and suffered other hardships. Another popular theme was the solidarity of children from all over the world in the struggle for peace.

Miner's Day was traditionally celebrated in Poland on St. Barbara's day (December 4th) since St. Barbara is the patron saint of miners in the Catholic Church. The communist regime did not change the date but deprived it of its religious character, at least in textbooks. The books simply concentrated all the readings and poems about the miners, previously dispersed throughout the textbooks, in one section to be read at the beginning of December. They encouraged pupils to find more publications dealing with miners: "Find a report on work in a modern coal mine in a weekly magazine and tell how the working conditions of miners have changed".[44]

The teaching profession was the only other one whose representatives celebrated their holiday in textbooks (which reflected the school reality of October 14th).

The anniversary of the October Revolution was commemorated until the late 1970s by readings about the life of Lenin or the history of the revolution and the Russian Civil War. The military parade in Moscow, organized yearly on this occasion, was sometimes mentioned, and Polish-Soviet friendship always emphasized. In the 1950s the whole month of November was presented as a month for deepening this friendship, hence sentences about a Soviet film festival or about special school events inserted into the grammar exercises.

Children

Children in textbooks were extremely serious, never just joyful and carefree. Even if they played, they were for example preparing paper figurines of the participants of a military parade at Red Square in Moscow, building a house, reloading the collier "Sołdek", reconstructing Warsaw or marching as soldiers (children-soldiers never actually fought in Polish textbooks). They could also try to prove that it was easier to build a snowman working together than apart. Most of the aforementioned examples come from the 1950s, but also later the children were presented at work rather than playing. They participated in the post-war reconstruction, saved textbooks, attended organizational meetings, published school newspapers, helped in the library, joined various interest circles, took care of younger children or of the school gardens, cleaned the school area, planted trees, fed animals, collected beetles that infested the fields or helped the farmers in state-owned or cooperative farms. Even during summer holiday, they combined rest with helping local people. Boys did some physical work while girls took care of the local children (so that their mothers could work in the fields), helped with the harvest or organized parties for the locals.

The textbooks promoted collective and organized forms of spending vacations, such as scouting camps or at least a half day spent on in-school activities. They were presented as much more interesting and advantageous for the children. These forms of spending free time were said to teach self-reliance and to supersede holidays spent with parents or extended family.

Children from textbook readings spent most of their time outside the home and family. The texts told the stories of mothers who left their infants at nurseries on their way to work. Older kids attended kindergartens and schoolchildren stayed in the afternoons in the day rooms at school. Apparently, this was the model promoted by propaganda, but was odd to most people since the readings showed a bias against those institutions and how it was overcome by both children and adults. They stressed the cleanliness of all forms of day care, their friendly and professional guardians, and the good atmosphere.

Most stories about children showed pupils whose main duty was learning. It was compared to the production work of their parents and regarded as a prologue to the future professional careers of the children. They should follow the same work discipline (this was why, the textbooks explained, one should not be late for school), develop work competitiveness (competition in coming to school on time or getting good grades), and engage in rationalization (e.g. little Walerka

100   Polish Language Instruction

was called a "rationalizer" when she went home and studied directly after her lessons and not just before the next one,[45] which took less time and brought better results, while another "rationalizer", Ewa, wrote a poem that helped her learn the alphabet[46]). The wording from the "general" propaganda of work was used, resembling newspaper articles of the time.

Good grades were not as important as school discipline and promotion. Those who were not promoted were presented as an economic problem for the whole country: they incurred extra education costs and delayed the "production" of a new cadre of workers. Every school class should have the ambition to achieve a level of 100% promoted students each year. In the early 1950s it was regarded as the pupils' contribution to the Six Year Plan. A 3rd grade textbook from 1952 published the oath of the children from one of the Warsaw schools, who swore to be promoted, to improve their grades and to bring plants to their classroom in order to help their parents fulfill the Six Year Plan.[47]

Textbooks also showed how the state authorities took care of schools. Opening and closing school year ceremonies were described at the beginning and end of many textbooks. Other official events attended by representatives of the Party and state apparatus or working foremen were also mentioned. The books proudly announced broad educational opportunities offered by the regime, which had not been available to workers' and peasants' children before the war. Young people from rural areas could now attend art schools and young capable workers were sent for further education. The state established new schools. Immediately after the war they were located in the former mansions acquired by the state as a result of the agrarian reform. Later they were constructed from scratch, especially within the project of "A Thousand Schools for the Millennium [of Poland in 1966]". The readings described how the pupils and their parents, with workers from the nearby factories, participated in the construction work. The opportunity of going to school was regarded as an honor and joy which poor children in the past were deprived of, as were all children during the Nazi occupation, but also the sons and daughters of partisans in Vietnam and young people in the colonies.

Of all the institutions of education, primary, vocational and technical schools enjoyed the most attention, since this was the desired model of education. The professions that the textbooks recommended to young readers were farmer, miner, metallurgist (sometimes called "the guard of great fire"[48] or "the cook of a great kitchen"[49]), tractor driver, car driver, electrician, constructor, fisherman, sailor, soldier and policeman (or rather a militiaman). One boy from the post-war books was going to be a "cooperative salesmen", and another one dreamt about being a typesetter. When his family did not share his enthusiasm for this profession and thought about his higher education, he explained that President Bierut also worked as a typesetter at the beginning of his career.[50] A girl of the 1960s wanted to become a milkmaid. Of the professionals, engineers enjoyed the highest esteem in the textbooks, while teachers and doctors were also mentioned. The files of the Ministry of Education and of the censorship office prove that the professions of the textbook adults were not freely chosen by the authors, but rather

Polish Language Instruction   101

were a political matter. The father of the main character from a reading primer in Stalinist times could not be an engineer but only a worker. The father of a friend of hers could be an architect. This would change only after 1956.[51]

Grades received at school determined the children's position both at school and at home. Parents did not love their children just because they were their children. A reading presented a father who smiled at his son for the first time in a long time when he finally got a passing grade. Another one could not enjoy his own achievements and his title of working foremen because his son failed a test at school.[52]

Fathers and mothers were first and foremost representatives of their professions, not just parents. Their family lives were dominated by their professional careers. In the 1940s they spent time together at a May 1st parade, or on reading and explaining a newspaper, or on discussion on the fulfilment of production plans. In the 1950s children were very proud when their parents were presented on the radio, during a school excursion to a factory, or invited to school ceremonies as working foremen.

In some readings the roles of parents and children were inverted. The children were better educated, especially politically, and explained various political issues to the adults. They could convince the adults to join a production cooperative (a collective farm) or to connect electricity to their homes and farms. The young people from the Union of the Polish Youth taught adults how to read and write. The super-smart members of the paramilitary organization "Service for Poland" from a 1951 textbook knew that when a horse was ill, one should call a vet instead of giving up and letting it die after home remedies were exhausted.[53]

Stalinist textbooks openly promoted "Service to Poland" as a place to learn many useful skills, such as to get a tractor-driver's or electrician's license, and at the same time to help reconstruct the country after the war: during the harvest, in the construction of bridges or earthworks, in digging ditches, in the melioration works in the fields or in the reconstruction of Warsaw and the construction of Nowa Huta near Cracow. The textbooks did not mention that these were exhausting and primitive jobs. They rather stressed that young people enthusiastically volunteered in "Service for Poland".

Other youth organizations from the textbooks included scouting for the youngest and the Union of Polish Youth for older ones. According to the textbooks, their organizational activities included attending (regular) meetings, excursions and summer camps, and participation in some communal work projects such as collecting reusable materials (paper, metals, clothes etc.), cleaning or aiding older people or neighbors. The members of the youth organizations were always enthusiastic and the younger children usually wanted to join them.

The pupils from the textbooks founded and operated school cooperatives, and saved money in School Savings Fund (*Szkolna Kasa Oszczędności*). To participate in the life of the collective and to take leadership positions was presented as an honor. Only one book, published in 1952, included a (fictitious) letter of an exhausted young activist to his friend where he complained that he could not fulfill all his social duties.[54]

The Image of the Post–World War II World outside Poland

The post-war world in the school textbooks was rather limited in scope. According to general tendencies it was presented through a black-and-white paradigm of the class struggle for the victory of socialism. Some countries had already achieved this stage of social development a long time ago such as the Soviet Union, or only very recently, as Vietnam or Cuba. Others were supposed to do it shortly and were presented in a positive, and sometimes even totally uncritical light, while in the capitalist countries there was nothing but problems and injustices to be found and the potential for a much-desired revolution.

The Soviet Union enjoyed the greatest attention of all the countries. It was presented as Poland's wartime ally, peacetime assistant and a model to follow. Soviet achievements in science, biology, chemistry and other books were presented again: the exploration of the Arctic (with Ivan Papanin, the organizer of one of the expeditions and Valeriy Tchkhalov, an aviator) and the development of the vast territories of Siberia. The enthusiasm of the young builders going into the wilderness was expressed in many texts. Ivan Michurin and his successors, who transformed plants and animals to better serve human needs, also attracted the attention of textbook authors.

Soviet pioneers were given as a model to follow by Polish pupils. They spent their free time in so-called pioneer palaces or houses where they enjoyed various interest circles that helped them find future professions. In the 1950s textbook readers were fascinated by the pioneers operating trains on the so-called pioneer railway in Leningrad. Other pioneers from Polish language textbooks did heroic deeds, not only during the war but also afterwards, such as rescuing people or the harvest from fire. There was a story, published in more than one textbook, about a Kazakh girl who went to school with a huge stone in her hands in order to stop the wind from blowing her away because she wanted to learn Russian.[55] Polish and Soviet children made friends and met one another in the Artek pioneer camp on the Crimean Peninsula.

Moscow was mentioned in the textbooks as a large, beautiful city. Moscow's subway was described as the most beautiful and comfortable in the world.

Among the Soviet people found in Polish language textbooks in the 1940s and 1950s, there were working foremen, especially females, such as the pioneer girl Nakhangova, and Mamlakat, who broke records for picking cotton, or a more anonymous Pelasia from a short story by Wanda Wasilewska. Pelasia was said to have received a medal for work in a collective farm.[56] Stalin also appeared in the textbooks of that period from time to time. Students could learn the biography of J. Dzhugashvili, starting from his childhood in a poor Georgian shoemaker's family. Young "Soso", as he was called, was an extremely capable pupil, but at the same one of the poorest ones. He could not afford to buy textbooks and borrowed them from his wealthier friends. He did not visit them at their homes, however, because he despised the rich. On the other hand, he became quite active when it came to games with his poor schoolmates. An episode from Stalin's meeting with revolutionaries in exile in Siberia was published (the same one found in

Russian language textbooks, but this time in Polish). His visit to the Polish city of Cracow in the pre-revolutionary period was also mentioned. Then he became an important figure of the October Revolution and the leader of the Soviet Union, a proponent of world peace and the creator of Soviet economic and military power. Stalin was also presented as a friend of children and of Poland. These were said to be the reasons why he enjoyed particular reverence in Polish textbooks. Some stories told Polish pupils how Soviet families celebrated Stalin's birthday (December 21st) and enumerated the gifts he received. They presented a Polish farmer who had planted fifty trees on the occasion of the 50th birthday of Stalin. Textbook characters were always eager to meet Stalin and even to learn that he had mentioned someone. Poems about Stalin were accompanied with pictures. Stalin disappeared from the textbooks in 1955. His immediate successors, Khrushchev or Brezhnev never appeared there.

In the 1960s the focus on the Soviet Union changed towards space flight. The flight of the first human in space, Yuri Gagarin, was covered in great detail. Fragments from Gagarin's memoirs were published (about the launching of his spaceship, the flight itself and landing in a Soviet kolkhoz field where he immediately recognized that, to his great joy, the people he met after landing were Soviet people). The Soviet dog Belka that spent a day in space in 1960 was presented in a textbook poem as an expert in astronomy explaining to other animals the nature of the moon (which was not a banana, nor cheese, nor a plate, Belka said).[57]

Other countries of the Soviet bloc did not appear as often as the Soviet Union. In the 1940s the Polish-Czechoslovak and Polish-Yugoslavian brotherhood was mentioned, within the pan-Slavic rather than communist perspective. In the 1950s Romanian, Bulgarian and Hungarian pioneers and working foremen appeared from time to time. They were presented in the same way as Polish or Soviet ones. It showed that all the countries of the bloc had similar problems, achievements and hierarchies. The Polish children made friends with children from other socialist countries.

Starting in 1950, a lot of space was devoted to the Far East: China, Korea and Vietnam, and to their leaders: Mao, Kim Il-Sung and Ho Chi Minh. A textbook from 1949 published a poem by Mao translated by Czesław Miłosz.[58] The textbooks claimed that communist rule in China ended corruption, the wasting of money and the exploitation of workers and peasants. Chinese children could go to school. Poems by well-known Polish authors expressed their support for North Korea. In one of them a newborn girl of the author's friends was going to be given the name Korea.[59] Vietnam was presented by prominent Polish journalists and writers who visited the country during the war. The sympathy of the authors was always with the partisans of the Vietcong and the civilian population of North Vietnam.

Cuba appeared in textbooks from the mid-1960s and early 1970s in a story of Fidel Castro visiting poor villages and trying to help people. At the same time, he explained that the authorities had a lot of urgent problems to solve and not all the needs could be fulfilled immediately. Thus, he recommended for example using leaves and sand instead of lamenting the shortages of soap.[60]

104 *Polish Language Instruction*

Western Europe was, generally speaking, beyond the scope of interest of textbook authors. In the 1940s England and France were sometimes mentioned as allies of Poland. In 1946, one of the children in a 5th grade grammar book was going to go to Denmark on summer holiday thanks to the offer of humanitarian assistance of the Danish government for Polish war victims.[61] In 1949, however, the same boy spent his holiday at the Artek pioneer camp on the Black Sea in the Soviet Union. In a story from the early 1950s a French dock worker came home from the night shift, where he and his comrades had dumped weapons overboard that were supposed to be shipped to the French army in Indochina.[62]

The United States appeared in textbooks more often than Western Europe, but always in a negative context, such as abuses of the black population and the weaknesses of an unplanned economy (e.g. devastation of the natural environment and exploitation of workers).

Periodically problems of the countries of the Third World also were discussed, mostly in textbooks for older children. The exploitation, especially of children, by local or white landlords was presented (e.g. in the rice fields in India or China, or cocoa plantations in South America). The children received little or no money for their extremely hard work, and were often beaten or defrauded.

In the 1960s a series of texts appeared that presented Polish aid for developing countries. Polish specialists went to exotic places to help: a doctor to Ghana, engineers constructing factories to Iraq and Vietnam or to coal mines in India. Another group helped rescue ancient monuments in Egypt. A few texts about reforms in Africa were published in the 1970s and 1980s.

Foreign countries, or at least their representatives, were associated with the "struggle for peace" under Soviet leadership. Other countries of the Soviet bloc were said to have joined it. It had also developed among the "progressive forces" in other countries. The textbooks showed young people engaged in this struggle. They prepared school newspapers, sometimes with the help of their peers from other countries, with whom they willingly corresponded. Peace conferences, congresses and speeches were also presented. The children were asked to write essays dealing with peace. The textbooks included a great variety of poems and other texts about the struggle for peace. In fact, some of them put more stress on "struggle" than on peace.

***

It is worth noting how propaganda content developed with the advancing age of pupils to whom it was addressed. It started as early as in reading primers. Already in these first textbooks, factories produced goods, the People's Army enjoyed widespread support and children expressed solidarity with other youngsters from all over the world. In the 1950s, President Bierut and Marshal Rokossovsky were presented in special readings (but not Lenin or Stalin, unlike in many other countries of the Soviet bloc).

However, in the first grades the readings dealt mostly with current domestic issues. Gradually, both the geographical and chronological scope was enhanced and the presentation of propaganda issues was more in-depth. Readings prepared

Polish Language Instruction 105

specifically for use at school were gradually replaced by excerpts from general literature and historical sources.

This is one of the reasons why the textbooks for older pupils in general contained more propaganda than those addressed to the younger learners. This situation changed in the 1980s when the first textbooks paid more attention to "educating" pupils to become better citizens, while in the final grades the primary schools concentrated mostly on literary education, practicing grammar and writing skills. However, in those last years of the People's Republic of Poland, the propaganda load of the school textbooks was generally much lower than in previous decades.

In the first grades textbooks depicted only the positive aspects of the world. Gradually, some negative aspects were also introduced. For example, the children in the People's Republic of Poland (according to the textbooks) were always happy, but in higher grades, the hardships of growing up in the past and in foreign countries were also mentioned.

Notes

1 The files of the Ministry of Education document a discussion on the inclusion of the classical poem by Juliusz Słowacki, one of the most eminent poets of Polish Romanticism, with a refrain "I am sad, oh God" (*Smutno mi, Boże*). The decision was eventually reached to move the poem from primary to secondary school.

2 Lausz, Karol, Kazimierz Staszewski and Zofia Zwierzchowska-Ferencowa. 1949. *O świcie. Czytanki dla klasy V szkoły podstawowej*. Warsaw: PZWS, 34–35.

3 Dembowska, Janina, Zygmunt Saloni and Piotr Wierzbicki. 1973. *Świat i my. Podręcznik do nauki języka polskiego dla klasy VI*. Warsaw: WSiP, 77.

4 Ibid., 135.

5 Lausz, Karol, Kazimierz Staszewski and Zofia Zwierzchowska-Ferencowa. 1949. *O świcie. Czytanki dla klasy V szkoły podstawowej*. Warsaw: PZWS, 261.

6 Pęcherski, Mieczysław. 1961. *Język polski. Wiadomości i ćwiczenia z gramatyki i pisowni. Klasa VI*. Warsaw: PZWS, 139.

7 Aleksandrzak, Stanisław, Józefa Rytlowa and Zbigniew Przyrowski. 1966. *W naszej gromadzie. Podręcznik do nauki języka polskiego dla klasy III*. Warsaw: PZWS, 94.

8 Sufin, Stanisława and Aniela Świerczyńska. 1965. *Mowa ojczysta. Wypisy z ćwiczeniami. Dla klasy VII*. Warsaw: PZWS, 19.

9 Wieczorkiewicz, Bronisław. 1950. *Mowa polska. Ćwiczenia gramatyczne. Klasa IV*. Warsaw: PZWS, 13, 18.

10 Nagajowa, Maria and Aniela Świerczyńska. 1969. *W naszej ojczyźnie. Podręcznik do nauki języka polskiego dla klasy V*. Warsaw: PZWS, 331.

11 Nagajowa, Maria and Aniela Świerczyńska. 1971. *W naszej ojczyźnie. Podręcznik do nauki języka polskiego dla klasy V*. Warsaw: PZWS, 375.

12 Sufin, Stanisława and Aniela Świerczyńska. 1965. *Mowa ojczysta. Wypisy z ćwiczeniami. Dla klasy VII*. Warsaw: PZWS, 277.

13 Ibid., 274.

14 Bielak, Franciszek, Władysław Szyszkowski and Artur Bardach. 1949. *Czytanki polskie. Dla VII kl. szkoły podstawowej*. Warsaw: PZWS, 316.

15 Rytlowa, Józefa. 1948. *Nauka pisania. Dla II klasy szkoły powszechnej*. Warsaw: PZWS, 18.

16 Even fairy tales were chosen that illustrated certain social problems, and the textbooks claimed that there was not much sense in reading fairy tales, if reality surpasses the fantasy: steppes are drained in the Soviet Union, great canals constructed and the Soviet machines can move mountains.

106 Polish Language Instruction

17 Wieczorkiewicz, Bronisław. 1946. *Ćwiczenia ortograficzne. Klasa VI.* Warsaw: PZWS, 22.

18 Dańcewiczowa, Jadwiga. 1948. *Ćwiczenia i wiadomości gramatyczne. Dla klasy V szkoły podstawowej.* Warsaw: PZWS, 46.

19 Dembowska, Janina and Zofia Strzelecka. 1977. *Książka życiu pomaga. Wypisy dla klasy VI.* Warsaw: WSiP, 132–134.

20 Usually the version by Wanda Wasilewska was published. Wasilewska was a pedagogue, but also a Communist activist who spent the World War II years in the Soviet Union and organized the pro-Stalinist Union of Polish Patriots in Moscow. She did not return to Poland after the war.

21 But at least one appeared also in 1971 (Kopczewski, Jan S. 1971. *Ta ziemia od innych droższa. Podręcznik do języka polskiego dla kl. VIII.* Warsaw: PZWS, 88–93).

22 Kubski, Benedykt and Jacek Kubski. 1960. *Wypisy. Dla klasy VII.* Warsaw: PZWS, 183–188.

23 Dembowska, Janina and Zofia Strzelecka. *Książka życiu pomaga. Wypisy dla klasy VI.* Warsaw: WSiP, 22–26.

24 Numerous memoirs prove the contrary (most recently Donna, Ubrikas. 2016. *My Sisters' Mother. A Memoir of War, Exile, and Stalin's Siberia.* Milwaukee, WI: University of Wisconsin Press).

25 Aleksandrzak, Stanisław and Zbigniew Przyrowski. 1966. *A czy znasz ty, bracie młody . . . Czytanki dla klasy IV.* Warsaw: PZWS, 64–66.

26 Kopczewski, Jan S. 1971. *Ta ziemia od innych droższa. Podręcznik do języka polskiego dla kl. VIII.* Warsaw: PZWS 316 and Nagajowa, Maria and Aniela Świerczyńska. 1980. *W codziennej pracy. Podręcznik do nauki języka polskiego. Dla klasy V.* Warsaw: WSiP, 72.

27 The Spanish Civil War was also mentioned on other occasions especially in the late 1940s and early 1950s.

28 Wieczorkiewicz, Bronisław. 1950. *Mowa polska. Ćwiczenia gramatyczne i słownikowe. Klasa I.* Warsaw: PZWS, 34.

29 Jaworski, Michał. 1984. *Język polski. Gramatyka i ortografia. Podręcznik dla klasy 7 szkoły podstawowej.* Warsaw: WSiP, 97, 105 respectively.

30 Falski, Marian. 1953. *Elementarz.* Warsaw: PZWS, 150.

31 Dembowska, Janina, Zygmunt Saloni and Piotr Wierzbicki. 1973. *Świat i my. Podręcznik do języka polskiego dla klasy VI.* Warsaw: WSiP, 135.

32 Aleksandrzak, Stanisław and Zbigniew Przyrowski. 1971. *Z bliska i z daleka. Wypisy dla klasy V.* Warsaw: WSiP, 90–92; Dembowska, Janina, Zygmunt Saloni and Piotr Wierzbicki. 1973. *Świat i my. Podręcznik do nauki języka polskiego dla klasy VI.* Warsaw: WSiP, 165–169; Dembowska, Janina, Zygmunt Saloni and Piotr Wierzbicki. 1976. *Nasz język, nasz świat. Podręcznik do nauki języka polskiego dla klasy VI.* Warsaw: WSiP, 184–188.

33 Dobraniecki, Stanisław, Mieczysław Kotarbiński and Stanisław Aleksandrzak. 1946. *Razem. Czytanki dla II klasy szkoły powszechnej,* Warsaw: PZWS, 158; Aleksandrzak, Stanisław and Zofia Kwiecińska. 1949. *Za progiem. Czytanki dla klasy II szkoły podstawowej.* Warsaw: PZWS, 15–16; Wieczorkiewicz, Bronisław. 1950. *Mowa polska. Ćwiczenia gramatyczne i słownikowe. Klasa I.* Warsaw: PZWS, 37 (in this case the boy is named Staś).

34 Wieczorkiewicz, Bronisław. 1953. *Mowa polska. Ćwiczenia gramatyczne, ortograficzne i słownikowe. Klasa IV,* Warsaw: PZWS, 155.

35 Kowalczewska, Anna and Zofia Mórawska. 1964. *Język polski. Ćwiczenia gramatyczne i stylistyczne dla klasy IV.* Warsaw: PZWS, 118–119.

36 Pęcherski, Mieczysław. 1972. *Nasz język ojczysty. Wiadomości i ćwiczenia z gramatyki i pisowni polskiej. Klasa VII.* Warsaw: PZWS, 48.

37 Sufin, Stanisława and Aniela Świerczyńska. 1965. *Mowa ojczysta. Wypisy z ćwiczeniami. Dla klasy VII.* Warsaw: PZWS, 282.

38 Aleksandrzak, Stanisław and Halina Koszutska. 1954. *Czytanki. Dla klasy III.* Warsaw: PZWS, 246–248.

Polish Language Instruction   107

39 Gawdzik, Witold. 1980. *Nasza mowa—nasz świat*. *Klasa 3*. Warsaw: WSiP, 172.
40 Słuszkiewiczowa, Maria. 1950. *Ćwiczenia ortograficzne*. *Dla klasy II*. Warsaw: PZWS, 18.
41 Dembowska, Janina, Halina Rudnicka and Teofil Wojeński. 1953. *Na drodze przemian*. *Czytanki dla klasy VII*. Warsaw: PZWS, 318–322.
42 Pauszer-Klonowska, Gabriela and Karol Lausz. 1951. *Dzień dzisiejszy*. *Wypisy dla klasy V*. Warsaw: PZWS, 291–295.
43 Przyłubska, Ewa and Feliks Przyłubski. 1976. *Litery*. *Ćwiczenia uzupełniające*. Warsaw: WSiP, 46.
44 Kopczewski, Jan S. 1971. *Ta ziemia od innych droższa*. *Podręcznik do języka polskiego dla kl. VIII*. Warsaw: PZWS, 273.
45 In Polish schools, the timetable for each day is different and most subjects are taught twice or even only once a week.
46 Aleksandrzak, Stanisław, Zofia Kwiecińska and Zbigniew Przyrowski. 1951. *Na szerokiej drodze*. *Czytanki dla klasy IV*. Warsaw: PZWS, 68–71; Aleksandrzak, Stanisław and Zbigniew Przyrowski. 1966. *A czy znasz ty, bracie młody . . . Czytanki dla klasy IV*. Warsaw: PZWS, 24–27; Aleksandrzak, Stanisław and Józefa Rytlowa. 1970. *W szkole i w domu*. *Podręcznik do nauki języka polskiego dla klasy II*. Warsaw: WSiP, 111.
47 Aleksandrzak, Stanisław and Halina Koszutska. 1952. *Czytanki*. *Dla klasy III*. Warsaw: PZWS, 259–262.
48 Aleksandrzak, Stanisław, Maria Bober and Hanna Zegadło. 1979. *Nasz dom ojczysty*. *Podręcznik do nauki języka polskiego*. *Klasa 2*. Warsaw: WSiP, 122.
49 Aleksandrzak, Stanisław, Józefa Rytlowa and Zbigniew Przyrowski. 1966. *W naszej gromadzie*. *Podręcznik do nauki języka polskiego dla klasy III*. Warsaw: PZWS, 270–272.
50 Zarembina, Ewa, Hanna Ożogowska and Zygmunt Batorowicz. 1947. *Czytanka*. *Dla IV klasy miejskich i wiejskich szkół podstawowych*. Warsaw: Nasza Księgarnia, 136–138.
51 Falski, Marian. 1953. *Elementarz*. Warsaw: PZWS; Falski, Marian. 1958. *Elementarz*. Warsaw: PZWS; Archiwum Akt Nowych, Warsaw. Files of the Ministry of Education (Ministerstwo Oświaty), file 5735, p. 29.
52 Dembowska, Janina and Halina Rudnicka. 1950. *Dom i świat*. *Wypisy dla klasy VI*. Warsaw: PZWS, 283–286.
53 Aleksandrzak, Stanisław, Zofia Kwiecińska and Zbigniew Przyrowski. 1951. *Na szerokiej drodze*. *Czytanki dla klasy IV*. Warsaw: PZWS, 159–161.
54 Klemensiewicz, Zygmunt and Janina Żlabowa. 1952. *Nasz język*. *Gramatyka języka polskiego z ćwiczeniami*. *Klasa VII*. Warsaw: PZWS, 18.
55 Aleksandrzak, Stanisław and Zofia Kwiecińska. 1949. *Za progiem*. *Czytanki dla klasy II szkoły podstawowej*. Warsaw: PZWS, 225–228.
56 Broniewska, Janina. 1949. *W naszej szkole*. Czytanki dla IV klasy szkoły podstawowej. Warsaw: PZWS, 44–48.
57 Aleksandrzak, Stanisław, Józefa Rytlowa and Zbigniew Przyrowski. 1966. *W naszej gromadzie*. *Podręcznik do nauki języka polskiego dla klasy III*. Warsaw: PZWS, 315–316.
58 Bielak, Franciszek, Władysław Szyszkowski and Artur Bardach. 1949. *Czytanki polskie*. *Dla VII kl. szkoły podstawowej*. Warsaw: PZWS, 318.
59 Wieczorkiewicz, Bronisław. 1952. *Pisownia polska w ćwiczeniach*. *Klasa VII*. Warsaw: PZWS, 72.
60 Dembowska, Janina, Zygmunt Saloni and Piotr Wierzbicki. 1973. *Świat i my*. *Podręcznik do nauki języka polskiego dla klasy VI*. Warsaw: WSiP, 102–107, 112; Kopczewski, Jan S. 1968. *Między dawnymi a nowymi laty*. *Wypisy dla klasy VIII szkoły podstawowej*. Warsaw: PZWS, 294–299.
61 Rytlowa, Józefa. 1946 and 1949. *Nauka pisania*. *Ćwiczenia ortograficzne, gramatyczne i przygotowanie do wypracowań dla V klasy szkoły powszechnej*. Warsaw: PZWS, 74–76.
62 Aleksandrzak, Stanisław and Halina Koszutska. 1952. *Czytanki*. *Dla klasy III*. Warsaw: PZWS, 225–227.

6 History

History textbooks were the most heavily loaded with propaganda of all the primary school textbooks in the People's Poland. School history is notorious for being used as a tool of indoctrination, not only in Poland and not only under Communism. The reasons for this lie in the very nature of the subject and of the academic discipline, as well as in the tradition of policymakers' practices. In the People's Republic of Poland history textbooks changed almost every year before 1955. In the 1960s they stabilized to some extent, though still changed more often than in the case of any other subject and mostly for political reasons. Policymakers influenced the selection of facts to be discussed and their assessments. The book by Gustaw Markowski for the 5th grade (dealing with ancient and medieval history) remained the same for more than ten years (1968–1978), but it was an exception. The higher the grade, the closer the material to the present times and therefore the less stable, more ideologically loaded and deceitful the textbook narratives.

The textbook authors also changed quite often. Markowski was a pre-war teacher, and after the war he became a Communist Party activist, working in the Ministry of Education and also taking charge of the history section of the National Center for Teaching Methodology. Most other authors were professional academic historians and/or teachers.

Indoctrination in history education was not just an addition to the core narrative, but an integral part of it. In order to eliminate propaganda from history education, one could not simply omit some parts of the textbooks. The textbook narratives themselves did leave out certain historical facts, figures, processes and phenomena (e.g. the Katyń massacre of about twenty thousand Polish officers by the Soviet NKVD,[1] the Soviet Gulag or the social role of the Catholic Church) but this did not significantly reduce the teaching material since many other unnecessary details were added, such as the names of minor left-wing organizations under Nazi occupation or of revolutionary activists in 19th century Russia. Eliminating the manipulated passages from the text could erase whole periods from history education; for example, if the interwar period was reduced in Stalinist textbooks to anti-Soviet policy, economic crises and social protests of the workers and peasants against the capitalist government, omitting propaganda would make the years 1919–1939 completely disappear.[2]

Propagandist interpretation further strengthened the indoctrinating role of the textbooks. Textbooks made clear judgments on everything from the past, and left children with no doubts or ambiguity. The presentation of a historical figure could start from an opinion; for example, "The new king [Sigismundus III] was tacit, obstinate and unchivalrous. The Poles did not like him".[3] The description of Calvinism was also far from being objective: "Stinginess, indifference to human misery, insensibility to the beauty of life—that was what the Calvinists regarded as the primary human virtues. Thus, Calvinism was an expression of the desires and goals of the wealthy bourgeoisie, and was the ideology of the emerging class of capitalists".[4] The labels "progressive", "backward" and "reactionary" were in constant use. Words and phrases from the communist newspeak of the time of publication also sometimes appeared, such as "brotherly help" from the Czechs for Poles in the Middle Ages, used by the propaganda of 1968 for the invasion of the Warsaw Pact in Czechoslovakia.

Attempts to bring the past closer to pupils' experiences could also be propaganda-oriented. For example, the tools of the 14th century were to be compared with contemporary ones. Turkish cannons from the siege of Constantinople "did not resemble those express and long-range cannons from the last war".[5] In the past "there were no vocational schools. Only master craftsmen prepared young people for their profession".[6]

This chapter will present only the general trends of propaganda in history textbooks. A detailed analysis of these books would overwhelm this study. There are separate monographs dealing with some individual aspects and periods, such as representations of Germany and Russia in the textbooks,[7] the indoctrinating role of history at schools in the Stalinist times,[8] or the organizational aspects of history education in post-war Poland.[9] New studies are still being undertaken.

Five propaganda areas can be distinguished in the presentation of the past. They closely correspond with the general scheme of textbook indoctrination, but were more deeply rooted in textbook narratives than in other subjects, changed slower, and to some extent survived the collapse of the communist regime before the textbooks were completely rewritten rather than just slightly modified.

First, **Marxist historiographical theory** was promoted from the issuing of the curriculum instruction of 1951. It replaced the traditional periodization (antiquity, Middle Ages, modern times, contemporary history) with primitive communism, slavery, feudalism, capitalism, socialism and prospective communism, and the class struggle was presented as the driving force of historical progress that moved humanity from one stage of development to the next.

Second, textbooks paid special attention to the development of **communist doctrine** and to the implementation of **socialism**, in accordance with guidance from the Soviet and Polish Communist Parties. The history of the revolutionary movement, the Soviet Union and the Soviet bloc occupied a great deal of space in textbooks.

Third, the **Catholic Church** was presented in an extremely negative light. Only the first Christians enjoyed a certain sympathy; later on the Church was only criticized, and its post–World War II history was not mentioned at all.

110   *History*

History teachers' journal *Wiadomości Historyczne* openly stated that history education should play a crucial role in the process of atheization of the youth.[10]

Fourth, the textbooks offered an entirely **presentist interpretation** of the geopolitical situation of Poland from its origins through recent times. Foreign policy, particularly relations with Germany and Russia, were seen from the perspective of post-war communist interests.

Fifth, the elements of "**polytechnization**" of history education can be found in stories about the development of mining and metallurgy through the ages, with details on technology and production volumes of ancient furnaces which were sometimes compared with contemporary steel mills.

Stalinist textbooks were the most heavily loaded with propaganda. In some of them, there was no neutral narrative at all. The themes mentioned earlier were taken to absurd extremes. For example, when the authors were not able to provide data on the class struggle in medieval Poland, they claimed that bourgeois historiography was to blame for deliberately omitting such data, and that future Marxist research would undoubtedly discover instances of rebellions. The whole 7th grade was devoted to learning the history of the working class movement, which covered left-wing political parties in Europe, America and Asia, including details on their fractions and the political views of particular leaders; these were assessed on the basis of their compatibility with Marxism-Leninism. The phrases "traitor" or "renegade" on the one hand and "a true revolutionary" on the other were not uncommon. The Church was said to play only a negative role. Even if the beginnings of Polish historiography or bringing Poland into European culture were attributed to the Church, they were assessed negatively: Latin, used by the Church, postponed the development of the Polish language for ages, and ties with Western Europe separated Poland from her Slavic roots.

The post-Stalinist "thaw" brought a revision of textbooks. With every major reform of education, new books became shorter, providing more information and fewer commentaries. In the 1980s they included more history of culture and of everyday life. Primary sources and pictures accompanied the main texts. However, the descriptions of some events, such as the Paris Commune and the Russian revolutions, as well as the biographies of figures such as Lenin and Marx, seem to have been written according to ideological guidance imposed by policymakers.

Periodization and Class Struggle

Already in the 3rd grade the presentation of pre-historical events stressed that from the earliest times people were organized in communities. All people were totally equal, duties fairly shared and work done collectively. The role of work in the separation of humans from the animal world and in founding civilization was stressed. According to Marxism, the differences in wealth and social positions that destroyed this system had been caused by a surplus of food, the development of crafts and the necessity to organize defense from invaders.

In all the "pre-socialist" political systems the ruling classes had legal instruments and a coercive apparatus to exploit the lower classes. Only they could benefit from the achievements of culture and civilization. The lower classes suffered from the increasing hardships of life, described emotionally and in detail, and from time to time fought to improve their living conditions. However, they did not know how do to it effectively and at the right time. Only Marxists could "scientifically" explain the victories and defeats of insurgents ("The millions of peasants [of the February Revolution of 1917 in Russia] did not have the consciousness or the experience that the vanguard of the revolutionary proletariat possesses"[11]). They knew, for example, that "unemployment could be liquidated only under socialism, when the working class takes power and deprives the capitalists of the means of production for the benefit of society"[12] or that "the communist ideas of Campanella could not have materialized in the socio-economic conditions of his times. The low level of productive forces could not secure an abundance of goods; only a contemporary socialist system could implement them".[13] On the other hand, changes were inevitable. A 1975 textbook read: "Working men rebelled, organized strikes. They were severely punished by the guild courts and municipal authorities. Outdated guilds **must** [emphasis mine— J. W.] have been replaced with the new forms of production".[14]

In the 1950s political history was regarded as pertaining to the ruling classes, and thus neglected in textbooks that dealt almost exclusively with revolutionary struggles. Thus, the history of the Roman Empire was reduced to the reasons for its collapse, the characteristics of its social classes and the rebellions of its slaves. No emperors were mentioned, no wars, no dates, no names nor places.

Among the rebellions that the academics looked for so carefully were the peasant uprising in ancient Egypt in 1750 BC (or "before our era", since communist historiography did not use the name of Christ) and the insurrection of the "Red Brows" in China in 18 AD ("of our era"). Spartacus's rebellion and the smaller revolts of Roman slaves enjoyed considerable attention.

In the Middle Ages the protests of peasants and townsmen were mentioned, such as in Saxony in 841 or in Normandy at the end of the 10th century. The division of the inhabitants of the city into two classes—patricians and ordinary citizens—was stressed, and the tensions between them also emphasized.

Other revolts of the poor mentioned by name were the rebellion of Etienne Marcel in Paris in 1357, of Wat Tyler in England in 1381, of Daniel Shays in the United States, the peasant revolts in Spain at the end of the 15th century and in France in the 18th century, as well as those in Russia under Peter the Great. A number of Polish rebellions were also presented. Many events were given a "class" interpretation; for example, the Polish Constitution of May 3rd, 1791, was regarded as "progressive" but "not revolutionary", and the textbook explained why it made only "a small breach" in the feudal system but did not remove its foundation.[15] World War I was labeled as an "imperialist" war and reference was made to Lenin's theory of imperialism.

Ordinary people were generally praised in the textbooks. They represented patriotic virtues in the Piast monarchy that, according to the textbooks, survived German invasions thanks to their attitude. Scenes of peasants cutting down trees in the forests in order to block the routes of the German army were described in

112   *History*

the 1950s and 1960s. The participation of the common people in famous battles like those of Legnica in 1241 and of Grunwald in 1410 was pointed out.[16] New heroes were promoted: Walenty Wąs, a coppersmith-apprentice from Lwów, was said to be the first to enter the city of Połock after its siege during the Polish-Russian war of the 16th century, while the peasant Kacper Wieloch was the first to enter another city during that war. The Silesian uprisings of 1919–1921 were characterized in a 1970 textbook as "a beautiful expression of patriotism of the miners, workers from the steel mills and the peasants of the Opole region".[17] In the 1958 edition the beautiful altar in St. Mary's Basilica in Cracow was said to be built "from the collections of poor townsmen and peasants" from the Cracow region.[18]

If the common folk did not join the right struggle, the upper classes were to blame. They were accused of merely looking after their selfish interests, not the good of the whole nation. Ordinary people were therefore right to refrain from worrying about their problems. Attitudes toward peasant rights were an important factor in textbooks' assessment of Polish leaders, political groups and events of the 19th century.

The upper strata of Polish society (the clergy, aristocrats and a part of the nobility) were held responsible for all the problems of Poland in the past. Already in the first centuries of Polish history its foreign policy was not sufficiently anti-German. In the 13th century the aristocracy was interested in Russian and Lithuanian lands instead of Silesia, which resulted in a negative turn taken by Poland's foreign policy, and in the long run led to the collapse of the country. The first symptoms of Poland's decay were observable as early as in the 14th century (though it collapsed more than four hundred years later). Textbooks dealing with the 19th century emphasized instances of collaboration between the nobility, aristocracy and bourgeoisie with the authorities of the empires that had partitioned Poland: Russia, Austria and Germany. Examples of servile letters and denunciations of Polish patriotic plots by these groups were presented. The aristocracy used its coercive apparatus in concert with the partitioning powers against the peasant revolts. It was not mentioned, however, that the leaders of the Polish patriotic societies which opposed the partitions also came from the nobility (and later from the intelligentsia). On the other hand, opinions were cited of intellectuals from all ages who appreciated the common people and criticized the existing social system.

The higher strata in Poland were said to refuse to support national uprisings, while their peers abroad instrumentally used people for their own interests. The people fought and the bourgeoisie took the profits, replacing feudal exploitation with its own system of exploitation, be it during the Reformation, the Dutch Revolt, the French Revolution or the revolutions in Russia before October 1917.

Interpretations of the French revolution in Polish textbooks are worth a closer look. In general it was regarded as "progressive", though the inviolability of private property in the Declaration of Human and Civil Rights was said to testify to its bourgeois character and to foretell further exploitation of the working people. The terror of the Jacobins was presented as understandable and even appreciated for its effectiveness, and the textbooks seemed to regret that it was not able to reach its conclusion.

The attitudes of ordinary people were often juxtaposed with the opinions of their leaders. In the Roman provinces, for example, the local aristocracy Romanized the inhabitants and profited from the occupation, while the common people opposed the occupiers and cultivated indigenous traditions. Several centuries later a similar situation occurred in Bohemia: the masses kept their national identity while the elites engaged in Germanization. After the battle of Vienna of 1683 the Austrian people were said to be grateful to the Polish king John Sobieski, who saved the city from the Turkish siege, as opposed to the emperor, who was afraid of Sobieski's growing power. During the 1848 "Spring of Nations" only the common people continued the struggle for Polish independence, while the nobility gave up quickly and was disarmed. Almost a hundred years later, in 1944, the enthusiasm of the Warsaw people was used by the leaders of the Home Army to evoke a purely political (anti-Soviet) uprising. The summary of the war between Russia and Japan in 1904–1905 is symptomatic: "Despite the bravery and endurance of the Russian soldiers and sailors Japan was victorious both on land and at the sea over the indecisive and corrupt generals".[19]

The Revolutionary Movement

The history of the "revolutionary movement" started from the Industrial Revolution and descriptions of the appalling working conditions of the first factories. Textbooks mentioned that initially the workers' anger was directed against the machines. Gradually, they came to understand that the organization of production was to blame and—depending on the textbook—the employer or the capitalist system directly. After the first, poorly planned protests, the working class came to understand that it was necessary to be organized and prepared their future actions more carefully. According to the textbooks, this was how the first trade unions emerged, and later the workers' parties, which were a more mature form of organization.

Workers' protests, small and large, of various countries, were noted in the textbooks. The revolts in Lyon in 1831 and 1834 were regarded as turning points in the revolutionary struggle, alongside the events of June 1848 in Paris and the Paris Commune (which was usually discussed in a separate chapter), the May 1st celebrations beginning in 1890, and the Russian revolutions of 1905 and 1917. All those events were presented with reverence. The October Revolution in Russia (called the Great October Socialist Revolution) was regarded until the last years of the People's Republic of Poland as the beginning of a new era in the history not only of Russia, but of the whole world. Until the collapse of the communist regime it was also presented as the turning point in the Polish struggle for independence before 1918.

The biographies of the leaders of the revolutionary struggle were described in detail. Priority was given to Marx, Engels and Lenin, and in the 1950s also to Stalin. Their works and speeches, especially pertaining to Polish issues, were

114   *History*

cited. Longer passages and even separate chapters were devoted to the political biographies of revolutionary activists who had some Polish connections, such as Ludwik Waryński, Rosa Luxemburg, Felix Dzerzhinsky and Julian Marchlewski.

The textbooks discussed the nuances of left-wing Polish parties from the 19th and 20th centuries. Those who were willing to cooperate with the Russian revolutionaries were praised, while others were criticized. Joseph Piłsudski came in for particularly strong condemnation. He was accused of cooperation with Germans and Austrians during World War I (which he found most effective for the struggle of the Polish independence in the first phase of the war, after which he changed his mind and was subsequently arrested and jailed in Magdeburg until November 1918; these facts did not save his reputation in the eyes of the ideologists of the Polish United Workers' Party). The war with Soviet Russia that he initiated in 1919 and the May coup d'état of 1926 further added to his negative perception by textbook authors.

Textbooks' presentations of Polish nationalists from the turn of the 19th and 20th centuries (national democracy) concentrated on their collaboration with the higher strata of Polish society (landlords and bourgeoisie) and their persecution of workers during the revolution of 1905. Little attention was paid to and little criticism expressed towards their nationalistic ideology.

The role of left-wing parties in the contemporary history of Poland was overemphasized. Some textbooks might have created the impression that the workers and their organizations were in charge of the struggle for Polish independence. In the interwar period the Polish Communist Party, marginal on the political scene of the time, was presented as if it were the dominant political force. According to the textbooks, the newly established Polish state was a disappointment to workers. The workers' councils of 1918 were presented as the legal Polish authority, and the social protests of 1923, sometimes even called a revolution, were depicted as the most significant events of the interwar period. Altogether, interwar Poland was said to be "one of the weakest links in the chain of the capitalist states".[20] It was dependent on foreign capital, poorly industrialized and incapable of defense. The Polish people were doomed to poverty, unemployment and ignorance and the country only pretended to be independent.

The members of the Communist Party were said to be the most active in the struggle with the German invaders and occupants during World War II. Marian Buczek was always mentioned in stories of the Polish campaign of September 1939. Buczek had been jailed for his political activities in the interwar period and was released only when the war started. Disregarding his earlier traumatic experiences, he sacrificed his life in defense of Poland, trying to save Warsaw. The presentation of other World War II figures corresponded with the content of Polish language textbooks.

The Catholic Church

In the 1940s some textbooks expressed appreciation of the role of the Church as the bearer of the heritage of antiquity and the only hope for the people during the troubled times after the collapse of Rome. From the very beginning the reluctance of the Church to openly protest against exploitation and postponing the realization of justice until eternity were regarded as weak points in Christian doctrine.

As soon as persecutions of the Church had stopped, the Church became a refuge for the "reaction", a pillar of the authorities, and one more exploiter of society. Both doctrinal and practical arguments were used against the Church, but practical ones dominated.

The doctrinal arguments included keeping people in ignorance, promoting dogmatic attitudes in science and concentrating research on theology while neglecting more practical disciplines, coupled with conservatism in all spheres of life.

The practical arguments concentrated on the economic exploitation of the faithful, the preoccupation of clergy with material issues rather than the development of spiritual life, the persecution of non-orthodox convictions (the activities of the Inquisition included) and using Latin instead of vernacular languages.

The popes and Jesuits were particularly detested. The former were accused of interfering in political issues, such as conspiring against orthodox Russia. Unsuccessful or unfair interventions by Rome regarding Poland were highlighted, while those in favor of Poland were neglected. They dated back to the conflict in the 14th and 15th centuries between Poland and the Teutonic Knights, particularly in 1440 when the pope encouraged the Polish king Władysław of Varna to continue the war with the Turks, which served the interest of Rome, but not of Poland, and resulted in the untimely death of the king as well as the weakening of his dynasty's international position. The attitude of the popes towards the Poles in the 19th century was also criticized. They asked the faithful to be obedient to the authorities of the partitioning empires and condemned the participants of the Polish uprisings (and were followed by bishops and ordinary priests[21]). In the 20th century Cardinal Ratti (the future Pope Pius XI) supported the Germans during the plebiscite of 1921 when the Polish-German boundary was being decided.

The human, not supernatural, origins of the institution of the papacy were stressed. It should be regarded as an element of the atheist education which can also be observed in other parts of history textbooks. For example, in a chapter on ancient Greece the question was asked: "Why did the people make up gods?"[22] The textbook mentioned that even in those ancient times, there were scientifically minded people who did not believe in gods. In the Far East, religion was said to help keep people obedient and give authority to the state. The political reasons for establishing Islam were given: the Arabs matured to replace the pedigree system with an organized state whose authority was confirmed by their religion. The authority of religion was questioned by scientific discoveries; for example, thanks to Darwin "the old medieval idea of the supernatural origin of the world of plants and animals and of the supernatural act of bringing humans to life was abolished".[23]

Jesuit education was completely condemned in the textbooks. It was described as concentrated on the memorization of incomprehensible, and nonsensical Latin texts, imposing corporal punishment, boredom and ignorance. Jesuit schools

116 *History*

were said to encourage intolerance, blind obedience to the Catholic Church and persecution of heathens. The entire Catholic system of education was presented as backwards and leading to ignorance. The fact that the Church had monopolized education was regarded as a failure, not to its credit. Only two Polish priests active in the field of education were appreciated: Szymon Konarski and more generally the order of the Piarists, and Grzegorz Piramowicz, the author of the first Polish textbooks, though it was not always mentioned that he was a Jesuit. Lay institutions of education were usually praised.

Jesuits tended to influence prominent political figures, including kings. Sigismund III was accused of following their advice too readily. Only in the mid-1970s were some positive aspects of Jesuit activities noticed, for example, that they preferred persuasion to repression, though in earlier textbooks blackmailing and provocations were presented as methods of achieving their aims at any price.

Taking into consideration the negative image of the Church presented in the textbooks, it comes as no surprise that protests against its power and doctrine were welcomed, and sometimes even exaggerated, by textbook authors. The Renaissance, which in Polish also goes by the name "rebirth" (*odrodzenie*), was explained literally as the rebirth of humans, who felt liberated from the influence of the Church that had been hampering and crushing the human mind and human abilities.[24]

Movements which combined national or social and anti-Church protests, such as the Czech Hussites, the Polish Arians and the French Albigenses, were particularly praised. In presenting the Reformation, Thomas Münzer was appreciated most for his idea of a social system with collective property and the abolishment of both material inequality and exploitation of some people by others. He was said to be the only reformation leader who cared for the interests of the peasants rather than the landlords or bourgeoisie.

On the other hand, links with the Church could add another negative dimension to judgements of people and groups already criticized on other issues. Within this scheme, the Germanization of Slavic lands in the Middle Ages was attributed to German bishops, and the peasant movement of the 19th century was said to be fiercely persecuted by landlords allied with the clergy.

Poland between Germany and Russia

The topic of the Polish-German and Polish-Russian relations in historiography and school history education has attracted significant attention from researchers, therefore this chapter discusses only its main points.

The post–World War II Polish borders were regarded as the only fair and safe ones. The post-war shape of Poland was compared to that of the Piast monarchy at the very beginning of the Polish state and to the territories occupied by the Slavs. Polish aspirations towards Silesia and Pomerania were thus regarded as absolutely justified, as was Polish expansion to the West. On the contrary, any interest in the Eastern territories was the subject of negative opinions from textbook authors. All the diplomatic and military activities of Polish history were assessed within this framework. The collapse of Poland in the 18th century was attributed to the turn towards the East by Casimir the Great back in the 14th century. Interwar Poland was accused of continuing this negative tradition in its anti-Soviet policy, which resulted in its defeat in 1939. Judgments were formulated from the perspective of the times when the textbooks were published.

Most post-war history textbooks were openly anti-German. The only Germans praised by the authors were Otto III (who visited Poland in 1000, planning to make it one of the four equal parts of his universal empire and to place a crown on the head of the Polish king), Karl Marx and Friedrich Engels. The list of negative German individuals is much longer and includes, among others, emperors, kings and dukes, especially of Brandenburg and Prussia, and Teutonic Knights (traitors, liars and exploiters of the local Polish population). Friedrich II and Bismarck were probably the most negatively portrayed figures besides Hitler.

The way the textbooks presented the nationalities of famous researchers is symptomatic:

> Charles Darwin was a famous English biologist [. . .] The French chemist Louis Pasteur was not only one of the greatest scholars of the 19th century, but also a true benefactor of mankind. [. . .] The discoveries of the eminent Russian chemist Dmitri Mendeleev had a profound impact on the development of science. [. . .] At the end of the 19th century the physicist Wilhelm Roentgen [with no nationality mentioned] discovered X-rays.[25]

Polish-German conflicts, in which the Germans were always to blame, were traced back to the times of the Slavs and the first dukes of the Piast dynasty, who had to defend themselves against invasions by their aggressive neighbors from the West. The textbooks stressed that the Northern March with its capital in Berlin was established on Slavic territory. They regretted the Germanization of patricians and the ruling elite in Silesia and argued that it originated in the recklessness of the local rulers, who married German princesses and allowed German settlers in their lands.

In the history of the 18th century Prussia was presented as an initiator of the partitions of Poland that had annexed the most valuable and most Polish territories of Poland, and later persecuted people for their Polishness. As in the case of the Church, national arguments were combined with social ones in laying out negative judgements: "The Prussian Junkers were the personification of militarism, breathing national hatred towards their neighbors while professing extremely backward social views", or "despite the brutal oppression from feudal-bourgeois Prussians. . . ".[26]

Russia was presented in a much more favorable light. During the partitions it was said to occupy Ukrainian and Belorussian lands which it in fact deserved, since they had been taken over by Lithuania, and later by greedy Polish landlords. The textbooks stressed that the Cossacks' religion and language were similar to that of Russians. Interwar Poland illegally came back into possession of these non-Polish lands, but justice was restored in September 1939, and confirmed after World War II.

118   *History*

The policies of the Russian authorities in the 19th century as presented in Polish textbooks appeared to be much more moderate than similar ones pursued by the Germans. Some textbooks put it openly:

> The tsarist system implemented the policy of Russification of the administration and schools and the political and cultural persecutions of the Polish population. It did not put up any larger obstacles, however, to the economic development of the country. In the Prussian partition, Germanizing activities encompassed political, cultural and economic life to an equal extent.[27]

Some textbooks simply did not mention Russification at all.

Conflicts between Russia and countries other than Poland were always presented in favor of Russia and from the Russian point of view. The textbooks lamented, for example, that Soviet diplomats were not allowed into the peace conference in Versailles in 1919, and praised the Russian resistance against Western influences in the 19th century which prevented Russia from becoming a colony of Western capitalists. All Soviet activities were regarded as right and just, their achievements outstanding and their sacrifices great. Among these achievements, the preparation of the first Five Year Plans (from the pre–World War II period) were enumerated. The crimes (or rather "political mistakes") of Stalin could not overshadow them. The Soviet Union was presented as the sole victor over Nazi Germany. After the war, the swift reconstruction of the country was praised, as well as achievements in the so-called conquest of space.

The exploration of space, according to a 1970 textbook, definitely had a national character. The launch of Sputnik was described as "a magnificent result of the achievements of socialist scientific thought—a visible sign of the progress which has been made since the victory of the Great October Revolution". The moon landing was "a magnificent achievement of human thought—the result of the work of tens of thousands of people".[28]

Coming back to narratives dealing with Russia, Polish textbooks started with the state of Kievan Rus', broken up by the Tartars. In the 1960s they mentioned that Russian resistance damaged the strength of the Tartars to move against other countries, including Poland (thus Poland was saved thanks to the sacrifice of its eastern neighbor). Relations between Poland and Kievan Rus' were characterized as generally positive. Conflicts were minimized and attributed to dynastic, not political issues. A 1951 textbook accused the German emperors of inciting attacks by the Kievan rulers on Eastern Poland in order to facilitate the German invasion of the West (so while Rus' attacked, Germany was blamed).[29] As mentioned earlier, the textbooks did not approve of Polish and Lithuanian expansion to the east. The revival of Russia and its growing power from the times from Ivan Kalita to Peter the Great were welcomed.

When Russia fell into conflict with Poland in the 17th century and became one of the partitioning powers in the 18th century, all negative aspects were attributed to the tsarist system, but not to Russia as a country, nor to the Russian people, who were said to harbor the most positive feelings towards the Poles.

The textbooks avoided the words "Russia" or "Russian" in reference to negative aspects of Russian policies. "Tsar" or "tsarist" were used instead. There was the tsarist army, tsarist officers and tsarist prisons, but Russian revolutionaries who supported Polish insurgents.

Plans for Polish-Russian cooperation were highlighted. This usually started with the Decembrist revolt of 1825, but Andriy Potebnya was an iconic figure in this regard. He was an officer of the Russian army who joined the Polish January Uprising of 1863 and was killed in action. Some textbooks gave the impression that the support of the Russian army for Poles was widespread. The cooperation between Polish and Russian revolutionaries in the socialist Internationals was mentioned. So were the Polish participants of the October Revolution. Soviet assistance to Poland during and after World War II was described in detail, while negative episodes were almost completely neglected.

***

As mentioned earlier, various propaganda motives, topics and techniques intertwined in the texts. One paragraph, sentence, or phrase could combine various elements and perspectives ("class", nationalist, atheist, etc.). They usually reinforced one another, but in some cases led to ambiguity. For example, Casimir the Great, the Polish king of the 14th century, was on the one hand praised as a good leader who developed the economy and culture of a growing country, and who protected the peasants with new laws that he introduced, but on the other hand he was criticized for strengthening the privileged position of the nobility and turning Polish foreign policy towards the Ukrainian and Russian territories in the east and south while giving up on the reinstatement of Polish dominance in Silesia and Pomerania. Some textbooks prioritized the positive elements of his rule, while others concentrated on critical remarks.

Notes

1 The first information on Katyń did not appear until 1984 in the 8th grade textbook by A. Szcześniak. (Szcześniak, Andrzej L. 1984. *Historia. Polska i świat naszego wieku. Książka pomocnicza dla kl. VIII szkoły podstawowej.* Warszawa: WSiP, 228). The perpetrators were not clearly identified.

2 The twenty years of interwar Poland occupy only 27 pages of the 1958 textbook for the 7th grade, while a few weeks of the Russian October Revolution—15 (Dutkiewicz, Józef, Gąsiorowska Natalia and Henryk Katz. 1958 *Historia. Dla klasy VII.* Warsaw: PZWS).

3 Markowski, Gustaw. 1962. *Historia. Dla klasy VI.* Warsaw: WSiP, 60.

4 Siuchniński, Mateusz (ed.). 1953. *Historia. Dla klasy VI.* Warsaw: PZWS, 112.

5 Ibid., 80.

6 Klubówna, Anna and Jadwiga Stępieniowa. 1961. *W naszej ojczyźnie. Podręcznik historii dla klasy IV.* Warsaw: PZWS, 47.

7 Mazur, Zbigniew. 1989. *Obraz Niemiec w polskich podręcznikach szkolnych do nauczania historii. 1945–1989.* Poznań: Instytut Zachodni; Składanowski, Henryk. 2004. *Stosunki polsko-sowieckie w programach nauczania i podręcznikach historii w szkole powszechnej (podstawowej) w Polsce w latach 1932–1956.* Toruń: Adam Marszałek.

120 *History*

8 Jakubowska, Barbara. 1986. *Przeobrażenia w szkolnej edukacji historycznej w Polsce w latach 1945–1956*. Warsaw: COM SNP; Hoszowska, Mariola. 2002. *Praktyka nauczania historii w Polsce 1944–1956*. Rzeszów: Wydawnictwo Uniwersytetu Rzeszowskiego.

9 Osiński, Zbigniew. 2006. *Nauczanie historii w szkołach podstawowych w Polsce w latach 1944–1989: uwarunkowania organizacyjne oraz ideologiczno-polityczne*. Toruń: Duet; Brynkus, Józef. 2014. *Komunistyczna ideologizacja a szkolna edukacja historyczna w Polsce (1944–1989)*. Kraków: Antykwa.

10 Podraza, Antoni. 1960. "Rola historii w kształtowaniu racjonalistycznego, laickiego poglądu na świat". *Wiadomości Historyczne* 3, no. 1: 1–9.

11 Dutkiewicz, Józef, Gąsiorowska Natalia and Henryk Katz. 1954. *Historia. Dla klasy VII*. Warsaw: PZWS, 173.

12 Siuchniński, Mateusz (ed.). 1953. *Historia. Dla klasy VI*. Warsaw: PZWS, 287.

13 Siuchniński, Mateusz (ed.). 1952. *Historia. Dla klasy VI*. Warsaw: PZWS, 117.

14 Kosman, Marceli. 1975. *Historia. Dla klasy VI*. Warsaw: WSiP, 164.

15 Missalowa, Gryzelda and Janina Schoenbrenner. 1951. *Historia Polski*. Warsaw: PZWS, 114.

16 In case of Grunwald the textbooks stressed that the Polish-Lithuanian army was supported by Russian detachments from Smolensk and some Czech military units. This made it a battle between Germans and Slavs.

17 Wojciechowski, Marian. 1970. *Historia. Dla klasy VIII*. Warsaw: PZWS, 55.

18 Hoszowska, Władysława. 1958. *Opowiadania z dziejów Polski. Część I (do roku 1505)*. Warsaw: PZWS, 146.

19 Dutkiewicz, Józef, Gąsiorowska Natalia and Henryk Katz. 1954. *Historia. Dla klasy VII*. Warsaw: PZWS, 79.

20 Ibid., 205.

21 Though many priests joined the uprisings but this was not mentioned. Only the 1987 textbook (Skowronek, Jerzy. 1987. *Historia. Do Niepodległej. Podręcznik dla klasy 7 szkoły podstawowej*. Warsaw: WSiP, 100, 130) admitted that Pope Pius IX supported the Poles in exile and appreciated the pro-Polish activities of the clergy in the Prussian partition.

22 Markowski, Gustaw. 1964. *Historia. Dla klasy V*. Warsaw: PZWS, 32.

23 Szostakowski, Stanisław. 1971. *Historia. Dla klasy VII*. Warsaw: PZWS, 131.

24 Siuchniński, Mateusz (ed.). 1953. *Historia. Dla klasy VI*. Warsaw: PZWS, 97.

25 Szostakowski, Stanisław. 1971. *Historia. Dla klasy VII*. Warsaw: PZWS, 130–132.

26 Dutkiewicz, Józef, Gąsiorowska Natalia and Henryk Katz. 1954. *Historia. Dla klasy VII*. Warsaw: PZWS, 46–47, 141 respectively.

27 Szostakowski, Stanisław. 1968. *Historia. Dla klasy VII*. Warsaw: PZWS, 186.

28 Wojciechowski, Marian. 1970. *Historia. Dla klasy VIII*. Warsaw: PZWS, 240–241.

29 Serejski, Marian H. 1951. *Historia. Dla klasy V*. Warsaw: PZWS, 193.

7 Foreign Languages and the Arts

Russian Language Instruction

The Russian language was for the majority of the existence of the People's Republic of Poland the only foreign language taught at primary schools. Immediately after the war schools (but not individual pupils) could choose a foreign language to be taught, from among English, German (which was not recommended, however), French and Russian, but a given school could choose only one language. Russian was not the most popular. According to data from the archives of the Society of the Polish-Soviet Friendship (*Towarzystwo Przyjaźni Polsko-Radzieckiej*), in 1947/48 only 5900 schools out of 10,287 had any foreign language classes at all. In 2855 (48.4%) French was taught, in 1127 (19.1%) English, in 793 (13.4%) German and only in 742 (12.6%) Russian. Some schools (383 or 6.5% altogether) chose two foreign languages.[1] The authorities encouraged Russian language instruction despite the shortage of qualified teachers, textbooks and other teaching aids. Already in 1945 the first teacher courses were organized. In 1946 the first textbook was published, authored by F. Sovetkin in Moscow but adjusted for Polish learners. In 1947/48 Russian became a compulsory subject in pedagogical upper secondary schools, which at that time were the main teacher training institutions for primary school teachers. The Ministry of Education sponsored the so-called research and methodological centers of the Russian language, which tried to popularize its teaching all over Poland. Two arguments were used in support of the Russian language as a school subject. The political justification emphasized the role of the Soviet Union as a liberator, ally and friend of Poland. Practical aspects were given as well: Russian, as a Slavic language, is quite similar to Polish and thus easier to learn for Polish pupils than any of the Western European languages. I was not able to find any document, however, that would explicitly make Russian the only foreign language taught at primary schools; but this became the common practice already at the beginning of the 1950s and lasted until the collapse of the communist regime. Only after 1989 was Russian abandoned as a compulsory foreign language.

The textbook by Sovetkin was approved by the Polish Ministry of Education for primary schools, but it was originally designed as a tutorial for adults. This is reflected, for example, in the grammatical forms used in the exercises. Although

122   *Foreign Languages and the Arts*

it was a textbook for beginners, the language skills of the pupils should have progressed rapidly, according to Sovetkin, so he included a set of stories and poems about the history of the Soviet Union. The book had 350–400 pages, depending on the edition. Another Soviet textbook, by Chistyakov, was published in 1948 and was more child-oriented. The book was thinner, progress slower, but the topics of the readings evolved quite quickly from everyday life to more general and propagandist issues. The Ministry of Education approved this book to be used in the 5th and 6th grade, and the textbook by Sovetkin in the 6th and 7th grade. Moreover, special "supplementary materials" were published for each grade in order to adjust the textbooks to the changing curricula. They consisted of excerpts from the works of Russian and Soviet writers and of educational readings written for those particular booklets.

The first Russian language textbooks authored by Poles were introduced in 1954/55 for the 5th grade (when the Russian language instruction started), in 1955/56 for the 6th grade, and in 1956/57 for the 7th grade. They were much thinner and included fewer readings than the Soviet books, but their propaganda content did not actually change until at least the early 1960s. The new generation of textbooks was designed for the 8-year school and remained in use until the mid-1980s. They dealt a bit less with Soviet history, politics and economy, but more with the everyday life of pupils in the Soviet Union and Poland. The last textbooks of the People's Republic of Poland were even more oriented towards everyday life, but it was still the everyday life of the pioneers who attended their pioneer meetings, helped in the kolkhozes and made friends with the Polish children whom they met in the famous pioneer camp in Artek at the Black Sea. They were fascinated with the space flights and watched the TV transmission of the May 1st parade from Moscow at 8 AM.

As mentioned earlier, all the textbooks provided information about life in the Soviet Union, which was in total accord with the school curricula. Most readings were set in Soviet realities, while Poland was mentioned only occasionally, usually in contacts with the USSR (e.g. Nowa Huta and the Palace of Culture and Science were presented as examples of Polish-Soviet friendship and cooperation).

Scenes from Russian history were presented especially in the 1950s, yet increasingly sporadically until the end of the 1970s. Textbooks described the beauty of Kievan Rus' and the admiration expressed by its foreign visitors. The Tartar-Mongol yoke over Rus' and the Russian liberation was mentioned. Readings about the settlement of the port and city of Arkhangelsk, about Peter the Great and his European travels, and about the Russian resistance against Napoleon's invasion testified to the Russian ability to deal with problems and take advantage of opportunities. The biographies of the Russian democrats and revolutionaries of the 19th century were presented, with the most space devoted to Lenin.

Many readings about Lenin (and about Stalin in the 1950s) were the Russian versions of stories that children must have also read in the Polish language textbooks. This might have been the result of the limited number of texts about Soviet leaders accepted for use at school. They presented Volodya Ulyanov as a beloved child, and an outstanding, laborious and diligent pupil who helped others. Others portrayed the adult Lenin in exile in Siberia where he celebrated May 1st by singing revolutionary songs during a walk with his comrades. Then pupils were introduced to Lenin in the Tatra mountain village of Poronin, where some local highlanders still remembered his visit from the beginning of the 20th century. After that, he was presented in the revolutionary St. Petersburg, when he crossed the bridge risking his life to assume the leadership of the Great October Socialist Revolution. After the revolution, Lenin explained its achievements to ordinary people, worked during a *subbotnik*, entertained children at a New Year's ball in the Moscow Sokolniki, and let himself be filmed after an illness so that all the Soviet citizens could see him.

Stalin's childhood did not appear in Russian language textbooks. However, his exile in Siberia and his role in the Russian civil war was presented. In the 1950s he was mentioned in readings dealing in general with other issues, as an inspiration for others or a person whom many would like to meet.

In the 1950s Lenin and Stalin were admired in numerous poems, songs and contemporary tales. Sovetkin cited their speeches and writings. The Stalinist textbooks also presented Vasily Chapayev, a hero of the Russian civil war, Felix Dzerzhinsky, the founder of the Soviet secret police (Cheka), Zoya Kosmodemyanskaya, a Komsomol activist murdered by the Nazis because, according to the textbooks, she refused to abandon hope of Stalin's victory in World War II (in fact, she was caught setting fire to buildings where Nazi occupants were stationed), and Alexandr Matrosov, who blocked a German pillbox with his body. Other Soviet heroes of World War II or rather of the "Great Patriotic War", also appeared later through the 1980s. The war was widely discussed in the textbooks. They admired the bravery, cleverness and sacrifice of the Soviets, both of soldiers and the civilian population, including children. The defense of Sevastopol, blockade of Leningrad and battle of Stalingrad were described, alongside the battle of Lenino, the liberation of Warsaw and the seizure of Berlin where the Poles and the Soviets fought together. Until the end of the People's Republic of Poland the textbook poems honored the sacrifice of the Soviet soldiers, who were said to fight for peace and whose deeds should be commemorated.

The peaceful life of the Soviet Union attracted the greatest attention of the textbooks. World War II was not a turning point in this case; the October Revolution was. The constant progress in all spheres of life under Soviet rule was stressed. The new bright perspectives for the young people, women, national minorities and all other Soviet citizens were drawn. The textbooks described Soviet investments, such as the Moskva-Volga and Volga-Don canals, irrigation of the deserts, new cities in the wilderness and new railroads. In the 1950s they were associated with particular Five Year Plans. The Soviet polar explorations were presented, and Soviet scientific achievements praised, particularly in agronomy. Textbooks by Soviet authors particularly praised Ivan Michurin and the Soviet system that employed his work. The peaceful implementations of nuclear energy (especially the icebreaker Lenin) and the space flights were presented through the very last editions.

All those achievements were presented as a result of good planning and management, as well as the devotion of the Soviet citizens, including the Soviet youth

124   *Foreign Languages and the Arts*

from Komsomol. The Soviet work foremen were regarded as the continuers of the idea of Alexey Stakhanov, whose biography was presented alongside details about other foremen. Life in collective and state-owned farms was praised. It was said to be much better and easier than in pre-revolutionary times. People were eager to work there, and the harvest exceeded their expectations. The Soviet textbooks also praised the political system of the USSR and its strength.

Textbook children were almost exclusively pioneers. Their life was concentrated on the struggle for learning, on attending meetings and various commemorative events, and community works. They spent their spare time in the "pioneer palaces" and their summer holiday in camps where they helped in the kolkhozes or admired their country. The schedule of a pioneer from a 1954 textbook can serve as an example: Monday—a meeting of the pioneer cell in the school club at 6 PM, Tuesday—an excursion to the Lenin Museum at 9 AM, Wednesday after lessons—a meeting of the editorial team of the school newspaper, Thursday—*The Young Guard*, a movie at the pioneer palace at 5 PM, Friday—visit Kolya in the hospital, bring him apples and *Timur and His Squad* by Arkady Gaydar, Saturday—visit grandfather at the kolkhoz, take a book on beekeeping, Sunday—a talk to the kolkhoz children about the great feats of communism.[2] Heroic deeds of the pioneers during the war and in peacetime were also mentioned. They helped extinguish fires, or warned that railway tracks were broken and thus prevented the derailing of a train.

Descriptions of the pioneer camp in Artek can be found, with details on its beautiful location, appearance, schedule and activities of the pioneers. They were accompanied by the enthusiastic opinions of Polish children who visited the camp and made friends there with peers from other countries, especially from the USSR. Other young Poles also corresponded and met (yet not as often) with Soviet children.

Moscow was another place in the Soviet Union that appeared in the Polish textbooks. Its long history was mentioned along with the beauty of its historical and contemporary buildings, many of which were enumerated by name. The books admired the Moscow underground with its escalators and rich ornaments of the palatial stations. New residential districts of tall blocks were admired. In the 1950s they were said to be built as an expression of care for the working people and had nothing in common with the "gloomy boxes of the American skyscrapers".[3] The Kremlin in the 1950s was presented as the working space of Generalissimo Stalin, and later as a historical monument. Military parades on Red Square on November 7th (the anniversary of the October Revolution) and February 23rd (Soviet Army Day) were described. The May 1st parade attracted the most attention. Other celebrations of this holiday at schools, in factories and on the streets were presented. Soviet poems about May 1st corresponded with the Polish ones that the children learned during their Polish language classes.

Other Soviet poems were also included in the textbooks. Pre-revolutionary Russian poets enjoyed less attention. Revolutionary songs, including *The International* and the anthem of the Soviet Union, were to be learned by heart. The pioneers' songs also appeared, together with excerpts from Soviet children's literature—the same as in Soviet schools (*Timur and His Squad, The Young Guard, Story of a Real Man, How the Steel Was Tempered*). The Russian translations of Polish children's poems by Julian Tuwim, Jan Brzechwa and Konstanty Ildefons Gałczyński were also published.

***

Soviet themes in Russian language textbooks repeated what the children could read in textbooks for other subjects. They were presented, however, in more detail and lasted longer. This can be justified by the very nature of the Soviet Union, which could not be separated from language instruction, but the propagandist character of those textbooks cannot be denied.

French, English and German

Western languages remained on the margins of primary school education in the People's Republic of Poland. Russian dominated foreign languages beginning in 1949. Only in the 1980s did French, German and English return as compulsory second foreign languages to be taught in the last two grades.

Between 1949 and 1981 the textbooks for these three languages were published in very small circulation (less than twenty thousand copies, while other textbooks reached over half a million). Documents approving circulations stated that the books would be used also in extracurricular education.

All the Western language textbooks were produced in Poland and underwent regular process of textbook approval. Some foreign publications were used at schools, at least in the 1980s, but they had a status of supplementary materials, not of the official textbooks.

Five phases can be distinguished in the overall form of Western language textbooks.

The Interim Period

Between 1946 and 1949 the main goal of textbooks was to help learn the language and get acquainted with the realities of the countries where they were used. There were usually a couple of readings about everyday life of workers or farmers, but it was presented in a factual and positive way, as something interesting and worth knowing. Farms were mechanized and well-organized, factories (Renault and Michelin appeared by name) offered fascinating jobs. Their owners took care of their workers. There was little (if any) propaganda. Most textbooks were reprints of pre-war editions and were published by small private publishers.

Stalinism

During the Stalinist period of 1950–1957 the concept of learning languages at school changed and so did the textbook authors, publishers and content. If a pupil learned material from the textbooks he would be able to speak in a foreign

126 *Foreign Languages and the Arts*

language about Poland building socialism. Therefore, the words such as *Vorarbeiter, travaillers de choc, schockworker, Wiederaufbau, la Pologne Populaire* and *collective farm* appeared. The readings dealt with the developing production cooperatives that were clean, well-equipped with machines and which provided their members with nice houses. Excursions to factories, labor competition in construction works and in coal mining, and celebrations of May 1st and July 22nd were also presented in all three languages.

The protagonists of those books were usually Polish families composed of a mother-shop assistant or spinner in a textile factory, father-worker, constructor or miner. Parents were often working foremen. At least one of their children was actively engaged in a youth organization and the other children tried to be as good. Professional or school achievements were their life goals. The families read newspapers, listened to the radio, discussed the problems of production or visited Warsaw to admire its reconstruction. Mothers visited "Public Department Stores", full of affordable goods, and thanks to the low prices in those shops could also go to the cinema.

The school life of the children, which was quite a typical topic in foreign language learning, took place in Poland, not abroad. The pupils competed with one another, organized and maintained school cooperatives, enrolled in scouting groups or in the Union of Polish Youth, participated in the reconstruction of Warsaw, prepared events to celebrate holidays or commemorate anniversaries. Only very rarely did they maintain any contact with their peers abroad. They usually exchanged letters in which the Polish pupils described what great things they had recently experienced in their country or neighborhood.

The information about foreign countries was usually concentrated on the foreign workers. Cities, such as Paris, London or New York, were, according to the textbooks, beautiful at first sight, but in fact they had vast areas of poverty and crime. The story of a former inhabitant of the London slums was cited and the tough life of black Americans presented. The poor neighborhood of Paris appeared as a place of traditional workers' demonstrations dispersed by the police. The citizens of the Western countries were usually poor sad children and their parents: workers who worked hard only to fill the pockets of their employers with money, or even worse, were unemployed. The hard life of the inhabitants of the former colonies was also described: children of Algeria who were forced to work for many hours and to learn in Koranic schools and were beaten for laziness; or black Africans treated like animals. An accident in a coal mine showed the solidarity of the workers who ran to rescue their suffering workmates, and the indifference of the owner who only wanted to avoid riots. Excerpts from the works of F. Engels and M. Thorez were cited which presented the tough life of the proletariat in England and France. Their biographies were discussed alongside events from the history of revolutionary movements, such as the Commune of Paris or the origins of the holiday of the 1st of May. Robert Owen and his idea of cooperatives was presented in the English language textbooks. They also portrayed the British inventors whose ideas were implemented in industry: Davy invented the mining lamp, Richard Arkwright—the spinning frame later improved thanks to James Watt. According to the textbooks, those inventions, however, did not improve the workers' lives; on the contrary, they only increased their exploitation. Various language versions of the anthem of the Soviet-dominated "World Federation of the Democratic Youth" were published.

German-language textbooks concentrated on the GDR. Other German-speaking countries were hardly mentioned. The description of East Germany followed the pattern set for the People's Republic of Poland and included production cooperatives, work productivity, new investments, the activities of young pioneers and state-controlled trade.

The Soviet Union also appeared in the textbooks for the Western languages. Its achievements were mentioned together with the assistance it offered to Poland and to the GDR (in the German-language textbooks) and the friendship between the USSR and other countries of the Soviet bloc. The history of the civilizational progress of a family from Uzbekistan was contrasted with the fate of African Americans.[4] The textbooks said that although the metro in Paris was very large, the metro in Moscow was the most beautiful or that the puppets from the Moscow theater were nicer than the French ones.

The language textbooks from the Stalinist period were very extensive. It looks as if the authors wanted to exhaust the scope of propaganda content regardless of whether it corresponded with the interests and language capabilities of the learners.

The Thaw

Between 1958 and 1960 the authors did not change, but their textbooks became much shorter. The 6th grade textbooks were now used in both 6th and 7th grade (one more proof that they had been too extensive and too difficult for the original audience) and those originally designed for the 7th grade were not used at primary schools at all. Most of the propagandist readings were removed. The Polish realities were replaced, though quite superficially, with the realities of the foreign countries concerned. The example family started to live in Germany, France or England, but the occupations of the parents or the activities of the children did not change. The descriptions of the schools or production cooperatives referred now to locations in France or the GDR. Even the reading about the reconstruction of Warsaw in the German-language textbook remained the same, except the name of the city, which was changed to Dresden.

The 1960s and 1970s

Textbooks introduced in the newly established 8-year primary school survived for twenty years (1961–1981) without any changes. New textbooks concentrated again on practical language use. Western realities were used, but quite a lot of readings dealt with the contacts of the foreigners with Poland. This gave an opportunity to present the achievements of the People's Republic of Poland: the reconstruction of Warsaw, economic development or the July 22nd celebrations.

128   *Foreign Languages and the Arts*

An English boy from the English-language textbook took some Polish ham for his picnic and commented: "We like Polish ham because it is good and not expensive".[5] The children from the French-language textbook were fascinated with the spaceflight of Yuri Gagarin. The German-language textbooks contained more propaganda than others because they presented the realities of the GDR: production cooperatives (*Landwirtschaftliche Produktionsgenossenschaft*) as model farms, factories as seen by the visiting children, cooperative shops, 1st of May celebrations, the friendship between Polish scouts and German pioneers, their meetings and camps, and the Peace Race (a bicycle race sponsored by the newspapers of the communist parties of the GDR, Czechoslovakia and Poland).

The 1980s

The textbooks used in the last decade of the People's Republic of Poland were free from propaganda. They were much more interesting than before. Concentrating on linguistic competences, they also presented foreign countries. The German-speaking world went beyond the GDR and FRG, and Austria and Switzerland were also portrayed.

Art

The first art textbooks for primary school in post-war Poland were prepared in the 1960s, for the 8-year school. All of them were authored by Stanisław Krzysztof Stopczyk. They were reprinted for almost twenty years with no changes. New editions were prepared in the 1980s with the extensive reform of education. The author did not change. His obituaries of 2013 mention him as a textbook author, and the revised versions of his textbooks are still in use in Poland.

Before the 1960s the school subject dealing with art was called "drawing" and concentrated on practical skills. The curricula suggested including propaganda content, for example, in the subjects of the pupils' sketches or paintings, such as May 1st parades, posters, workers. However, due to a lack of available textbooks it remains out of the scope of my research.

Art textbooks were rather thin because, according to the curriculum, practical drawing still dominated in this school subject. Propaganda content was rather limited. It was reflected in the selection of pictures that illustrated certain artistic phenomena. Pupils would see a picture of Lenin in the Smolny Institute, the revolutionary struggle in St. Petersburg, a statue of general Świerczewski or posters promoting peace. They would not see any religious paintings, which must have distorted their idea of the history of European art. The Catholic Church was presented not as a promoter of art, but as the institution that limited its development. Art in the past was said to have served the ruling social classes. Utilitarian criteria of assessing art were promoted: the purposes that a certain piece served was the most important factor. "In art truth and beauty always go together"—read one of the textbooks.[6]

Medieval art was totally marginalized. The Church was accused of dominating art as a whole, and particularly architecture. The Renaissance was presented as

Foreign Languages and the Arts   129

the liberation of humanity from the pressure of the Church. Only then did people start to think, to search for truth and to make their dreams come true. Residential buildings were built and churches were sponsored not for the glory of God or as places for prayers, but in order to promote the family of the founder. Baroque art also served its sponsors: the Church and aristocracy. Art of the 19th and 20th centuries received a "class" interpretation. Neo-Romanesque and Neo-Gothic buildings were said to express the wealth of the upstart bourgeoisie, were overloaded with ornaments that were selected with "no taste, no care of harmony, but with the intention to impress with the wealth". They were "not very creative" and "repetitive".[7] Romanticism, on the contrary, supported revolutions and was praised. So was Realism that corresponded with Marxism. 20th century art, as it presented the poverty of the working people, the struggle for peace, and thus promoted the "good cause" was appreciated.

Art textbooks did not leave pupils any freedom in their artistic judgments. They left no doubt what pupils should and should not like. They praised folk art (which the People's Republic of Poland was said to cultivate) and contemporary mass production of practical and comfortable everyday life utilities.

> Imagine a cubic vacuum cleaner painted in orange flowers. Both the form is irrelevant, unsuitable for the purpose of the product, and the colored pattern inappropriate, bizarre. Looking at such a product we would just shrug. The similar product presented in picture 76 is another story.

Picture 76 presented a real Zelmer vacuum cleaner, designed and made in Poland.[8]

Art textbooks claimed that the "people's government" took care even of the aesthetics of the life of its citizens. Not only did it organize the production of all the necessary (and nice) goods, but also constructed beautifully arranged cities that did not have rich and poor or nice and ugly districts anymore. There were only rationally designed residential districts for the working people. The government co-financed the housing.

Art textbooks did not avoid polytechnization, though it was usually limited to a short call for creative work, regardless of area. Workers were compared in this regard to researchers and artists. Inventors in the factories were presented as "artists" of the working class.

In the 1980s propaganda content was further limited. The critical attitude towards the Catholic Church remained (though it was expressed with more brevity), as did the assessment of art based on its sponsors and the interests of its audiences. The artistic achievements of the People's Republic of Poland were still praised. More space was devoted to the interpretation of various visual symbols, including the logo of the Centre of Children's Healthcare in Warsaw and the textbook publisher (WSiP).

> The wide-open book could mean an invitation to read, to deepen your knowledge. Together with the head of the eagle from our coat of arms, it means much more: that the aim of the publishing house is to publish books that will enrich your civic knowledge, essential for good service to the country, that

130　*Foreign Languages and the Arts*

the publisher wants to contribute to the education of generations of Poles whose knowledge will bring profit to the homeland.[9]

Posters promoting peace and environmental protection were also analyzed.

Music

The first music textbooks in post-war Poland were simple song books that helped teachers choose an appropriate repertoire for their lessons. The subject itself was called "singing". Only the 8-year school changed its name to "music" and the curriculum (and textbooks) included some theory and history of music. Musical instruments were presented as well as styles of music, music in various countries and in various times. The textbooks of the 1980s continued this trend, but all the books contained quite a lot of songs (both lyrics and music), either as illustration of theory or on their own.

The selection of songs was influenced by propaganda. Classical communist songs—such as *The International, The Red Banner, Warszawianka, On to the Barricades, O Working People!, The Shackles Mazurka* by Ludwik Waryński (a Polish Social-Democrat) and the anthem of the World Federation of Democratic Youth adopted in 1949—were always taught. The introductions to the songs presented their authors and the circumstances in which the songs were written.

There were quite a lot of military songs, predominantly those connected with the "people's" Polish Army. They presented the military route of the First Polish Army during World War II (which fought alongside the Soviet Army), praised the Polish-Soviet friendship in arms and life in the army in general. The most famous was *Oka*, dealing with the beginnings of the Polish Army in the Soviet Union in 1943, at the Oka River. It was taught in the 3rd grade until the collapse of the communist regime. *The March of the People's Guard* appeared in the 5th grade. In the 1950s the *General's Heart* was placed in the textbooks for all grades between 5 and 7. It was devoted to General Karol Świerczewski, a communist activist famous for his participation in the Spanish Civil War (and portrayed by Hemingway in *For Whom the Bell Tolls*), supporting the communist regime in Poland and killed by the Ukrainian Insurgent Army in 1947.

In the 1950s, so-called production songs were published. They were related to fulfilment of production plans, labor competition, construction works (such as the reconstruction of Warsaw or the construction of Nowa Huta in Cracow). Some songs about Warsaw and about miners' work survived until the late 1970s. In the 1960s, 7th graders were supposed to learn a song *The Guard on the Odra River* that praised the post-war Polish-German border. Another one from the same time period, *A Thousand Schools*, was related to the Millennium of Poland celebrated in 1966 and to the project of the government to build a thousand schools to commemorate this anniversary. The song about a militiaman (policeman) appeared in the 1970s. It presented him as a friend who takes care of everyone. Songs about peace, friendship between nations, the cooperation of children and adults, enthusiasm for work and for the construction of the country can be found in textbooks for all grades and in all editions. The same can be said about

Foreign Languages and the Arts   131

May Day songs. Almost every textbook contained one of them. The 22nd of July was not as popular as May 1st.

Scouting songs were not propagandist per se, but if we take into consideration that encouraging pupils to enroll in the scouting organization was one of the educational goals of school, we cannot ignore the role of music textbooks in fulfilling this task.

The books also contained a lot of Soviet and Russian songs. Not all of them were propagandist, but the very fact that they appeared in Polish textbooks was symptomatic, especially since most of them were not masterpieces of music. American music was represented by the African American lyrics expressing sorrow and longing for freedom.

Two kinds of songs did not appear in the music textbooks of the People's Republic of Poland, despite the fact that the pupils must have been familiar with them. First, popular music—both Polish and foreign—was despised by textbook authors. Its lack of any ideology and concentration on pure entertainment was unacceptable for educational purposes according to communist decision-makers. Second, all sacred music, both historical and contemporary, was completely omitted. Religious songs appeared only in the books published in the first post-war years. This choice must have been part of the "lay education", but it distorted the history of music and the role it had played for ages.

Other Subjects

Practical Technical Training

Only one textbook for this subject was published, for the 5th grade, in the 1970s. It concentrated on instructions for the projects that the pupils were supposed to complete. There were also theoretical passages about wood, paper and textiles. The origin of the raw materials was explained as well as the way they were processed and later used. Polish factories involved in production were proudly enumerated and the development of certain branches of industry mentioned.[10]

Physical Education

Textbooks for physical education for grades 1, 2 and 3 were destined for the proposed 10-year-school of the 1980s. Each had a circulation of about 600,000 copies. The book for grades 4 to 6 (one for all three years) had only 50,000 copies. They were lavishly illustrated. The books presented descriptions and pictures of exercises and the rules of different sports. The only elements of propaganda they included were slogans urging pupils to save money in SKO (School Savings Fund) for sport equipment[11] and to participate in summer scouting and sport camps.[12]

Notes

1 Piliszek, Ekaterina V. 1977. *Radziecko-polska współpraca w dziedzinie nauki i oświaty 1944–1950*. Wrocław: Ossolineum, 87.

132   Foreign Languages and the Arts

2 Zieliński, Antoni and Jerzy Żurawski. 1954. *Język rosyjski. Klasa V.* Warsaw: PZWS, 53.
3 Zieliński, Antoni and Jerzy Żurawski. 1954. *Język rosyjski. Klasa VI.* Warsaw: PZWS, 233–234.
4 Prejbisz, Antoni, Janina Smólska, Zofia Siwicka and Stanisław Helsztyński. 1955. *Nauka angielskiego. Learning English. I rok nauczania.* Warsaw: PZWS, 75.
5 Mickunas, Jan. 1967. *My English Book. II rok nauki.* Warsaw: PZWS, 145.
6 Stopczyk, Stanisław. 1968. *Wiadomości o sztuce. Podręcznik wychowania plastycznego dla klasy V szkoły podstawowej.* Warsaw: PZWS, 56.
7 Stopczyk, Stanisław. 1969. *Wiadomości o sztuce. Podręcznik wychowania plastycznego dla klasy VII szkoły podstawowej.* Warsaw: PZWS, 75.
8 Stopczyk, Stanisław K. 1981. *Plastyka. Klasa 4.* Warsaw: WSiP, 53.
9 Ibid., 26.
10 Czyżycki, Walenty, Antoni Marek and Jadwiga Zabierowska. 1971. *Zajęcia praktyczno-techniczne. Klasa V.* Warsaw: PZWS.
11 Liedke, Andrzej. 1978. *Ćwicz razem z nami. Klasa II.* Warsaw: WSiP, 4.
12 Mieczkowski, Tadeusz. 1977. *Wychowanie fizyczne—podręcznik dla klas IV-VI.* Warsaw: WSiP, 166.

8 Civic and Defense Education

Civic Education

There were very few primary school textbooks for civic education published in the People's Republic of Poland, although the subject was taught in the last year of primary education throughout the entire period in question. However, for the most part there was no officially approved textbook and the teachers were asked to use either "auxiliary materials" or teachers' journals and current press. The proposed textbooks usually turned out to be either overly complex for pupils, or did not exactly match the ideological expectations of Party officials. The most striking example of the first case were textbooks from the late 1940s and early 1950s by Józef Barbag and Władysław Bieńkowski.[1] Both authors were ideologists of the Polish United Workers' Party and their books were originally addressed to a more general audience of young adults, which the authors noted in the prefaces. Despite the fact that, for ideological reasons, the books were approved as official textbooks for the 7th grade, their language and depth must have been overwhelming for pupils.

This chapter is based on analysis of textbooks from the 1960s and early 1970s by Tadeusz Szymczak of the University of Łódź, and by Jan Gajewski and Kazimierz Kąkol. Kąkol was a high-ranking Communist Party official dealing with the Church, while Gajewski was a professor at Warsaw University and specialized in economic issues, particularly socialist agriculture.

The main theme of civic education textbooks was the superiority of socialism over capitalism in all spheres of life: political, social, economic and moral.

The socialist economy was said to develop faster than the capitalist one. The textbooks noticed that socialist countries lagged behind capitalist countries in absolute numbers, but this was attributed to much worse starting points, caused by the deficiencies of their capitalist past and by the devastation of war. The economic growth of post-war Poland was particularly stressed. Both pre- and post-war statistical data was used. Sometimes Poland was compared to other countries—but only when the results supported the goals of the propaganda. The textbook by Kąkol and Gajewski included 37 diagrams depicting various aspects of economic growth, stressing the role of the government in these processes.

134   *Civic and Defense Education*

Industrial development was particularly emphasized, while in the case of agriculture excuses for its problems were presented. The main cause of all these problems was said to be private ownership of agriculture that prohibited the implementation of planning and thoughtful large-scale investments. Private property was classified as the worst kind of property. Cooperative property was ranked higher, and state property was at the top of the textbook hierarchy. The pupils were assured that the government took great care to prevent the exploitation of workers, including in private property that was permitted to exist on the margins of the socialist economy.

As for political issues, socialist countries were said to make the desires of the previously exploited working and peasant class come true. Western democracy was fake and superficial, according to the textbooks. Despite the declarations of those in power, broad masses of people were deprived of rights. The black population of the United States served as the most striking example of this. In fact, the Western countries were ruled by monopolies of great capital. Only rich people had real influence on political issues. Ideologically loaded language was used in those narratives: "The formal features of the political systems of the pre-socialist states have only served to mask the exploitative character of those states".[2] (Pre-socialist according to Marxist ideology meant that all countries were supposed to follow the same path of development whereby capitalism would eventually be replaced by socialism, and then by communism).

The socialist system was praised as efficient and just. The realities of the People's Republic of Poland were used to illustrate its features. Every citizen was said to be able to participate in the life of the country on various levels. He could vote, could present his questions and postulates to his representatives, could submit petitions and grievances, and even exercise judicial power as an assessor. The public was said to be consulted in the course of planning—contrary to the capitalist system, where such decisions were limited only to the richest financial spheres.

On the other hand, limitations on freedom of speech, print or gatherings were presented as natural. Pupils were taught that they could not question the political system. These aspects were not compared to Western solutions. The role of the Church was usually mentioned in chapters dealing with civic rights. It was supposed to concentrate only on pastoral issues, while the authorities should safeguard religious tolerance.

The textbooks tried to justify such elements of the political system of the People's Republic of Poland as the leading role of the Polish United Workers' Party or the dual dependence of the local "national councils" (which were subordinated to both the central government and local administration).

The superiority of the socialist system in the social sphere was illustrated using solutions adopted in the Soviet Union and in other countries of the Soviet bloc, such as the elimination of unemployment and socialist work discipline. The costs of creating new jobs were presented to stress the efforts of the authorities. Work discipline under the socialist system was "not, as in exploitative societies, a discipline of carrot and stick, but a conscious discipline of the people who control their own property".[3] It included efforts to exceed the production norms, workers' initiatives in labor competition, as well as participation in "socialist labor brigades" and in the "rationalistic movement".

The development of education and its accessibility for all social groups was presented as one of the primary achievements of the People's Republic of Poland. The successful "struggle with illiteracy" opened access to culture for the masses. Culture could flourish thanks to the careful protection and inspiration of the government. The working people were provided access to free healthcare and summer holidays. The People's Republic of Poland managed to successfully deal with these issues in spite of their seeming unsolvable in the pre-war times—yet another manifestation of the superiority of socialism, also illustrated in statistical tables and diagrams.

The "shortcomings" and "temporarily difficulties" of the economy of the People's Republic of Poland, which pupils must have encountered in their everyday lives, were explained and excused. Housing shortages were apparent, but a lot had already been done, as the textbooks assured. Meat shortages in the shops were presented as a result of the export of meat, which was absolutely necessary in order to import more important goods. Besides, meat consumption increased considerably in the post-war years despite all the difficulties, and the textbooks informed the pupils that the pre-war population ate mostly bread and cereals.

The moral superiority of socialism was manifested first and foremost in the abolishment of the exploitation of "every man for himself". Capitalism, according to the textbooks, was based on injustice, where greedy capitalists captured the majority of the profits produced by the working people.

On the world political stage the Soviet bloc (or rather the "socialist camp") aimed at introducing peace, while the "imperialist camp" wanted to start a new war. The Warsaw Pact was juxtaposed with NATO and other American military alliances. The United States and West Germany enjoyed the worst opinions in Polish textbooks. They were accused of aggressive, revisionist policies, of neo-colonialism and the violation of human rights. Socialist countries helped one another and cooperated under Soviet leadership in order to achieve harmonious development. The Soviet Union was always presented with the utmost reverence as the first socialist state, the one world power which could boast military and other achievements, and was ready to help others.

Soviet peace initiatives were discussed in detail. The Soviet Union and its allies had a monopoly on the proper interpretation of Marxist doctrine. Thus, the Soviet concept of the peaceful co-existence of various political systems that would eventually prove the superiority of socialism was justified, while the Chinese or Albanian tendencies to immediately spread socialism using all possible means, war included, were condemned. Proof of the effectiveness of Soviet policies were sought and the prompt victory of communism expected. The economic stagnation of the Western world was one of them, accompanied by the rapid development of socialist countries. Former colonies chose a "non-capitalist path of development".[4]

Civic education textbooks were the quintessence of political education. The People's Republic of Poland was presented as a model country and excuses were

136 *Civic and Defense Education*

found for its apparent deficiencies and problems. The socialist authorities took care of their citizens, who were expected to be indulgent, patient, and to help the government in the implementation of its plans. Poland was on the "right" side of the world. It enjoyed the friendship of its neighbors and the protection of its allies, especially the Soviet Union. Pupils should only wait for the global triumph of socialism, whose superiority should never be doubted. Communism would follow and bring complete happiness to the Earth.

Defense Training

Defense training was introduced as a primary school subject in 1971. Earlier, "military training" with similar content was taught at secondary schools. Defense training was scheduled for the second semester of the 7th grade and the first semester of the 8th grade. In 1974, it was moved entirely to the 8th grade (both semesters). The curriculum stressed the educational values of the subject and its emotional influence on young people. The first textbook for military training was not published until 1975.

Patriotic education was established as the primary goal of the subject. It included the forming of a positive attitude towards the People's Republic of Poland and the People's Army, as well as encouraging pupils as prospective conscripts to join the army. A basic course in civil defense formed another part of the subject matter.

Chapters devoted to military aspects, such as the presentation of contemporary armies and weapons, and instructions on how to react in emergencies, dominated the textbooks and remained unchanged in all editions, over a period of twenty years. They were very informative, of a practical orientation, and precise.

The politicized introduction, of a propagandist nature, was rewritten multiple times. In general, it dealt with three issues: the traditions of Polish struggles for liberation, with particular attention paid to World War II and the input of the left-wing political parties and the People's Army; the role of the army in post-war peacetime life in Poland; and the international military and political situation of Poland. Despite all the changes, this part of the defense training textbook always presented a distorted image that resembled the textbooks for other subjects from the Stalinist times.

Let us start with the interpretation of the history of Poland. It was most briefly formulated in the defense training textbook of 1975: "The People's Republic of Poland is a historical achievement of the patriotic, progressive and revolutionary forces of the Polish nation".[5] This sentence combined nationalist and communist rhetoric and was (most positively) oriented towards present-day Poland. Pre-war history was summarized in just three sentences, presenting the Polish past as a period of exploitation of the masses by an aristocracy and nobility who did not serve the nation and whose policies eventually resulted in the partition of Poland. The 19th century struggle for independence was treated as a part of the revolutionary movement, and the Soviet revolution was said to have played a crucial role in its success. Interwar Poland was criticized for the privileges that proprietors enjoyed at the expense of the working class. It was labeled as a country of bourgeoisie and landowners with a reactionary political system, which must have had a negative impact on any chances of preserving independence. It would seem, therefore, that the textbook narrative was dominated by propaganda and had very little in common with historical research or with reality.

The People's Republic of Poland was said to be the fulfilment of the dreams of the workers and youth. In the 1970s the reforms of the communist authorities were enthusiastically enumerated, just as in the Stalinist times: agrarian reform, the nationalization of industry, depriving capitalists and landlords of their power, providing healthcare and social security for all citizens, and development of education.

The Polish-Soviet alliance was presented as the cornerstone of the post-war Polish foreign policy. The dominating role of the Polish United Workers' Party, which united all of society, was also stressed.

The historical narrative in the defense training textbooks concentrated on the history of Polish military struggles. In 1982 they were just enumerated, but in 1987 an anti-German interpretation appeared: "One of the reasons that Poland faced an almost constant threat was German pressure, which dates back to the very beginning of our statehood".[6] Anti-German accents appeared also in other parts of the historical introduction to the book.

The main point of the historical part of the textbooks was that World War II was the cradle of the People's Republic of Poland and of the "people's" Polish Army. The main organizer of the Polish Resistance seemed to be the Polish Workers' Party (the Communist Party), which in reality played only a marginal role. Pro-communist groups were characterized in great detail, their military actions were described while the Home Army and Grey Ranks (the underground scouting movement) were only briefly mentioned in the last paragraphs. Only in 1987 were Resistance activities presented in chronological order with approximately the same amount of space allotted to each political group. Even those proportions did not reflect the actual participation of particular political factions and the narrative was still biased, but it was a new way of dealing with the war.

The military contribution of Poles to World War II was represented in the defense training textbooks almost exclusively by the activities of the "people's" Polish Army. In the 1980s its first battle (at Lenino in 1943) was presented in detail, with an accompanying map. The heroism of Polish soldiers on other fronts was also mentioned—in Africa, Italy and Western Europe—but they were only briefly discussed, and the textbooks claimed that only the struggle alongside the Red Army let them make true use of their devotion, brought real benefits, and was the most direct path to the liberation of their country.

The contributions of the army to the successes of the People's Republic of Poland were also discussed. It started with post-war defense from internal enemies. This euphemism was used for the struggle against anti-communist partisans labeled as "a reactionary military underground, the forces of an internal counter-revolution".[7] And instead of the brutal military actions that actually had taken place, textbooks mentioned "thousands of rallies, lectures and meetings with the

138 Civic and Defense Education

populations of towns and villages" to promote "the truth about the new Poland".[8] This theme enjoyed particular attention in the period 1975–1979. Later on, textbooks concentrated on the assistance that the army provided to farmers at harvest time or to the civilian population in general in times of natural disasters. In the 1980s textbooks also mentioned the achievements of the military research institutes and praised the army for securing specialists in various fields.

Military preparations for a possible future war were also mentioned. They were usually preceded by a short description of the war itself and of the international situation in general. According to the textbooks, the imperialist countries (the term was used even as late as in 1987) affiliated with NATO posed a threat to peace in the world. The United States and West Germany in particular spent more and more money on the arms race, fueling hatred among nations, and in the 1980s on the sabotage of détente. Their policies forced the peace-loving Warsaw Pact to act in defense of world peace, according to the interpretation presented in the textbooks.

The world as shown in defense training textbooks was thus black and white. Friends and foes were clearly defined, and war was always just about to break out. Only in the case of space exploration was cooperation between the two blocs mentioned.

Poland, as an important and strong member of the Warsaw Pact, also had to be prepared for possible military struggle. The Polish Army was, according to the textbooks, well-equipped, organized and trained. Military equipment was either designed or produced in Poland or in other allied countries. The army guaranteed the safety of the country and its citizens.

The educational role of the army was constantly stressed. It instilled moral virtues alongside the correct ideological attitude. The ideology of the "people's" Polish Army was in many instances typical of military training in general, but it was still ideology. All textbooks claimed, for example, that

> military conscription is an honor for a young citizen and is proof of the deep trust put in him by the people's authorities and by society as a whole. Young people in the ranks of the army learn how to act collectively, be disciplined, respect the social effort and social property, to be generous, courageous and persistent in achieving their goals; [they learn] entrepreneurship, endurance and mental strength, readiness to sacrifice and order.[9]

Soldiers were said to represent "the highest qualities of ideology, education, professionalism and mental strength".[10] If someone was not convinced by those arguments, he should at least obey the law. The Act on Compulsory Enrolment for the Defense of the People's Republic of Poland was cited, which *inter alia* mentioned that defense education was a compulsory school subject.

Notes

1 Bieńkowski, Władysław. 1948. *Nauka o Polsce współczesnej*. Warsaw: PZWS; Barbag, Józef, Julian Lider, Walentyna Najdus, Kazimierz Mariański and Edward Słuczański,

Civic and Defense Education 139

1949. *Nauka o Polsce i świecie współczesnym. Książka do użytku szkolnego.* Warsaw: PZWS.

2 Gajewski, Jan and Kazimierz Kąkol. 1969. *Wychowanie obywatelskie. Klasa VIII.* Warsaw: PZWS, 5.

3 Ibid., 140–142.

4 Szymczak, Tadeusz. 1964. *Wiadomości o Polsce i świecie współczesnym.* Warsaw: PZWS, 12.

5 Gajewski, Jan, Franciszek Kusztelak and Ryszard Szadkowski. 1975. *Przysposobienie obronne dla klasy VIII szkoły podstawowej.* Warsaw: WSiP, 12.

6 Kusztelak, Franciszek. 1987. *Przysposobienie obronne. Podręcznik dla klasy ósmej szkoły podstawowej.* Warsaw: WSiP, 5.

7 Gajewski, Jan, Franciszek Kusztelak and Ryszard Szadkowski. 1975. *Przysposobienie obronne dla klasy VIII szkoły podstawowej.* Warsaw: WSiP, 18.

8 Ibid.

9 Gajewski, Jan, Franciszek Kusztelak and Ryszard Szadkowski. 1981. *Przysposobienie obronne dla klasy VIII szkoły podstawowej.* Warsaw: WSiP, 17; Kusztelak, Franciszek. 1987. *Przysposobienie obronne. Podręcznik dla klasy ósmej szkoły podstawowej.* Warsaw: WSiP, 8.

10 Gajewski, Jan, Franciszek Kusztelak and Ryszard Szadkowski. 1981. *Przysposobienie obronne dla klasy VIII szkoły podstawowej.* Warsaw: WSiP, 17.

9 Conclusion

Primary School Textbooks, Propaganda and the Totalitarian State

Let us return to the definition of propaganda as the deliberate and systematic attempt to shape perceptions, manipulate cognitions and direct behavior to achieve a response that furthers the desired intent of the propagandist.

Deliberate and Systematic Attempt

There is no doubt that politically loaded content was inserted into Polish primary school textbooks on purpose and in a systematic way. Not only textbooks, but also school curricula, pedagogical journals, official and unofficial documents of the Ministry of Education, of the Polish United Workers' Party and of the censorship office testify to the existence of a propaganda canon to be pursued by schools.[1]

Since the publication of the Polish version of this book, research on the political aspects of Polish education under communism has progressed significantly. It now includes studies on particular schools, on teachers and their training, on school curricula and practices. No matter what perspective the canon is analyzed from, researchers arrive at similar conclusions: that schools were supposed to instill communist ideology and positive attitude towards the Soviet Union, the Communist Party and its rule over Poland in the minds of pupils. Both the model and the manner in which it was implemented were strictly controlled. Elements of propaganda were to be included in all school subjects. The school was part of the totalitarian state.

Textbooks proved to be an important way to implement the model in everyday practice. Their content corresponded closely to the regulations and recommendations of policymakers. The sheer amount of textbook propaganda is yet another argument in favor of the theory of a "deliberate and systematic attempt".

The total percentage of textbook pages with propaganda (Figure 9.1, medium line) was calculated, as well as sub-totals for humanities (top line; geography included) and mathematics and sciences (bottom line). They confirm the saturation of textbooks with propaganda. The degree of indoctrination peaked in the early 1950s, and from the mid-1950s slowly but noticeably decreased. The humanities were always more indoctrinated, while the sciences maintained a generally constant level. The drop in the 1970s was caused by reforms in mathematics teaching.

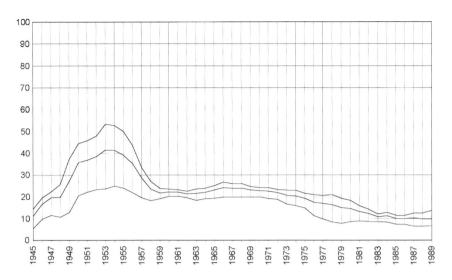

Figure 9.1 Total Amount of Propaganda in Primary School Textbooks by Year

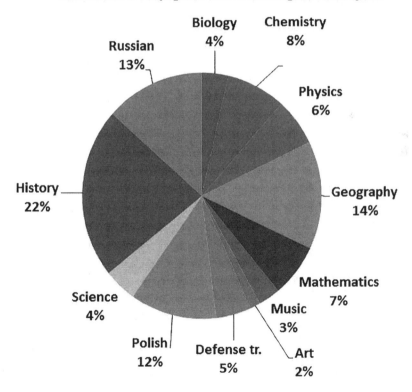

Figure 9.2 Distribution of Propaganda Content Among School Subjects

142   *Conclusion*

History had the largest share of school indoctrination. Together with Polish, Russian and geography, it provided at least half of all propaganda, and the proportion even grew in the 1980s when mathematics and sciences were almost completely free of ideology.

Textbook propaganda was distributed almost equally among grades, as shown on Figure 9.3. Only the youngest pupils were exposed to a lesser extent. However, in the Stalinist period, attempts were made to saturate their textbooks as well— yet more proof that policymakers of the time were so preoccupied with ideology that they paid no attention to the pedagogical aspects of textbooks.

The list of the textbooks most heavily loaded with propaganda (Figure 9.4) confirms the domination of history and of the Stalinist period in the process of indoctrination of younger generations. The examples listed should be regarded as propaganda books rather than school textbooks.

The graph of total propaganda per pupil starting education in each year of the People's Republic of Poland includes those pupils who could complete their

	1	2	3	4	5	6	7	8
1945–48	2%	7%	10%	14%	12%	15%	15%	25%
1949–55	6%	15%	12%	21%	12%	17%	17%	–
1956–64	3%	9%	18%	21%	15%	17%	17%	–
1965–79	2%	6%	14%	17%	13%	16%	14%	18%
1980–89	4%	7%	13%	14%	8%	13%	19%	22%
1945–89	**3%**	**8%**	**13%**	**17%**	**12%**	**16%**	**15%**	**16%**

Figure 9.3 Distribution of Propaganda Content Among the School Grades

1.	J. Dutkiewicz, N. Gąsiorowska, H. Katz, *Historia. Kl. VII* (1953–55) [History. 7]	96–98%
2.	G. Missalowa, J. Schoenbrenner, *Historia Polski* (1950–53) [History. 4]	95%
3.	*Historia. Dla klasy VII* (1956–58) [History. 7]	90%
4.	*Materiały pomocnicze do nauczania geografii. Klasa VII. ZSRR i kraje demokracji ludowej* (1949) [Geography. 7]	89%
5.	M. Dłuska, J. Schoenbrenner, *Historia. Dla klasy IV* (1953–56) [History. 4]	84–85%
6.	*Historia. Dla klasy VI. Pod red. M. Siuchnińskiego* (1950–57) [History. 6]	75–79%
7.	J. Dembowska, H. Rudnicka, T. Wojeński, *Na drodze przemian. Czytanki dla klasy VII* (1951) [Polish readers. 7]	76%
8.	Z. Klemensiewicz, J. Żlabowa, *Nasz język. Podręcznik gramatyki języka polskiego z ćwiczeniami. Dla klasy VII* (1950) [Polish grammar. 7]	76%
9.	M. Dłuska, *Z naszych dziejów. Podręcznik dla IV kl. szkoły podstawowej* (1949) [History. 4]	72%
10.	S. Aleksandrzak, H. Koszutska, *Czytanki. Dla klasy III* (1952–55) [Polish reader. 3]	72%

Figure 9.4 Textbooks with the Largest Percentage of Pages with Propaganda

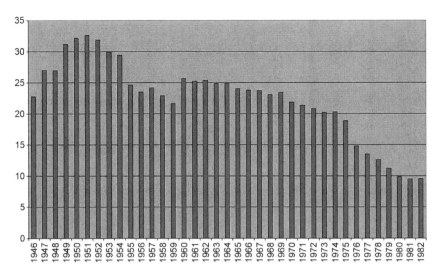

Figure 9.5 Total Amount of Propaganda in Primary School Textbooks for Pupils Starting Their Education in Each School Year

primary education before the collapse of the communist regime, and who attended school on a regular basis. The graph again confirms the peak of indoctrination in the Stalinist period. However, it did not stop with the death of Stalin. Only those who started education in the mid-1970s or later experienced significantly less ideological pressure.

Interestingly, similar propaganda content and similar patterns of change can be observed in other countries of the Soviet bloc. This has been noticed by many Western researchers, and illustrated in detail by John Rodden in his *Textbook Reds*. Rodden analyzed a set of textbooks from the GDR and his conclusions were very similar to mine. He seemed to be impressed by the scope and content of textbook propaganda in East Germany and regarded it as something exceptional—which apparently was not the case. The transnational study of textbooks under communism reveals not only similarities and each country's specifics[2] but also common inspirations as well as decision-makers.

Shaping Perception and Manipulating Cognition

In shaping perception, textbooks constructed their realities according to Marxist ideology, including the theory of the stages of history, materialism, knowledge of the world, evolutionary theory and the omnipotence of man, especially in transforming the environment. No contradictory opinions were allowed. Textbook narratives affirmed those concepts and ignored cases that could raise any doubts.

144   *Conclusion*

They manipulated the selection of examples and illustrations in order to prove the superiority of communism and socialism over capitalism or of the People's Republic of Poland over earlier periods of Polish history. Lies were also used, especially in history textbooks.

The language of textbooks was used as a tool of manipulation. Many phrases and even whole passages came directly from newspapers and propaganda brochures. Facts were seldom left without comments and were often dominated by them. The same messages—words, phrases, examples—were repeated over and over again in textbooks for various subjects. Propaganda was, in general, related to knowledge of the discipline, but sometimes inserted without any particular connection to introductions, citations or separate chapters. Subject or grade had little impact on textbooks, either on vocabulary or on overall content, especially in the Stalinist times. Disregarding the age of the readers, all pupils were treated the same—as "little adults".[3] Children were not to be careless. They were to be involved in the real problems of the real world, and in the victory of socialism. What distinguished primary school textbooks from other propaganda materials was the fact that they concentrated on positive messages. The world of textbooks was optimistic. There was a lot of wishful thinking, but little criticism and very few instances of hatred.

Directing Behavior

Many tasks formulated in the textbooks referred to the school and extracurricular activities of the readers. They asked pupils to perform certain activities, to become involved or interested in certain issues from the current propaganda framework of the regime. The textbooks suggested how to organize school and family life. They presented desirable actions, events, meetings, and promoted models of behavior and career paths. This corresponded completely with Hannah Arendt's opinion that the ultimate goal, in this case of education under the communist regime, was to transform propaganda lies into a functioning reality.

The Propagandist and its Intent

The system of post–World War II education in Poland was directed and controlled by the Communist Party. As I wrote in an article on the process of textbook approval:

> On the lowest level, the traditional power of a teacher as an educator was to be replaced by a power of a textbook. The power of a textbook author as a creator of a book was limited by the guidance and control of the ministry and publishing house. The publishing house had its monopoly guaranteed by the state but was often itself an object of influence and control of ministerial supervisors. However, formulating educational policy and making strategic decisions about the textbooks' contents was not in the realm of the ministry. It was the Communist Party leadership that lead the decisions, while

the governmental institutions only implemented its directives. The Party influenced all other stages of textbook productions as most authors and editors were its systematically trained and controlled members. Although the censorship office had the last word in the approval process, in fact it was only implementing the guidelines received from the Party officials.[4]

The propagandist intended to make pupils identify with the People's Republic of Poland, with the policies of its authorities, and also with the authorities of the Soviet Union, who were in charge of the whole "progressive world". Young Poles were supposed to follow the ideas and support the actions of the authorities. Those objectives were voiced openly in the official speeches of the Party and state dignitaries, in published documents, as well as in the school curricula and teachers' press.

There is a question as to whether school propaganda in the People's Republic of Poland changed significantly over time. Some scholars argue that the intent of the Communist Party was constant and any modifications in the content of education were purely tactical. They aimed to achieve better indoctrination, but not to limit it.[5] Others distinguish the Stalinist period as "purely" totalitarian and often stop their narratives in 1956 claiming—explicitly or implicitly—that afterwards the situation returned to a kind of normalcy.[6] The content of primary school textbooks shows that the quantity of propaganda did change (and mostly diminished). However, the main ideas and themes continued throughout the whole period.

Achieving a Response

The question of the effectiveness of textbook propaganda is the most problematic, if not irresolvable, one. On the one hand, already under communism ideologists complained that teachers were reluctant to include ideological elements in their lessons, that too often such issues were attached only superficially and as an afterthought to lessons, if at all. Pupils' performance on surveys concerning so-called socio-political knowledge was never satisfactory. They could repeat some propaganda clichés, but apparently did not reflect on them— for example, in the 1950s claiming that in pre-war Poland workers worked 24 hours a day and peasants were serfs. Was this a success or a failure of school propaganda?

Pupils who participated in research on historical consciousness in the 1970s and 1980s in private talks with researchers confessed that they lied in the (anonymous) questionnaires and wrote what they thought they were expected to answer.[7] Such a split personality can be regarded as a side effect of propaganda at school. In the 1990s Rev. Józef Tischner used the term "homo Sovieticus"[8] to characterize the mentality of Polish society. He claimed that people who lived under communism developed personal features to adjust to it and cultivated those features even after the collapse of the communist regime. Possibly, school education, including textbooks, had its share in that process.

Unsatisfactory educational results led to the reduction of school propaganda in the mid-1950s, early 1970s and 1980s. In the 1950s, besides general political

146   *Conclusion*

changes, it became apparent that the curricula and textbooks were so overloaded that pupils were unable to absorb either ideological or general content. The large-scale students' protests of 1968 came as a big surprise to the authorities. The regime could not believe that a generation brought up entirely under communist rule did not follow the propaganda principles of the curricula and textbooks. It was decided to present those principles in a more attractive and communicative way. However, the widespread support of the young people for the Solidarity movement in 1980 and 1981 again proved the ineffectiveness of official propaganda. This time the authorities decided to bring difficult facts and controversial issues into the textbooks, since pupils would learn about them anyway. "Proper" commentaries were supposed to assure interpretations favorable to the regime. Apparently, these measures did not improve the overall situation, and the younger generation actively supported the collapse of the regime in 1988–1989.

Studies on the systems of values of Polish secondary school pupils and their parents have shown general continuity since the pre-war years. Traditional values were deeply rooted and young people dreamt about stability and happy family lives[9]—though their textbooks promoted activism, careers and progress.

However, one should also keep in mind the negative results of a total rejection of school propaganda. Pupils could reject not only ideological elements of education, but also the general values promoted by schools, such as patriotism, selflessness, cooperativeness and others.

Here we come to another discussion: on the extent of school propaganda. One can claim, as Mariusz Mazur, that the regime's goal—at least in the Stalinist times—was to raise "a new man".[10] His features were similar to the "new men" of other ideologies (e.g. fascism and Nazism,[11] but also of the Enlightenment and the Progressive Era). Some of them referred to the new ideology, but many were simply general virtues that adults would like their children to cultivate to become better grown-ups in the future. They started with being polite and washing teeth, telling the truth and helping people older and weaker than themselves. Should pieces promoting those general virtues be regarded as propaganda? What would education be without them? I did not classify such instances as propaganda, unless they directly referred to communist ideology—for example, when a boy gave up his place in a train to a woman, I did not classify it as indoctrination, but if the boy was a pioneer I did.

Looking at the issue from another point of view, one could suggest, as some do, that all education is propaganda for it promotes certain values and serves the interests of certain groups.[12] The world is portrayed and judged from their point of view. Moreover, individual biases of textbook authors seem to be inevitable. However, democracies usually allow teachers and pupils to choose their textbooks. There are plenty of publications available to be used at school. In many Western countries they need not be accepted by any governmental body.[13] This was not the case in the People's Republic of Poland, where not only textbooks had to be approved according to a strict multi-level procedure, but the same principles applied to all books to be acquired by school libraries. The policy of one textbook per subject and grade eliminated any competition and divergent interpretations. Moreover, in democratic countries in the post–World War II period teachers were asked to encourage their pupils to identify the bias of textbook authors as a way of dealing with this inevitable phenomenon (instead of futile attempts to eliminate any bias).[14] In Poland, on the contrary, ideology in textbooks was not only tolerated, but also encouraged and promoted. Both teachers and pupils were supposed to strictly follow the books. Their content was to be memorized, not criticized or questioned.

Despite these demands, textbooks were never the only source of information nor the only pedagogical tool at Polish schools. Many teachers completely disregarded textbooks and pupils were supposed to learn by heart what the teacher had told them (sometimes turning the lessons into mundane dictating).[15] What were they saying then? Some researchers regard teachers as loyal servants of the regime. There is evidence, however, such as in the memoirs of former pupils, that this was not universally true. Many teachers either avoided communist ideology or even openly questioned it.[16] Moreover, education was not limited to school. Family, friends, the Church and other bodies had their role in raising new generations. This must have weakened the impact of the textbooks.

The unattractiveness of the textbooks also played a role. The authorities' preoccupation with the ideological content of textbooks led to neglecting other aspects, such as their communication value or aesthetics. As a result, the books turned out to be boring and incomprehensible, also (or sometimes particularly) in their ideological content.

This is not to say that Polish pupils were totally immune to textbook propaganda. In the words of Joseph Goebbels, "If you tell a lie [. . .] and keep repeating it, people will come to believe it". Some would even deny inheriting their attitudes from school textbooks. But being unaware did not insulate them from the influence of textbook propaganda. The influence manifests itself in a certain sentiment towards the People's Republic of Poland among those who spent their childhood in that period. A reading primer from the 1960s reprinted in 2005 became a best-seller, despite the fact that it contained pro-regime stories and images, such as a reading about a May 1st parade. Other elements of communist heritage addressed to young people also enjoy considerable popularity, even if they are obviously propagandist, for example, the TV serial *Czterej pancerni i pies*, telling the story of four tank crew members and their dog who fought against the Nazis alongside the Red Army. Apparently, the communist system has not been totally and universally rejected by the school graduates of the People's Republic of Poland. However, I am not aware of any systematic research on its impact on the attitudes held by people today.

Notes

1 For a detailed presentation of the steps of textbook production and approval see: Wojdon, Joanna. 2015. "The system of textbook approval in Poland under communist rule (1944–1989) as a tool of power of the regime". *Peadagogica Historica: International Journal of the History of Education* 51, no. 1–2: 181–196.

148 Conclusion

2 My study of the reading primers from the Soviet bloc confirms that such common patterns existed. The mechanisms, however, were not revealed by mere comparison of the final products: the textbooks (Wojdon, Joanna. 2015. *Świat elementarzy. Obraz rzeczywistości w podręcznikach do nauki czytania w krajach bloku radzieckiego*. Warsaw: IPN.)

3 Radziwiłł, Anna. 1981. *Ideologia wychowawcza w Polsce w latach 1948–1956. Próba modelu*. Warsaw: Nowa.

4 Wojdon, 2015. "The system of textbook approval", 195.

5 E.g. Brynkus, Józef. 2014. *Komunistyczna ideologizacja a szkolna edukacja historyczna w Polsce (1944–1989)*. Kraków: Antykwa.

6 E.g. Kosiński, Krzysztof. 2000. *O nową mentalność. Życie codzienne w szkołach 1945–1956*. Warsaw: TRIO.

7 Rulka, Janusz. 1991. *Przemiany świadomości historycznej młodzieży*. Bydgoszcz: WSP, 108.

8 The term came from the book by the Soviet sociologist Alexandr Zinovyev.

9 Nowak, Stefan (ed.). 1989. *Ciągłość i zmiana tradycji kulturowej*. Warsaw: PWN.

10 Mazur, Mariusz. 2009. *O człowieku tendencyjnym. Obraz nowego człowieka w propagandzie komunistycznej w okresie Polski Ludowej i PRL 1944–1956*. Lublin: UMCS.

11 Alessio Ponzio claims that for both ideologies, the vision of a new man was quite similar, so were the methods of his upbringing (Ponzio, Alessio. 2015. *Shaping the New Man: Youth Training Regimes in Fascist Italy and Nazi Germany*. Milwaukee: University of Wisconsin Press.

12 Apple, Michael. 1979. *Ideology and Curriculum*. New York: Routledge.

13 Cajani, Luigi. 2009. "History Textbooks Between Teachers' Freedom and State Control". Paper presented at the Annual Meeting of International Society for History Didactics in Braunschweig, Germany.

14 Marsden, William. 2004. *The School Textbook: History, Geography and Social Studies*. New York: Routledge.

15 Hoszowska, Mariola. 2002. *Praktyka nauczania historii w Polsce 1944–1956*. Rzeszów: Wydawnictwo Uniwersytetu Rzeszowskiego, 190–192.

16 Grzybowski, Romuald (ed.). 2013. *Zaangażowanie? Opór? Gra? Szkic do portretu nauczyciela w latach PRL-u*. Toruń: Adam Marszałek.

Bibliography of the Textbooks Cited

Note

The full bibliography of textbooks can be found in the Polish version of the book (Wojdon, 2000, 292–318) and at www.wojdon.net.

Art

Stopczyk, Stanisław K. 1968. *Wiadomości o sztuce. Podręcznik wychowania plastycznego dla klasy V szkoły podstawowej.* Warsaw: PZWS.

Stopczyk, Stanisław K. 1969. *Wiadomości o sztuce. Podręcznik wychowania plastycznego dla klasy VII szkoły podstawowej.* Warsaw: PZWS.

Stopczyk, Stanisław K. 1981. *Plastyka. Klasa 4.* Warsaw: WSiP.

Biology

Feliksiak, Stanisław and Włodzimierz Michajłow. 1950. *Zoologia dla kl. VI.* Warsaw: PZWS.

Feliksiak, Stanisław and Włodzimierz Michajłow. 1952. *Zoologia dla kl. VI.* Warsaw: PZWS.

Feliksiak, Stanisław and Włodzimierz Michajłow. 1955. *Zoologia dla kl. VI.* Warsaw: PZWS.

Feliksiak, Stanisław and Włodzimierz Michajłow. 1963. *Zoologia. Dla klasy VI.* Warsaw: PZWS.

Kołodziejczyk, January. 1950. *Botanika. Dla klasy V.* Warsaw: PZWS.

Kołodziejczyk, January. 1955. *Botanika. Dla klasy V.* Warsaw: PZWS.

Kołodziejczyk, January. 1961. *Botanika. Dla klasy V.* Warsaw: PZWS.

Podgórska, Aniela, Tadeusz Gorczyński and Halina Pomirska. 1975. *Botanika. Dla klasy VI.* Warsaw: WSiP.

Podgórska, Aniela, Tadeusz Gorczyński and Halina Pomirska. 1976. *Botanika. Dla klasy VI.* Warsaw: WSiP.

Raabe, Henryk. 1950. *Biologia. Kl. VII. Nauka o człowieku.* Warsaw: PZWS.

Stępczak, Kazimierz. 1981. *Biologia. 4.* Warsaw: WSiP.

Wernerowa, Janina and Jan Żabiński. 1950. *Nauka o człowieku. Podręcznik dla kl. VII szkoły podstawowej.* Warsaw: Nasza Księgarnia.

Wójcik, Zofia. 1976. *Zoologia dla klasy VII.* Warsaw: WSiP.

Wójcik, Zofia. 1982. *Zoologia dla klasy VII.* Warsaw: WSiP.

150　　*Bibliography of the Textbooks Cited*

Chemistry

Bogucki, Anatoliusz. 1959. *Chemia. Podręcznik dla uczniów klasy VII szkoły ogólnokształcącej*. Warsaw: PZWS.
Lewicki, Władysław. 1949. *Chemia. Dla klasy VII szkoły jednolitej stopnia podstawowego.* Warsaw: PZWS.
Lewicki, Władysław. 1950. *Chemia. Dla klasy VII szkoły ogólnokształcącej*. Warsaw: PZWS.
Lewicki, Władysław. 1953. *Chemia. Dla klasy VII*. Warsaw: PZWS.
Lewicki, Władysław. 1955. *Chemia. Dla klasy VII*. Warsaw: PZWS.
Matysik, Jan. 1951. *Chemia. Dla klasy VII szkoły ogólnokształcącej*. Warsaw: PZWS.
Matysik, Jan and Anatoliusz Rogowski. 1966. *Chemia. Dla klasy VIII*. Warsaw: PZWS.

Civic Education

Barbag, Józef, Julian Lider, Walentyna Najdus, Kazimierz Mariański and Edward Słuczański. 1949. *Nauka o Polsce i świecie współczesnym. Książka do użytku szkolnego*. Warsaw: PZWS.
Bieńkowski, Władysław. 1948. *Nauka o Polsce współczesnej*. Warsaw: PZWS.
Gajewski, Jan and Kazimierz Kąkol. 1969. *Wychowanie obywatelskie. Klasa VIII*. Warsaw: PZWS.
Szymczak, Tadeusz. 1964. *Wiadomości o Polsce i świecie współczesnym*. Warsaw: PZWS.

Defense Education

Gajewski, Jan, Franciszek Kusztelak and Ryszard Szadkowski. 1975. *Przysposobienie obronne dla klasy VIII szkoły podstawowej*. Warsaw: WSiP.
Gajewski, Jan, Franciszek Kusztelak and Ryszard Szadkowski. 1981. *Przysposobienie obronne dla klasy VIII szkoły podstawowej*. Warsaw: WSiP.
Kusztelak, Franciszek. 1987. *Przysposobienie obronne. Podręcznik dla klasy ósmej szkoły podstawowej*. Warsaw: WSiP.

English

Mickunas, Jan. 1967. *My English Book. II rok nauki*. Warsaw: PZWS.
Prejbisz, Antoni, Janina Smólska, Zofia Siwicka and Stanisław Helsztyński. 1955. *Nauka angielskiego. Learning English. I rok nauczania*. Warsaw: PZWS.

Geography

Brzozowska, Felicja and Maria Kanikowska. 1969. *Geografia. Dla kl. IV*. Warsaw: PZWS.
Czekańska, Maria. 1951. *Geografia Polski. Klasa VI*. Warsaw: PZWS.
Czekańska, Maria. 1953. *Geografia Polski. Dla klasy VI*. Warsaw: PZWS.
Czekańska, Maria. 1980. *Geografia. Klasa 6*. Warsaw: WSiP.
Czekańska, Maria and Halina Radlicz-Ruehlowa. 1950. *Wiadomości z geografii. Dla klasy V szkoły podstawowej*. Warsaw: PZWS.
Czekańska, Maria and Halina Radlicz-Ruehlowa. 1951. *Wiadomości z geografii. Dla klasy V szkoły podstawowej*. Warsaw: PZWS.
Czekańska, Maria and Halina Radlicz-Ruehlowa. 1963. *Geografia. Dla klasy V*. Warsaw: PZWS.

Bibliography of the Textbooks Cited   151

Czekańska, Maria and Halina Radlicz-Ruehlowa. 1965. *Geografia świata. Klasa VII*. Warsaw: PZWS.

Czekańska, Maria and Halina Radlicz-Ruehlowa. 1980. *Geografia. Dla klasy V*. Warsaw: WSiP.

Czekańska, Maria and Halina Radlicz-Ruehlowa. 1983. *Geografia 6. Europa. Azja*. Warsaw: WSiP.

Golec, Barbara, Marianna Nowak and Ewa Przesmycka. 1987. *Geografia. Europa. Azja. Podręcznik dla klasy 7 szkoły podstawowej*. Warsaw: WSiP.

Kądziołka, Jan. 1981. *Geografia. 4. Krajobrazy Polski*. Warsaw: WSiP.

Kondracki, Jerzy and Wiesława Richling-Kondracka. 1951. *Geografia Polski. Dla klasy VI. Cz. II szczegółowa. Gospodarka i ludność*. Warsaw: PZWS.

Ministerstwo Oświaty. 1949. *Program nauki w 11-letniej szkole ogólnokształcącej. Projekt. Geografia*. Warsaw: PZWS.

Mordawski, Jan. 1984. *Geografia 7. Afryka, Ameryka, Australia. Podręcznik dla klasy 7 szkoły podstawowej*. Warsaw: WSiP.

Mordawski, Jan. 1986. *Geografia. Ameryka, Afryka, Australia i Oceania. Podręcznik dla klasy 6 szkoły podstawowej*. Warsaw: WSiP.

Piskorz, Sławomir and Stanisław Zając. 1982. *Geografia. 5. Krajobrazy ziemi*. Warsaw: WSiP.

Radliński, Tadeusz and Jan Zaćwilichowski. 1948. *Nasz kraj i jego przyroda. Podręcznik dla klasy IV szkoły podstawowej*. Kraków: Księgarnia Stefana Kamińskiego i Tadeusza Radlińskiego.

Staszewski, Józef. 1950. *Geografia. Klasa VII. Na rok szkolny 1950/51*. Warsaw: PZWS.

Staszewski, Józef. 1952. *Geografia. Klasa VII*. Warsaw: PZWS.

Staszewski, Józef. 1953. *Geografia. Klasa VII*. Warsaw: PZWS.

Wuttke, Gustaw. 1949. *Poznaj swój kraj. Podręcznik geografii dla klasy IV szkoły podstawowej*. Warsaw: PZWS.

History

Dutkiewicz, Józef, Gąsiorowska Natalia and Henryk Katz. 1954. *Historia. Dla klasy VII*. Warsaw: PZWS.

Hoszowska, Władysława. 1958. *Opowiadania z dziejów Polski. Część I (do roku 1505)*. Warsaw: PZWS.

Dutkiewicz, Józef, Gąsiorowska Natalia and Henryk Katz. 1958. *Historia. Dla klasy VII*. Warsaw: PZWS.

Klubówna, Anna and Jadwiga Stępieniowa. 1961. *W naszej ojczyźnie. Podręcznik historii dla klasy IV*. Warsaw: PZWS.

Kosman, Marceli. 1975. *Historia. Dla klasy VI*. Warsaw: WSiP.

Markowski, Gustaw. 1962. *Historia. Dla klasy VI*. Warsaw: WSiP.

Markowski, Gustaw. 1964. *Historia. Dla klasy V*. Warsaw: PZWS.

Missalowa, Gryzelda and Janina Schoenbrenner. 1951. *Historia Polski*. Warsaw: PZWS.

Serejski, Marian H. (ed.). 1951. *Historia. Dla klasy V*. Warsaw: PZWS.

Siuchniński, Mateusz (ed.). 1952. *Historia. Dla klasy VI*. Warsaw: PZWS.

Siuchniński, Mateusz (ed.). 1953. *Historia. Dla klasy VI*. Warsaw: PZWS.

Skowronek, Jerzy. 1987. *Historia. Do Niepodległej. Podręcznik dla klasy 7 szkoły podstawowej*. Warsaw: WSiP.

Szcześniak, Andrzej L. 1984. *Historia. Polska i świat naszego wieku. Książka pomocnicza dla kl. VIII szkoły podstawowej*. Warsaw: WSiP.

152 Bibliography of the Textbooks Cited

Szostakowski, Stanisław. 1968. *Historia. Dla klasy VII*. Warsaw: PZWS.
Szostakowski, Stanisław. 1971. *Historia. Dla klasy VII*. Warsaw: PZWS.
Wojciechowski, Marian. 1970. *Historia. Dla klasy VIII*. Warsaw: PZWS.

Mathematics

Abramowicz, Tomasz and Mieczysław Okołowicz. 1948. *Arytmetyka z geometrią.*
Podręcznik dla klasy IV szkoły podstawowej. Warsaw: PZWS.
Abramowicz, Tomasz and Mieczysław Okołowicz. 1959. *Arytmetyka z geometrią. Dla klasy*
V. Warsaw: PZWS.
Abramowicz, Tomasz and Mieczysław Okołowicz. 1967. *Matematyka. Dla klasy V*. Warsaw:
PZWS.
Rusiecki, Antoni M., Adam Zarzecki, Zygmunt Chwiałkowski and Wacław Schayer. 1953.
Arytmetyka I. Warsaw: PZWS.
Rusiecki, Antoni M., Adam Zarzecki, Zygmunt Chwiałkowski and Wacław Schayer. 1948
and 1949. *Arytmetyka II*. Warsaw: PZWS.
Rusiecki, Antoni M., Adam Zarzecki, Zygmunt Chwiałkowski and Wacław Schayer. 1951.
Arytmetyka II. Warsaw: PZWS.
Rusiecki, Antoni M., Adam Zarzecki, Zygmunt Chwiałkowski and Wacław Schayer. 1951.
Arytmetyka VI. Warsaw: PZWS.
Rusiecki, Antoni M., Adam Zarzecki, Zygmunt Chwiałkowski and Wacław Schayer. 1951.
Arytmetyka z geometrią. IV. Warsaw: PZWS.
Rusiecki, Antoni M., Adam Zarzecki, Zygmunt Chwiałkowski and Wacław Schayer. 1953.
Arytmetyka z geometrią. V. Warsaw: PZWS.
Białas, Aleksander. 1967. *Matematyka. 8*. Warsaw: PZWS.
Białas, Aleksander and Stanisław Straszewicz. 1972. *Matematyka. Kl. 6*. Warsaw: PZWS.
Iwaszkiewicz, Bolesław. 1950. *Algebra. Klasa VII*. Warsaw: PZWS.
Iwaszkiewicz, Bolesław. 1953. *Algebra. Klasa VII*. Warsaw: PZWS.
Rusiecki, Antoni M. and Wacław Schayer. 1964–1976 (all editions). *Arytmetyka z*
geometrią. IV. Warsaw: PZWS.
Rusiecki, Antoni M. and Wacław Schayer. 1965. *Arytmetyka III*. Warsaw: PZWS.
Rusiecki, Antoni M. and Wacław Schayer. 1968. *Arytmetyka z geometrią. IV*. Warsaw:
PZWS.

Physical Education

Liedke, Andrzej. 1978. *Ćwicz razem z nami. Klasa II*. Warsaw: WSiP, 4.
Mieczkowski, Tadeusz. 1977. *Wychowanie fizyczne—podręcznik dla klas IV-VI*. Warsaw:
WSiP, 166.

Physics

Bąkowski, Stefan. 1949. *Fizyka i chemia. Wiadomości wstępne. Podręcznik dla V klasy*
stopnia podstawowego szkoły jednolitej. Warsaw: PZWS.
Bąkowski, Stefan, Czesław Fotyma and Czesław Ścisłowski. 1957. *Fizyka dla klasy VII*.
Warsaw: PZWS.
Bąkowski, Stefan, Czesław Fotyma and Czesław Ścisłowski. 1961. *Fizyka. Dla klasy VI*.
Warsaw: PZWS.

Bibliography of the Textbooks Cited   153

Fotyma, Czesław and Czesław Ścisłowski. 1948. *Fizyka. Podręcznik dla VII klasy szkoły podstawowej*. Warsaw: PZWS.

Fotyma, Czesław and Czesław Ścisłowski. 1950. *Fizyka. Dla klasy VI szkoły ogólnokształcącej*. Warsaw: PZWS.

Fotyma, Czesław and Czesław Ścisłowski. 1951. *Fizyka. Dla klasy VII*. Warsaw: PZWS.

Fotyma, Czesław and Czesław Ścisłowski. 1952. *Fizyka. Dla klasy VI szkoły ogólnokształcącej*. Warsaw: PZWS.

Fotyma, Czesław and Czesław Ścisłowski. 1971. *Fizyka. Dla klasy VI*. Warsaw: PZWS.

Mazur, Bolesław and Marian Wessely. 1981. *Fizyka. Dla klasy VIII*. Warsaw: WSiP, 159.

Polish

Aleksandrzak, Stanisław, Maria Bober and Hanna Zegadło. 1979. *Nasz dom ojczysty. Podręcznik do nauki języka polskiego. Klasa 2*. Warsaw: WSiP.

Aleksandrzak, Stanisław and Halina Koszutska. 1952. *Czytanki. Dla klasy III*. Warsaw: PZWS.

Aleksandrzak, Stanisław and Halina Koszutska. 1954. *Czytanki. Dla klasy III*. Warsaw: PZWS.

Aleksandrzak, Stanisław and Zofia Kwiecińska. 1949. *Za progiem. Czytanki dla klasy II szkoły podstawowej*. Warsaw: PZWS.

Aleksandrzak, Stanisław, Zofia Kwiecińska and Zbigniew Przyrowski. 1951. *Na szerokiej drodze. Czytanki dla klasy IV*. Warsaw: PZWS.

Aleksandrzak, Stanisław and Zbigniew Przyrowski. 1966. *A czy znasz ty, bracie młody . . . Czytanki dla klasy IV*. Warsaw: PZWS.

Aleksandrzak, Stanisław and Zbigniew Przyrowski. 1971. *Z bliska i z daleka. Wypisy dla klasy V*. Warsaw: WSiP.

Aleksandrzak, Stanisław and Józefa Rytlowa. 1970. *W szkole i w domu. Podręcznik do nauki języka polskiego dla klasy II*. Warsaw: WSiP.

Aleksandrzak, Stanisław, Józefa Rytlowa and Zbigniew Przyrowski. 1966. *W naszej gromadzie. Podręcznik do nauki języka polskiego dla klasy III*. Warsaw: PZWS.

Bielak, Franciszek, Władysław Szyszkowski and Artur Bardach. 1949. *Czytanki polskie. Dla VII kl. szkoły podstawowej*. Warsaw: PZWS.

Broniewska, Janina. 1949. *W naszej szkole. Czytanki dla IV klasy szkoły podstawowej*. Warsaw: PZWS.

Dańcewiczowa, Jadwiga. 1948. *Ćwiczenia i wiadomości gramatyczne. Dla klasy V szkoły podstawowej*. Warsaw: PZWS.

Dembowska, Janina and Halina Rudnicka. 1950. *Dom i świat. Wypisy dla klasy VI*. Warsaw: PZWS.

Dembowska, Janina, Halina Rudnicka and Teofil Wojeński. 1953. *Na drodze przemian. Czytanki dla klasy VII*. Warsaw: PZWS.

Dembowska, Janina, Zygmunt Saloni and Piotr Wierzbicki. 1973. *Świat i my. Podręcznik do nauki języka polskiego dla klasy VI*. Warsaw: WSiP.

Dembowska, Janina, Zygmunt Saloni and Piotr Wierzbicki. 1976. *Nasz język, nasz świat. Podręcznik do nauki języka polskiego dla klasy VI*. Warsaw: WSiP.

Dembowska, Janina and Zofia Strzelecka. 1977. *Książka życiu pomaga. Wypisy dla klasy VI*. Warsaw: WSiP.

Dobraniecki, Stanisław, Mieczysław Kotarbiński and Stanisław Aleksandrzak. 1946. *Razem. Czytanki dla II klasy szkoły powszechnej*. Warsaw: PZWS.

154 Bibliography of the Textbooks Cited

Falski, Marian. 1953. *Elementarz*. Warsaw: PZWS.

Falski, Marian. 1958. *Elementarz*. Warsaw: PZWS.

Gawdzik, Witold. 1980. *Nasza mowa—nasz świat. Klasa 3.* Warsaw: WSiP.

Jaworski, Michał. 1984. *Język polski. Gramatyka i ortografia. Podręcznik dla klasy 7 szkoły podstawowej.* Warsaw: WSiP.

Klemensiewicz, Zygmunt and Janina Żlabowa. 1952. *Nasz język. Gramatyka języka polskiego z ćwiczeniami. Klasa VII.* Warsaw: PZWS.

Kopczewski, Jan S. 1968. *Między dawnymi a nowymi laty. Wypisy dla klasy VIII szkoły podstawowej.* Warsaw: PZWS.

Kopczewski, Jan S. 1971. *Ta ziemia od innych droższa. Podręcznik do języka polskiego dla kl. VIII.* Warsaw: PZWS.

Kowalczewska, Anna and Zofia Mórawska. 1964. *Język polski. Ćwiczenia gramatyczne i stylistyczne dla klasy IV.* Warsaw: PZWS.

Kubski, Benedykt and Jacek Kubski. 1960. *Wypisy. Dla klasy VII.* Warsaw: PZWS.

Lausz, Karol, Kazimierz Staszewski and Zofia Zwierzchowska-Ferencowa. 1949. *O świcie. Czytanki dla klasy V szkoły podstawowej.* Warsaw: PZWS.

Nagajowa, Maria and Aniela Świerczyńska. 1969. *W naszej ojczyźnie. Podręcznik do nauki języka polskiego dla klasy V.* Warsaw: PZWS.

Nagajowa, Maria and Aniela Świerczyńska. 1971. *W naszej ojczyźnie. Podręcznik do nauki języka polskiego dla klasy V.* Warsaw: PZWS.

Nagajowa, Maria and Aniela Świerczyńska. 1980. *W codziennej pracy. Podręcznik do nauki języka polskiego. Dla klasy V.* Warsaw: WSiP.

Pauszer-Klonowska, Gabriela and Karol Lausz. 1951. *Dzień dzisiejszy. Wypisy dla klasy V.* Warsaw: PZWS.

Pęcherski, Mieczysław. 1961. *Język polski. Wiadomości i ćwiczenia z gramatyki i pisowni. Klasa VI.* Warsaw: PZWS.

Pęcherski, Mieczysław. 1972. *Nasz język ojczysty. Wiadomości i ćwiczenia z gramatyki i pisowni polskiej. Klasa VII.* Warsaw: PZWS.

Przyłubska, Ewa and Feliks Przyłubski. 1976. *Litery. Ćwiczenia uzupełniające.* Warsaw: WSiP.

Rytlowa, Józefa. 1946 and 1949. *Nauka pisania. Ćwiczenia ortograficzne, gramatyczne i przygotowanie do wypracowań dla V klasy szkoły powszechnej.* Warsaw: PZWS.

Rytlowa, Józefa. 1948. *Nauka pisania. Dla II klasy szkoły powszechnej.* Warsaw: PZWS.

Słuszkiewiczowa, Maria. 1950. *Ćwiczenia ortograficzne. Dla klasy II.* Warsaw: PZWS.

Sufin, Stanisława and Aniela Świerczyńska. 1965. *Mowa ojczysta. Wypisy z ćwiczeniami. Dla klasy VII.* Warsaw: PZWS.

Wieczorkiewicz, Bronisław. 1953. *Mowa polska. Ćwiczenia gramatyczne, ortograficzne i słownikowe. Klasa IV.* Warsaw: PZWS.

Wieczorkiewicz, Bronisław. 1946. *Ćwiczenia ortograficzne. Klasa VI.* Warsaw: PZWS.

Wieczorkiewicz, Bronisław. 1950. *Mowa polska. Ćwiczenia gramatyczne. Klasa IV.* Warsaw: PZWS.

Wieczorkiewicz, Bronisław. 1950. *Mowa polska. Ćwiczenia gramatyczne i słownikowe. Klasa I.* Warsaw: PZWS.

Wieczorkiewicz, Bronisław. 1952. *Pisownia polska w ćwiczeniach. Klasa VII.* Warsaw: PZWS.

Zarembina, Ewa, Hanna Ożogowska and Zygmunt Batorowicz. 1947. *Czytanka. Dla IV klasy miejskich i wiejskich szkół podstawowych.* Warsaw: Nasza Księgarnia.

Russian

Zieliński, Antoni and Jerzy Żurawski. 1954. *Język rosyjski. Klasa V.* Warsaw: PZWS.

Science

Gąsiorowska, Zofia and Jadwiga Wernerowa. 1952. *Biologia. Dla klasy III*. Warsaw: PZWS.

Krośkiewicz, Wiesława and Elwira Szylarska. 1980. *Poznaję swój kraj. Środowisko społeczno-przyrodnicze. Kl. 3*. Warsaw: WSiP.

Rościszewska-Gąsiorowska, Zofia. 1949. *Poznajemy rośliny i zwierzęta. Podręcznik dla klasy III. Książka ucznia*. Warsaw: PZWS.

Wernerowa, Jadwiga. 1951. *Biologia. Dla klasy III*. Warsaw: PZWS.

Zalewska, Zofia and Gustaw Wuttke. 1951. *Poznaj swój kraj. Podręcznik przyrody i geografii dla klasy III szkoły podstawowej*. Warsaw: PZWS.

Ziemecki, Stanisław. 1956. *Nauka o przyrodzie. Dla klasy IV*. Warsaw: PZWS.

Technical Training

Czyżycki, Walenty, Antoni Marek and Jadwiga Zabierowska. 1971. *Zajęcia praktyczno-techniczne. Klasa V*. Warsaw: PZWS.

General Bibliography

Note

An overview of the secondary literature as of 2000 has been provided in its original Polish version. Due to the fact that the literature has been almost entirely published in Poland and in Polish and therefore remains unavailable to most English-language readers, I chose not to provide the details here and to give bibliographical references only to the works directly cited. For further references see Propaganda polityczna and Wołoszyn, Jacek Witold. 2015. Szkoła jako instrument politycznej legitymizacji władzy partii komunistycznej w Polsce (1944–1989). Lublin: IPN.

Bibliography of the Books Cited

Ackerman, Diane. 2007. *The Zookeeper's Wife*. New York: W. W. Norton.

Apple, Michael. 1979. *Ideology and Curriculum*. New York: Routledge.

Brynkus, Józef. 2014. *Komunistyczna ideologizacja a szkolna edukacja historyczna w Polsce (1944–1989)*. Kraków: Antykwa.

Cajani, Luigi. 2009. "History Textbooks Between Teachers' Freedom and State Control". Paper presented at the Annual Meeting of International Society for History Didactics in Braunschweig, Germany.

Choińska-Mika, Jolanta, Jakub Lorenc, Krzysztof Mrozowski, Aleksandra Oniszczuk, Jacek Staniszewski and Klaudia Starczynowska. 2014. "Nauczyciele historii". In *Liczą się nauczyciele: Raport o stanie edukacji 2013*, edited by Michał Federowicz, Jolanta Choińska-Mika and Dominika Walczak. Warsaw: IBE.

DeJong-Lambert, William. 2014. "The New Biology in Poland After the Second World War: Polish Lysenkoism". *Paedagogica Historica* 45, no. 3: 403–420.

Dziennik Urzędowy Ministerstwa Oświaty [Journal of the Ministry of Education], 1948, no. 7; 1949, no. 12; 1950, no. 13; 1951, no. 11.

Frycie, Stanisław (ed.). 1985. *Programy szkoły podstawowej. Zbiór dokumentów*. Warsaw: WSiP.

Głowiński, Michał. 1990. *Nowomowa po polsku*. Warsaw: OPEN.

Grzybowski, Romuald (ed.). 2013. *Zaangażowanie? Opór? Gra? Szkic do portretu nauczyciela w latach PRL-u*. Toruń: Adam Marszałek.

Hłasko, Marek. 1966. *Piękni dwudziestoletni*. Paris: Instytut Literacki.

Hoszowska, Mariola. 2002. *Praktyka nauczania historii w Polsce 1944–1956*. Rzeszów: Wydawnictwo Uniwersytetu Rzeszowskiego.

General Bibliography 157

Jabłoński, Henryk. 1949. Zarządzenie Ministra Oświaty z 2 sierpnia 1949 r. w sprawie przejściowego programu nauczania w 11-letniej szkole ogólnokształcącej na rok szkolny 1949/50. *Dziennik Urzędowy Ministerstwa Oświaty*, no. 12, item 209.

Jabłoński, Henryk. 1950. Zarządzenie Ministra Oświaty z 28 lipca 1950 r. w sprawie programu nauczania w 11-letniej szkole ogólnokształcącej na rok szkolny 1950/51. *Dziennik Urzędowy Ministerstwa Oświaty*, no. 13, item 173.

Jakubowska, Barbara. 1986. *Przeobrażenia w szkolnej edukacji historycznej w Polsce w latach 1945–1956*. Warsaw: COM SNP.

Jarosiński, Witold. 1951. Zarządzenie Ministra Oświaty z 16 czerwca 1951 r. w sprawie instrukcji programowej i podręcznikowej dla 11-letnich szkół ogólnokształcących na rok szkolny 1951/52. *Dziennik Urzędowy Ministerstwa Oświaty*, no. 11, item 135.

Johnsen, Egil. 1993. *Textbooks in the Kaleidoscope: A Critical Survey of Literature and Research on Educational Texts*. Oslo: Scandinavian University Press.

Jowett, Gareth and Victoria O'Donnell. 2006. *Propaganda and Persuasion*. Thousand Oaks, CA: Sage.

Kosiński, Krzysztof. 2000. *O nową mentalność. Życie codzienne w szkołach 1945–1956*. Warsaw: TRIO.

Kosiński, Krzysztof. 2008. *Historia pijaństwa w czasach PRL. Polityka—obyczaje—szara strefa—patologie*. Warsaw: Neriton.

Maciaszek, Maksymilian. 1980. *Treść kształcenia i wychowania w reformach szkolnych PRL*. Warsaw: Książka i Wiedza.

Marsden, William. 2004. *The School Textbook: History, Geography and Social Studies*. New York: Routledge.

Mauersberg, Stanisław. 1974. *Reforma szkolnictwa w Polsce w latach 1944–1948*. Wrocław: Ossolineum, 239.

Mazur, Mariusz. 2009. *O człowieku tendencyjnym. Obraz nowego człowieka w propagandzie komunistycznej w okresie Polski Ludowej i PRL 1944–1956*. Lublin: UMCS.

Mazur, Zbigniew. 1989. *Obraz Niemiec w polskich podręcznikach szkolnych do nauczania historii. 1945–1989*. Poznań: Instytut Zachodni.

Ministerstwo Oświaty. 1949. *Program nauki w 11-letniej szkole ogólnokształcącej. Projekt. Matematyka*. Warsaw: PZWS.

Ministerstwo Oświaty. 1951. *Program nauki w 11-letniej szkole ogólnokształcącej. Biologia. Projekt*. Warsaw: PZWS.

Ministerstwo Oświaty. 1959. *Program nauczania w szkole podstawowej*. Warsaw: PZWS.

Ministerstwo Oświaty. 1964. *Program ośmioklasowej szkoły podstawowej (tymczasowy)*. Warsaw: PZWS, 2nd ed.

Nowak, Stefan (ed.). 1989. *Ciągłość i zmiana tradycji kulturowej*. Warsaw: PWN.

Osiński, Zbigniew. 2006. *Nauczanie historii w szkołach podstawowych w Polsce w latach 1944–1989: uwarunkowania organizacyjne oraz ideologiczno-polityczne*. Toruń: Duet.

Paczkowski, Andrzej. 2003. *The Spring Will Be Ours—Poland and the Poles from Occupation to Freedom*, trans. by Jane Cave. University Park: Pennsylvania State University Press.

Papazian, Elizabeth. 2013. "Literacy or Legibility: The Trace of Subjectivity in Soviet Socialist Realism". In *The Oxford Handbook of Propaganda Studies*, edited by Jonathan Auerbach and Russ Castronovo. Oxford: Oxford University Press.

Pęcherski, Mieczysław and Antoni Tatoń. 1963. *Więź szkoły z życiem w krajach socjalistycznych*. Warszawa: PZWS, 5–35.

Piliszek, Ekaterina V. 1977. *Radziecko-polska współpraca w dziedzinie nauki i oświaty 1944–1950*. Wrocław: Ossolineum.

158   General Bibliography

Pine, Lisa. 2010. *Education in Nazi Germany*. Oxford, New York: Berg.

Podraza, Antoni. 1960. "Rola historii w kształtowaniu racjonalistycznego, laickiego poglądu na świat". *Wiadomości Historyczne* 3, no. 1: 1–9.

Ponzio, Alessio. 2015. *Shaping the New Man: Youth Training Regimes in Fascist Italy and Nazi Germany*. Milwaukee: University of Wisconsin Press.

Radziwiłł, Anna. 1981. *Ideologia wychowawcza w Polsce w latach 1948–1956. Próba modelu*. Warsaw: Nowa.

Rodden, John. 2006. *Textbook Reds: Schoolbooks, Ideology and Eastern German Identity*. University Park: Pennsylvania State University Press.

Rulka, Janusz. 1991. *Przemiany świadomości historycznej młodzieży*. Bydgoszcz: WSP, 108.

Składanowski, Henryk. 2004. *Stosunki polsko-sowieckie w programach nauczania i podręcznikach historii w szkole powszechnej (podstawowej) w Polsce w latach 1932–1956*. Toruń: Adam Marszałek.

Skrzeszewski, Stanisław. 1948. *Podstawowe zadania oświatowe*. Warsaw: PZWS.

Skrzeszewski, Stanisław. 1948. Zarządzenie Ministra Oświaty z dnia 10 czerwca 1948 r. w sprawie przejściowego program nauczania w szkole średniej na rok szkolny 1948-1949. In: *Dziennik Urzędowy Ministerstwa Oświaty [Journal of the Ministry of Education]*, no. 7, item 127, 271–272.

Ubrikas, Donna. 2016. *My Sisters' Mother: A Memoir of War, Exile, and Stalin's Siberia*. Milwaukee: University of Wisconsin Press.

Wojdon, Joanna. 2000. *Propaganda polityczna w podręcznikach dla szkół podstawowych Polski Ludowej (Political Propaganda in Primary School Textbooks of the People's Poland (1944–1989))*. Toruń: Adam Marszałek.

Wojdon, Joanna. 2015. "The System of Textbook Approval in Poland Under Communist Rule (1944–1989) as a Tool of Power of the Regime". *Peadagogica Historica International Journal of the History of Education* 51, no. 1–2: 181–196.

Wojdon, Joanna. 2015. *Świat elementarzy. Obraz rzeczywistości w podręcznikach do nauki czytania w krajach bloku radzieckiego*. Warsaw: IPN.

Wołoszyn, Jacek Witold. 2015. *Szkoła jako instrument politycznej legitymizacji władzy partii komunistycznej w Polsce (1944–1989)*. Lublin: IPN.

Index

aeronautics *see* space exploration

Africa 77, 104, 126

agriculture 18–21, 24–5, 30–2, 33, 35, 38–40, 44–5, 50, 56–7, 64, 69, 72, 77–9, 82, 92–5, 116, 124, 126, 128, 138; agrarian reform in Poland 6, 12, 19, 20, 86, 92, 137

Albania 23, 135

Albigenses 116

alcohol 31, 59

Algeria 126

aluminum 30, 50, 73

Anders Władysław, general 87

apartments 22, 34, 36, 42–4, 58–9, 91, 93, 94

apple trees *see* Michurin

Arctic Circle *see* polar expeditions

Arendt, Hannah 4, 144

Arkwright, Richard 126

army 23, 31–2, 49, 83, 96, 99, 100, 130, 136–8; French 104; German 111; Home (Polish) 87, 113, 137; Polish ("people's") 14, 23, 41, 44, 45, 68, 86–8, 96, 97, 104, 130, 136–8, 147; Russian 86, 113, 119; Soviet (Red) Army 14, 16, 41, 44, 65, 68, 73, 82, 87, 88, 96, 123–4, 130, 137; Ukrainian Insurgent 130; Yugoslavian 73

Artek pioneer camp 102, 122, 124

atomic theory 27, 47–9, 52

authorities, image of 17–25, 37, 43, 86, 90, 93, 95, 100, 136, 137, 145

automotive industry 19, 22, 31, 32, 37, 39, 40, 43, 45, 50, 65, 68, 92, 125

aviation 43, 45, 47, 50

Baku 71

Baltic Sea 14, 65–7, 88; Polish access to 13, 44, 65

Bata, Tomas 73

Bautzen 88

Belgium 77

Belomor Canal *see* canals

Berlin 84, 88, 117

Bierut, Bolesław 7, 12, 23, 49, 68, 81, 83, 86, 91, 95, 96, 100, 104

Bismarck, Otto von 117

Boleslaus the Brave 89, 117

borders of Poland 12–15, 18, 65, 78, 84, 88, 89, 116, 130

bourgeoisie 15, 76, 109–17, 129, 137

Bratsk 71

Brezhnev, Leonid 103

bricklayer 25, 37, 44, 91

Broniewski, Władysław 81, 86

Bruno, Giordano 26

Brzechwa, Jan 90, 125

Buczek, Marian 114

Bulgaria 9, 72, 73, 103

Calvinism 109

Cambodia (Kampuchea) 74

Campanella 111

Canada 75, 89

canals 45, 71, 75, 123

Casimir the Great, king 117, 119

Castro, Fidel 103

cement 31, 33, 40, 51, 52, 64, 68; factory in Opole 14, 67

Censorship Office 2, 29, 43, 44, 51, 60, 100, 140, 145

central planning 16, 18, 21, 22, 30, 33, 39, 45, 50, 56, 57, 64, 71, 72, 74, 75, 78, 90, 123, 134

Chapayev, Vasily 123

Chełm 36, 87

Chicago 76

childcare *see* kindergarten; nursery

160   *Index*

China 17, 73, 75, 103, 104, 111, 135
Christianity 3, 4, 26–7, 36, 47–8, 63, 82, 88–9, 97–8, 108–10, 114–17, 128–9, 131, 134
cinema 94, 99, 126
coal 14, 18, 19, 31, 33, 34, 37, 41, 43, 44, 50, 51, 52, 57, 64–8, 70, 72, 77, 91, 98, 126
collective farms *see* agriculture
Communist Party *see* Polish United Workers's Party
Constantinople 109
Constitution: of the People's Republic of Poland 8, 95; of Poland 3rd May, 1791 97, 111; of USSR 72
construction work 13, 19, 22, 25, 32, 34, 35, 37, 41, 44–5, 51, 90–2, 94, 100, 101, 104, 126, 130
cooperative (farm) *see* agriculture
cooperative (shop) 7, 20, 25, 30–2, 35, 38–9, 83, 93–4, 128
Copernicus 27, 47, 63, 88
cosmonauts *see* space exploration
Cossacks 117
cotton 15, 55, 70, 71, 102
Cracow 112; Nowa Huta 16, 19, 24, 31, 49, 68, 92, 101, 122, 130
craftsmen's workshops 18, 32, 38, 110
Cuba 40, 75, 102, 103
Curie-Skłodowska Marie 88
Cyrankiewicz, Józef 81, 96
Czech *see* Lech, Czech and Rus
Czechoslovakia 14, 18, 30, 65, 72–3, 103, 109, 128
czyny (campaigns) 25, 39, 98

Dąbrowski, Jarosław *see* Paris, Commune
Darwin, Charles 115, 117
Darwinism 27, 54
Davy, Humphry 126
Decembrist Revolt (of 1825) 119
Democritus 48
Denmark 76–7, 80, 104
department stores 20, 31, 39, 42, 93, 126
Displaced Persons 88
Długosz, Jan 89
Dneproges 45, 70
doctors 24, 34, 42, 94, 100, 104
Donetsk coal basin 77–8
Dresden 127
Dutch Revolt 112
Dzerzhinsky, Felix 85, 114, 123

Edison, Thomas 45, 46
Egypt 47, 84, 104, 111

electrification 7, 15, 21–3, 25, 29, 32, 35, 39, 42–3, 45, 50, 64–5, 71, 95, 101
emigration 78, 89
Encyclopedistes 85
energy production 17, 18, 46, 70, 72: citizens' enagement 12, 18, 24–5, 31, 35, 39, 90, 99, 126, 144
Engels, Friedrich 52, 85, 113, 117, 126
engineer 23, 24, 37, 41–2, 97, 100–1, 104
England 17, 104, 111, 126–8
enthusiasm 7, 12, 17, 20, 68, 72, 88, 92, 94, 98, 102, 113, 130
environment devastation 17–18, 46, 57–8, 67, 76–7, 104; protection 18, 39, 52, 57, 67; transformation 15, 26, 64, 143
exploitation of workers and peasants 7, 8, 14–20, 28, 47, 71, 73, 75, 77, 82, 84, 86, 92, 103, 104, 110, 112–16, 127, 134–6

Fadeev, Alexander 87
fantasy, non-existence 27, 83, 105
Faraday, Michael 46
farmers *see* agriculture
fertilizers 14, 21, 31, 34, 35, 50, 51, 56, 68, 69, 92
Finland 76
fishing 7, 31, 57, 79
forerunners *see* working foremen
forest festivals 25, 39, 58, 61
foresting 15, 17, 26, 35, 39, 46, 56–8
France 17, 74, 77, 89, 104, 111, 116, 117, 126–8; French Revolution 46, 112
Friedrich II, king 117
Friendship pipeline 16, 22, 40, 50, 72

Gagarin, Yuri 16, 34, 103, 128
Galileo 26
Gaydar, Arkady 87, 124
Gdańsk 13, 22, 45, 66, 68
Germany 13, 14, 46, 59, 66–7, 82–4, 89, 111–20, 128, 138; Federal Republic of 15, 78, 135, 138; GDR 2, 6, 9, 14–15, 55, 59, 65, 69, 72, 84, 127, 128, 143; Nazi 14, 29, 43, 84; WWII 14, 19, 73, 77, 86–8, 98, 123
Ghana 104
Gierek, Edward 10, 96
Głogów *see* Legnica
Goebbels, Joseph 147
Gomułka, Władysław 96
Great Britain 17, 46, 70, 74–5, 77, 104, 111, 126–7
Greece 27, 78, 115
Grunwald 84, 112, 120

healthcare 16, 22, 23, 34, 39, 58–9, 82, 91–3, 129, 135, 137
highlanders 69, 123
Hitler, Adolf 117
Ho, Chi Minh 103
Holiday 25, 16, 97, 126; All Saints' Day 96; Christmas 36, 97; July 22nd 30, 36, 98; May 1st 36, 98, 124, 126; Miners' Day 97; Mother's Day 97; November 7th (October Revolution) 98, 124; St. Nicholas Day 97; summer 14, 22, 23, 35, 58, 66, 67, 99, 104, 124, 135; Teachers' Day 98
Home Army see army
Homo Sovieticus 145
household appliances 21, 22, 38, 95
housing 22, 32, 34, 36–8, 44, 51, 58, 59, 73, 99, 126, 129, 135
Hungary 9, 103: Dunaujvaros (Hungary) 73; Szekesfehervar 73
Hussites 65, 116

Iceland 76
Igarka 71
Imperialism 7, 8, 9, 17, 42, 46, 52, 73–8, 111, 135, 138
India 70, 74–5, 77, 104
industrialization of Poland 18, 20, 29, 67, 72
Industrial Revolution 113
Inquisition 115
internationalism 7, 8, 9, 28
interwar Poland 43, 66, 84, 86, 108, 114, 117, 119, 136–7
Iran 77, 87
Iraq 40, 104
Islam 115
Italy 78, 137
Ivan Kalita 118

Jagiellonian period 66
January Uprising of 1863 86, 119
Japan 73–4, 82, 113
Jaroszewicz Piotr 96
Jesuits 115–16
Jews 86
July Manifesto 6, 13, 26, 36, 68, 95, 98

Kampuchea see Cambodia
Karaganda 71
Kashubians 66
Kasprowicz, Jan 89
Katowice 67, 92; Stalinogród 67
Katyń 108, 119
Kemerovo 71

Khrushchev, Nikita 103
Kievan Rus' 118, 122
Kim, Il-Sung 102
Kindergarten 23, 56, 89, 93, 99
Kirovsk 71
Komsomolsk 71
Konarski, Szymon 116
Konopnicka, Maria 89
Korea 17, 73–4, 103
Kościuszko, Thaddeus 85–6
Kościuszko Division 86, 87
Kosmodemyanskaya, Zoya 123
kulak 93

labor competition 16, 18, 25, 32, 35, 36, 37, 41, 44, 52, 67, 81, 87, 91, 95, 96, 97, 100–3, 124, 126, 130, 135
Lafargue, Pierre 85
Laos 73–4
Latin (language) 110, 115
Lech, Czech and Rus – legend of 14, 84
Legnica; battle 112; Legnica-Głogów copper basin 14, 22, 67, 72, 92
Lenin (icebreaker) 46, 123
Leningrad (St. Petersburg) 71, 79, 102, 123
Lenino 87, 123, 137
Lenin, Vladimir 1, 15, 42, 69, 83, 85, 95, 99, 104, 110, 111, 113, 122, 123, 128
Liebknecht, Karl 85
Lithuania 84, 112, 117, 118, 120
Lodygin, Alexandr 16, 45–6
Łódź 66, 68, 92
Lomonosov, Mikhail 16
London 126
Los Angeles 76
Lublin 45, 68, 87, 98
Łukasiewicz, Walerian 88
Lusatians 84
Luxemburg, Rosa 114
Lyon revolts 113
Lysenko, Trofim 16, 53–5

Magadan 71
Magdeburg 114
Magnitogorsk 49, 71
malaria 58
Mao, Zedong 103
Marcel, Etienne 111
Marchlewski, Julian 114
Marconi, Guglielmo 46
Marxism 2, 7, 8, 52, 54, 78, 85, 109, 110–13, 129, 134, 135, 143
Marx, Karl 77, 78, 85, 110, 113, 117
materialism 8, 26, 27, 48–9, 143

162   *Index*

Matrosov, Alexandr 123
Mendeleev, Dmitri 16, 117
Mendel, Gregor 55
metallurgy 7, 14, 16, 18–20, 22, 25, 31–2, 37, 43, 49–52, 64, 67–9, 73, 77, 91–2, 100, 110
metro *see* subway
Michurin, Ivan 15–16, 39–40, 54–5, 102, 123
Mickiewicz, Adam 86
Middle Ages 47, 49, 63, 65, 66, 84, 89, 109–11, 115–16, 128
Miłosz, Czesław 103
Minc, Hilary 52, 91
mining 3, 14, 18–20, 22, 25, 26, 31–3, 34, 37, 43–4, 47, 50–2, 57, 64, 66–9, 77, 81–3, 89, 91, 95, 97, 98, 100, 110, 112, 126, 130
Ministry of Education 2, 3, 6, 7, 41, 43, 48, 29, 53, 63, 100, 105, 121, 140, 144
Moczar, Mieczysław 96
Model living conditions 22, 25
Mongolia 73
Monte Cassino 88
Moscow 71, 76, 99, 102, 123, 127; May 1st parade 99, 122, 124; subway 102, 124, 127
Münzer, Thomas 116
Murmansk 70

Narvik 88
nationalization of industry 12, 19–20, 72, 77, 91, 94, 137
NATO 135, 138
Netherlands 77, 112
new man concept 146, 148
newspapers 31, 95, 99, 101, 104, 124, 126
Newton, Isaac 46
New Year 36, 86, 96, 97, 123
New York 76, 126
Niagara Falls 70
Novokuznetsk 71
Nowa Huta *see* Cracow
nuclear energy 17, 26, 46, 49, 74, 123
nursery 23, 58, 89, 93, 99
Nysa River 14, 65

October Revolution 6, 15, 25, 36, 46, 71, 72, 82, 83, 85, 97, 99, 102–3, 109–14, 118–19, 123, 124, 128, 136
Odra river 14, 65, 84, 92, 130
Ohm, Georg 46
Oil refinery *see* Płock refinery
Opole 13, 14, 67, 112
Osowa Sień 93

Otto III, emperor 117
Owen, Robert 46

PaFaWag *see* Wrocław
Panama Canal *see* canals
Paris 111, 113, 126, 127; Commune 85, 110, 126
Partitions of Poland 86, 112, 115–18, 136
Pasteur, Louis 117
peace, struggle for 9, 28, 41–2, 46, 71, 76, 78, 79, 98, 103, 104, 123, 128, 129, 130, 135–8
Peace Race 128
Peter the Great 111, 118, 122
Petrov and Yablochkov 46
Piarists friars 116
Piast dynasty 66, 67, 111, 116–17
Piłsudski, Józef 114
pioneers 15, 29, 102–4, 122, 124, 127, 128, 146
Piramowicz, Grzegorz 116
Pius XI, pope 115
plastics 49, 51
Płock refinery 19, 22, 31, 50, 68, 92
polar expeditions 71, 102; Papanin and Cheluskin expedition 16, 122
police (militia) 23, 100, 130
Police fertilizer-producing plant 14, 92
Polish-German textbook commission 15
Polish United Workers' Party 2, 7–11, 19, 24, 30, 36, 56, 68, 81, 82, 95, 96, 98, 100, 134, 137, 140, 144–5
Polkowice *see* Legnica
Połock siege 112
polytechnization 33, 40, 41, 44–7, 49–52, 64, 91, 110, 129
Polzunov, Ivan 46
Pomerania 65, 66, 88, 89, 116, 119
popes 115, 120
Popov, Alexander 16, 46
Poronin *see* Tatra Mountains
ports 14, 22, 30, 31, 65–6, 70, 89, 91, 122
Portugal 78
post-war and pre-war *see* pre-war and post-war comparison
potato beetle 25, 39, 55, 99
Potebnya, Andriy 86, 119
Poznań 68–9
pre-war and post-war comparison 18, 19, 21–3, 30, 34, 39, 40, 43, 50, 52, 56–9, 65–9, 72–3, 77, 89–92, 94, 100, 111, 133, 135–6, 145, 146
progress 6–9, 12, 15, 21, 22, 26–7, 31–5, 38, 39, 43, 45–7, 54, 57, 58, 64, 67,

71–6, 88, 95, 109, 111, 112, 118, 123, 127, 136, 145, 146
property – collective vs. private 8, 16, 39, 71, 73, 93–4, 112, 116, 134, 138
Prussia 14, 117, 118, 120
Pushkin, Alexander 86

Rąblów, battle of 87
radio 16, 21, 22, 35, 45, 46, 53, 68, 88, 91, 93, 95, 101, 126
Railway 14, 33, 39, 41, 67, 68, 70, 78, 95, 124
Rationalization 25, 33, 91, 99–100
reading primers 3, 17, 20, 92, 97, 101, 104, 147, 148
reconstruction, post-war 12, 14, 19, 21, 24, 29, 41, 43, 45, 46, 65, 66, 71, 89–90, 96, 99, 101, 118, 126, 127, 130
Recovered Territories (Poland) 13, 14, 25, 89
Reformation 112, 116
Renaissance 116, 128–9
Reymont, Władysław 86
Richmann, Georg 46
Rodden, John 2, 29, 49, 59, 69, 70, 143
Roentgen, Wilhelm 117
Rokossovsky, Konstantin 7, 88, 90, 95, 104
Romania 73
Roman myths 27 empire 111, 113
Roma people 86
Rus see Lech, Czech and Rus

Sandomierz 88
Saudi Arabia 77
saving 35–6, 51, 59; School Savings Fund 35, 101, 131
Scandinavia 76
scientific world view see materialism
scouts 10, 15, 35, 36, 83, 87, 89, 90, 99, 101, 126, 128, 131, 137
Second Polish Republic (1918–1939) see interwar Poland
Service for Poland (Służba Polsce) 35, 101
Sevastopol 123
Shays, Daniel 111
shipyards 14, 19, 22, 43, 44, 65, 66
shop see cooperative
shortages: food 57, 59, 72, 135; housing 135; paper 51; soap 103
Siberia 16, 50, 70, 71, 79, 102; Lenin or Stalin in 85, 102, 123
Siberian rivers, reversing 26, 71
Sigismudus III, king 109, 116
Silesia 13–14, 66–7, 88, 89, 90, 92, 112, 116–19

Silesian uprisings (1919–1921) 66, 112
Six Year Plan 7, 8, 12, 16, 17, 20–1, 25, 33, 37, 43, 49, 51, 52, 57, 64–5, 67, 68, 83, 90–2, 96, 100
Skierniewice Institute 56
SKO see saving, School Savings Fund
Skopenko, Vasyl 88
Slavs 6, 7, 13, 14, 65–7, 83–4, 98, 103, 110, 116–17, 120, 121
Służba Polsce see Service for Poland
Sobieski John, king 113
Solidarity trade union 10, 13, 146
South America 75, 104
Soviet bloc 7, 9–11, 71–6, 78, 79, 97, 103, 104, 109, 127, 134–5, 143, 148
space exploration 16, 26, 34, 46, 63, 71, 103, 118, 122, 123, 128, 138; Sputnik 34, 118
Spain 78, 111; Civil War 88, 106
Spartacus 111
sport 56, 131
Spring of Nations (1848) 113
Sputnik see space exploration
Stakhanov see labor competition
Stalin 12, 15, 23, 25, 42, 73, 81, 87–8, 102–3, 118, 122–3; peak of 70
Stalingrad 123
Stalinism 6–8, 24, 32, 35, 37, 44, 48–50, 54, 75–7, 86, 92, 95, 101, 108–10, 123, 124–7, 142–6
state farms see agriculture
State Machinery Center 31, 38, 93
Stephenson, Robert L. 46
Stołczyn steelworks 14, 66
subway 90, 102, 124, 127
Suez Canal see canals
sulfur 50, 51, 72, 92
Świerczewski, Karol (general) 7, 88, 128, 130
Świętokrzyskie Mountains 69
Szczecin 13, 30, 45, 65

Tacitus 83
Tarnobrzeg 50, 72, 92
Tartars 118, 122
Tatra Mountains 69, 85, 123
Tchkhalov, Valeriy 102
teachers 1, 6, 7, 10, 13, 144–7; in textbooks 23, 24, 41–2, 97, 100
television 14, 66, 82, 122
Tereshkova, Valentina 34
Teutonic Knights 14, 65, 84, 114, 117
textile industry 31, 38, 52, 64, 68, 91. 126, 131
Thorez, Maurice 126

164   *Index*

Three Year Plan 21, 33, 43, 52, 90
Tito, Josip 7, 23, 73
Titov Herman 34
Tobruk 88
Trachoma 58
tractor 2, 21, 34, 35, 38, 45, 47, 51, 65, 70,
    82, 91, 93, 96, 97, 100, 101
trade 19, 20, 21, 40, 64, 93, 127; *see also*
    cooperative; department stores
transportation 2, 19, 31–3, 37, 45, 69
tsarism 15, 16, 71, 118–19
tuberculosis 58
Turks 109, 113, 115
Tyler, Wat 111

Ukraine 71, 88, 117, 119, 130
underground *see* subway
Union of Polish Youth (ZMP) 24, 81,
    101, 126
United States of America 9, 17, 46, 54, 55,
    59, 70, 71, 73–8, 85, 104, 111, 124, 135,
    138; black population 17, 76, 104, 126,
    127, 131, 134
Urals 70, 71
utopian socialism 85
Uzbekistan 127

vacation *see* holiday
venereal diseases 58
veterans 96
Vienna, battle of (1863) 113
Vietnam 17, 73, 74, 100, 102–4
Vistula River 69, 85, 89, 92
Voltaire 85
Vorkuta 71

Warsaw 19, 24, 31, 33, 37, 42, 45, 50, 85,
    68, 88–9, 96, 99–101, 113, 114, 123,

126, 127, 129, 130; Constitution Square
30; East-West Route 30, 42; Palace of
Culture and Science 16, 19, 42, 51, 68,
90, 122
Warsaw Pact 73, 109, 135, 138
Warsaw Uprising 53, 63, 87
Waryński, Ludwik 86, 114, 130
Wasilewska, Wanda 102, 106
waste paper collecting 25, 26, 35, 51,
83, 90
Wąs, Walenty 112
Watt, James 46, 127
welfare (social care) 12, 17, 22–3, 37,
43, 44, 47, 50, 67, 91, 124–5, 129,
134, 136
Western Europe 3, 7, 16–17, 41–2,
60, 73, 75–8, 104, 110, 118, 125, 127,
134–7
White Eagle (Polish coat of arms) 84,
95, 129
Wieloch, Kacper 112
Władysław of Varna, king 115
women 23, 25, 26, 33, 38, 56, 58, 91, 97,
102, 123
working foremen *see* labor competition
World War I 114
World War II 7, 12, 14, 16–17, 39,
41, 45, 68, 71, 73–4, 83, 87, 88, 95–6,
98, 102, 114, 119, 123, 124, 130,
136, 137
Wrocław 13, 88; PaFaWag 14, 19, 67, 89

Yugoslavia 7, 23, 72–3, 103

Zabrze-East coal mine 30, 31, 67, 81
ZMP *see* Union of Polish Youth
Żuławy, Wiślane 89
Zvorykin, Vladimir Kosma 16, 46